11C

CODE NUMBER 72/BEN FRANKLIN: PATRIOT OR SPY?

By the same author

ROAD TO REVOLUTION:
Benjamin Franklin in England,
1765–1775

CODE
NUMBER
72
BEN FRANKLIN

Patriot or Spy?

———•———

CECIL B. CURREY

PRENTICE-HALL, INC.
Englewood Cliffs, N.J.

Code Number 72/Ben Franklin: Patriot or Spy?
By Cecil B. Currey
Copyright © 1972 by Cecil B. Currey

Printed in the United States of America

Prentice-Hall International, Inc., London
Prentice-Hall of Australia, Pty. Ltd., North Sydney
Prentice-Hall of Canada, Ltd., Toronto
Prentice-Hall of India Private Ltd., New Delhi
Prentice-Hall of Japan, Inc., Tokyo

Library of Congress Cataloging in Publication Data

Currey, Cecil B
    Code number 72/Ben Franklin; patriot or spy?

    Bibliography: p.
    1. Franklin, Benjamin, 1706–1790. I. Title.
E302.6.F8C798   973.3'2'0924 [B]   72–7497
ISBN 0–13–139493–2

For my family . . .
Laura
Samuel
Anne
Laura

PREFACE

————•◦•————

I make no pretense that the story which follows is a "balanced" picture of the life of Benjamin Franklin. His interests were so broad, his activities so far-ranging that for the sake of clarity I have neglected almost any mention of his social friends, his amusements and recreations, his inventiveness, his scientific and literary endeavors, and other such things. Other more general appraisals should be read as well, and then the reader will begin to appreciate just how multi-faceted and intricate was Franklin's career. Additionally, I have used and relied upon the records of several men who, for various reasons, have usually been dismissed out of hand whenever they criticized Benjamin Franklin. When biographers extoll Franklin for his service to the United States while on a diplomatic mission to France during the Revolutionary War, they usually do not point out that some believed "the political salvation of America depends upon the recalling of Dr. Franklin." [1] Sam Adams, who once had thought highly of Franklin, argued that it was one thing to honor Franklin's "Wisdom of the Philosopher," and quite another to remember "that in the different Character of a Politician he may be lyable to human Frailties at the age of more than three Score and ten." [2] Both John Jay and John Adams shared doubts as to Franklin's ability as a

---

[1] Ralph Izard to Richard Henry Lee, 15 October 1780, in E. C. Burnett (ed.), *Letters of the Members of the Continental Congress* (8 vols., Washington, D. C., 1921–1936), V, 362n.
[2] Sam Adams to James Warren, 24 March 1779, *ibid.*, IV, 207n.

diplomat. It was then charged that although Franklin was a great man in science, his "knowledge in electricity does not prove him to be acquainted with the politics of the courts of Europe; nor does his leading the lightning with a thread prove that he had lead us into any secrets of the British court." [3] The theme of this book is an investigation into the activities of Franklin which brought about these misgivings toward him.

For their courtesy and never-failing helpfulness, I would like to thank the staffs of the English, French, and American archives in which I have worked. I have also appreciated the comments and criticisms of this manuscript by two colleagues in my own department: Professor Edward Silbert and Professor John Belohlavek, Department of History, University of South Florida. I wish to thank publicly three of my graduate student assistants who have labored with me on this study: Michael Pfeifer, Carol Lindsey Barnett, and June Dombrova. I have also appreciated the enthusiasm, helpfulness, and determination of my editor, Dennis Fawcett.

Of great importance has been the aid given to me by my wife, Laura Gene Currey, who has read this material through every draft and who has taken my writing habits to task again and again. She has been wise enough to smooth the way for me to have as much time as possible in which to write. Her care has been prized.

Cecil B. Currey

---

[3] *Ibid.*, IV, 412n.

CONTENTS

———•—•—•———

"*I am sure it cannot be my duty, nor the interests of my country, that I should conceal any of my sentiments of him [Benjamin Franklin], at the same time that I do justice to his merits. It would be worse than folly to conceal my opinion of his great faults.*"

—John Adams, Wednesday, 23 June 1779, aboardship for America on his return from France. From John Adams' *Diary*, in *The Works of John Adams*, ed. Charles Francis Adams (1865), III, 221.

CODE NUMBER 72/BEN FRANKLIN: PATRIOT OR SPY?

CHAPTER ONE

———•◆•———

Envoy in Paris

On the dark water of the North Sea crews of enemy ships sighted one another, unfurled their battle flags. Each sought the weather gauge for the advantage it would give. Cannon were made ready, galley fires were smothered, seamen scattered sand on the decks in hopes of better footing during the desperate moments ahead. In heavy seas, courses and t'gallants were reefed so the ships would ride the waters more easily. The smaller ship, *Bonhomme Richard*, passed on the lee side of its larger opponent, *Serapis*. Cannon came to bear and starboard guns sang their screaming cacophony. The winds carried away the cries of wounded and dying men on the *Serapis*. They would not see the end of this Thursday, 23 September 1779. *Bonhomme Richard* tacked about and fired into the stern of the two-decker. But the *Serapis* now had the advantage of the weather gauge.

Serapis swung and hurtled toward the smaller ship. As they passed, both fired broadsides, and then again. Cut rigging tumbled toward deck and water. Splintered masts crashed upon men and guns. Cannon hurled death while men, staring incoherently at suddenly smashed limbs, vomited blood. On *Serapis* was a palpitating mass, half a carronade crew. Breaking waves drenched desperate sailors with spray as the decks on which they stood were pounded by cannon. In the water were the flotsam and jetsam of death and feebly swimming men. John Paul Jones sailed his injured *Bonhomme Richard* alongside the *Serapis*, so close that the remaining rigging tangled and cannon muzzles touched. Called on to surrender, Jones shouted "I have not yet begun to fight!" Three hours later the *Serapis* was his. Those who were still standing after the hand-to-hand battle gazed insensately at the fallen. Two days later, the little *Bonhomme Richard*, abandoned and bruised beyond repair, sank into foaming water.

The sun rode the skies like burnished copper. Exhausted men crouched fearfully behind earthworks thrown up Friday night. Now it was Saturday morning, 17 June 1775, and amateur soldiers lay spent upon the ground. The hill upon which they lay admirably commanded the town below them. But they were only a handful, and three thousand of the enemy were preparing an assault. Each of those British professionals would march up that hill, rank upon firmly disciplined rank. Every man would have thirty-six inches of polished steel fixed to the end of his musket, ready to thrust the point into softly yielding flesh. The June heat became more insufferable. Insects flickered through the air and swarmed in the body sweat of those who waited. There was little water and throats thickened and clogged. Below, drums began to beat, the sprightly sound of fifes drifted upward. Columns of men began the deadly march toward the earthworks. Those who waited made ready, checked powder, lead, wadding, and flint. Fusiliers seized ramrods and slow match. Heat from the cloudless sky lay like an invisible weight upon both attackers and defenders. Twice the British were beaten back from Bunker's Hill. On the third assault, late in the evening, the American positions were overrun.

A world away and separated by months from these two events, another scene unfolded. In Paris, Conrad Alexandre Gérard de Rayneval, the French Foreign Minister's secretary, had a slight cold. His head stuffy, bothered by an occasional cough, Gérard felt too ill to attend a scheduled meeting and so postponed it until the next day, a Friday. While he struggled with this gross infirmity, a people in America fought for nationhood. The colonists needed French troops, French arms, munitions, equipment, and ships. They would have to wait twenty-four more hours.

It was the second month of the year 1778. Americans fought their former mother country, Great Britain, for freedom from colonial control and for independence. Revolution had sundered a unified society and while the English fought a civil war with their American brethren, the citizens of the new states sought recognition from Europe that they were truly a new country.

The sixth of February 1778 was one of the most fateful dates in all American history. On the evening of that day, the representatives of France and the United States of America met in Paris in the Hôtel de Lautrec, on the Quai des Théatins, the headquarters for the French Ministry of Foreign Affairs. Gérard, having recovered sufficiently from his ills of the previous day, headed the delegation for his nation. For the United States there appeared Benjamin Franklin of Philadelphia, Silas Deane of Connecticut, Arthur Lee of Virginia. Present also that evening was Dr. Edward Bancroft, physician, friend of Franklin and Deane, sworn enemy of Arthur Lee, and secretary for the American legation.

The Intolerable and Coercive Acts were now ancient history. British Major John Pitcairn and his men had long since marched through Lexington Green, momentarily slowed by Captain John Parker and his sixty militiamen. The shot heard round the world had blossomed into repeated and staccato gunfire in battle after battle. General George Washington, the Virginia gentleman, answering the call of the colors, had assumed command of the available American troops. The Second Continental Congress hastily assembled in May 1775 rather than in September as the members had anticipated a year earlier. England had won its pyrrhic victories at Bunker's and Breed's Hills, British soldiers had pitted themselves successfully against the Americans at the Battle of Long Island, and red-coated buglers had sounded fox-hunting calls as the British regulars routed the terrified colonials.

A startled and sleepy commandant of Ticonderoga had been rudely awakened to hear Ethan Allen command him to surrender "in the name of the Continental Congress and the Great God Jehovah." Many of the battles of our birthing had already been fought, and won or lost: Trenton, Princeton, Bennington, Brandywine, Camden, and Saratoga.

The Congress, split by quarreling factions and lacking authority, taxing power, organization, and an army or navy, had performed masterfully in its administration of the war. Congress knew that open alliances with European powers had been America's greatest need from the beginning. Since 1775 the United States Congress had urged its agents in Europe to work for treaties of alliance with royal governments there. On 6 February 1778 that hope was about to be realized.

Two treaties were to be signed that Friday in the Hôtel. One was a treaty of amity and commerce, the other a treaty of alliance. The first document was based mainly on the "Plan of 1776" set forth two years before the Franco-American alliance by Congress as a guide for its European agents. The ideas contained in that two-year-old plan had not even been new when it was drawn up. A congressional committee, of which Benjamin Franklin was a member, selected its ideas from various practices then current among trading nations. The Plan of 1776 called for free ships, free goods; the trading rights of neutral nations carrying cargoes between belligerent ports; contraband lists which excluded food and naval stores.

Much of the Plan of 1776 was now to be activated in the Hôtel de Lautrec. According to the unsigned treaty, France and the United States would treat one another as "most favored nations." Their ports would be open, to be freely used by the other.

The second document, the Treaty of Alliance, was even

more important. France was to avow openly that she was the pledged ally of the United States. She would support America's efforts at independence and commit her own troops and navy if and when war broke out between France and Great Britain. Reciprocally, the neophyte United States pledged to aid the French to the best of its ability in case of conflict. Neither nation was to sign a truce or make peace without the other's consent. France, moreover, promised not to begin peace negotiations until Britain had recognized the independence of the United States.[1]

Certainly without French aid, given secretly before 1778 and openly thereafter, the United States of America could not have won its war with Britain. The representatives of the new states were already finding it difficult to hang together, and without France, the ringleaders of revolution might well have "hung separately."

Gérard had earlier told the Americans in Paris that his government had agreed to an alliance. The intervening weeks were devoted to working out details and drafting the documents themselves. The French also attempted to bring Spain into the alliance. American paperwork progressed slowly, Arthur Lee complained, because of Benjamin Franklin's insistence upon dining out daily in evening-long soirées. Still the work was completed. The documents would have been signed on the fifth save for Gérard's headcold. On the evening of 6 February 1778 the men came together in a room at Ministry headquarters.

The ceremony was brief. Franklin dressed as he had the day before, when he still believed the signing would occur then, in an old, too-tight, faded coat of blue Manchester velvet. Franklin had once remarked that he "never put himself to any trouble or inconvenience to retaliate." To Silas Deane that night, however, he commented that wearing the old coat was "to give it a little revenge." Five years earlier he had been publicly scolded by a British official, and now Franklin got his "revenge," he told Deane, because "I wore this coat on the day [Alexander] Wedderburn abused me at White-hall." [2]

Gérard was the first to sign. Franklin followed. The two men then walked over to a nearby fireplace to talk while the other Americans signed the documents. Lee wondered whether he should sign his name twice, once as commissioner to France and a second time as well since he was also a commissioner to Spain. Deane, as usual, scorned both Lee and his suggestion so the Virginian, as had the others, signed but once. Edward Bancroft remained throughout the ceremony, silently watching. At the conclusion of the signing, the papers were given to Franklin for safekeeping while he made the necessary arrangements to send them to America for congressional ratification.[3] He silently handed them to Bancroft.

Forty-two hours later the ministers of King George III were reading copies of the Franco-American treaties clandestinely sent them from the American mission at Paris. Louis XVI had not yet officially received at Versailles, as he planned, the representatives of the newly recognized United States of America. The French ship *Sensible*, which would carry the treaties, had not yet sailed to deliver the tidings to the New World. Yet the English Secret Service had procured every detail of the arrangements and had already disseminated them throughout the proper offices of Lord North's cabinet.

Edward Bancroft, into whose hands Franklin had passed the French treaties, was not only the secretary for the legation but was also a close friend of Franklin's, who described Bancroft as "a gentleman of character and honor," and said of him that he was "an intelligent, sensible man whom I esteem most highly." [4] In addition to his administrative and secretarial duties, Bancroft was a traitor and spy, the chief of a British intelligence cell organized within the American embassy.[5]

For over 190 years the activities of Benjamin Franklin have been accepted at face value—that is, at the value he himself put on them. His many biographers and adulators, and they are legion, have had only laudatory comments to make concerning his career, accomplishments, and reputation. Most of the written tales about Franklin depict his life in France during the Revolutionary War as the zenith of his career. All the years that went before, like an arrow, drove straight toward this mark. They were but preparatory, molding him for this task. The years that followed, we are told, were restful ones as the declining old man basked in the glory of his fame as his life "melted away like butter hardened in the sun." [6]

Benjamin Franklin, his biographers write, was the Constitution-Maker from America gone to France to secure help for his embattled countrymen. The people of that foreign land greeted him with open arms, welling hearts, and glad cries. He captivated the French Foreign Minister, the compte de Vergennes, and swayed him to America's cause. He stole a march on the British by inventing a new word for dishonesty, *"stormonter"*—"to lie"—so called after the English Ambassador, Lord Stormont. He met Voltaire and the French shouted that Solon and Sophocles had just embraced. The American busied himself endlessly writing letters for the public press in support of his nation's position, sending various adventurers to aid the cause of Washington's army, issuing letters of marque authorizing privateers to attack British shipping, designing colonial currency, printing bagatelles and satires at his press in Passy. We are reminded that Franklin converted the *physiocrats* to advocacy of New World revolution, that he twisted the tail of Albion's lion with his shrewd advice to French officials. The stories are repeated of Franklin's "compleat" dedication to the mission which had brought him to the Old World and of the success that crowned his labors when the Franco-American treaties were signed on 6 February 1778.

Franklin biographers further declare Franklin to have been an astute debater and unconquerable defender of his nation's aspirations when peace negotiations began late in the war. In spite of the best trained minds that England could send to the peace table, Franklin, undaunted by possible trickery within the French government, stood head and shoulders above his peers and was able to safeguard the claims of the United States. He was, it is said, the architect of the Peace of Paris, 1783.

Authors have delighted in chronicling Franklin's joys during those years in France. We are shown how he was called *"mon cher papa"* by the ladies of Paris, young and old. Writers regale us with accounts of his dreams, his romances with Mme. Helvétius, Mme. Brillon de Jouy, and more passing flirtations with others. We are gladdened with anecdotes about his gout, his chess-playing, his wigs, the Franklin miniatures that were sold everywhere. Both diplomatic achievements and the maintenance of Franklin's *joie de vivre* were managed in the most difficult of circumstances. Was not his comrade, Silas Deane, recalled by a petulant Congress? Didn't Franklin have to contend, almost daily, with the petty nagging, malicious gossip, and near madness of the other commissioner, Arthur Lee? Many have written of the influence which Franklin brought to bear on the French Court. Ben, too bulky to be cast in the role of hero on horseback, is characterized by his eulogists as the absolutely necessary man of the hour without whose aid France might not have committed herself.

But let the biographers speak for themselves. Phillips Russell called him the "midwife at the birth of the world's first great republic." The popularizer, Bernard Faÿ, noted that "He was bound to the cause, body and soul. . . . Just as Abraham, at the age of seventy-five, left for Egypt, the wise old Franklin, now turned sixty-nine, prepared to leave for France." Verner W. Crane, a Franklin historian, told how "the burden of exploiting all the possible advantages of French benevolent neutrality fell mainly on Franklin, who alone commanded the confidence of Vergennes." Paul C. Phillips wrote categorically that "Franklin . . . was undoubt-

edly the great statesman of the Revolution." The famous
nineteenth century historian, George Bancroft, felt that
Franklin was "the greatest diplomat of his century." Or
again, we are told that Franklin "won a diplomatic campaign
equal in results to Saratoga." [7]

The listing of such "evaluations" of Benjamin Franklin
could be indefinitely extended, but there would be little
point. Enough has been said already to reveal their flavor.
There seems to be a general agreement among historians on
the fact that Franklin considerably aided the American cause.
And yet there is reason to suspect that this was not his primary purpose on his mission to France. Those who have
made him central in the drama which culminated in the delivery of French aid to America have heavily glossed over the
background of European power politics and continental intrigue within which he operated. To be sure, Franklin did
emerge from the war years as an American hero, but those
who have praised his life in France could do so only by wink-
ing at bits and pieces of evidence which simply do not fit into
the usual Franklin mold. Writers have been able to uphold
Franklin as a paragon of moderation, wisdom, and virtue only
by suppressing or ignoring comments by his peers which
were often bitter, pointed, and possibly quite close to the
mark. Franklin repudiated and dismissed as sheer madness
critical descriptions of himself by those who best knew him,
and through the years the voices of his critics have been
muted while Franklin's own voice still booms forth. Ben's defenders have carefully steered away from detailed analysis of
several projects in which he involved himself while in France.

The popular picture of Franklin as a hero remains uncor-
rected only because so few have been interested in examining
the frame in which it hangs. As one author has suggested:

> So great is the reputation of [Franklin] that almost no
> modern writer has undertaken to question the upright-
> ness of his actions or failed to accept his testimony at

face value, while the evidence given by [others] so far as
it relates to Franklin, though supported in many instances by . . . other reliable authorities, has been
thrown out of court without serious consideration. Such
historical practice is, of course, not justifiable. A discard-
ing of hero worship and a careful weighing of all contemporary evidence would produce a conclusion quite
different from that which has been reached.[8]

Past authors have not always checked Franklin's words
against contemporary descriptions of his activities made by
his peers. Some have been unwilling to give an honest hearing to Franklin's critics. When these things are done, the results are startling. The shadowy phase of Franklin's life that
emerges here does not fit easily into the accepted view of
Benjamin Franklin. To be sure, there remain large gaps
which have had to be bridged by speculations and supposi-
tions. Where such speculations are interposed upon the available records, their speculative nature is explicitly acknowledged rather than carefully hidden, as is too often the case in
other works on Franklin.

Getting at the truth about Benjamin Franklin is no easy
matter. One modern interpreter has suggested that at times
Franklin resembled a chameleon.[9] A chameleon blends with
its background as a defense, hiding itself from careful investigation and known dangers. The allusion to Franklin is apt.
His adulators tend to make us forget that Franklin was not always praised. A contemporary described him as a man of
"talents without virtue." [10] His old enemy Alexander Wedderburn thought of him as the most "hypocritical, abandoned
old rascal that ever existed—a man who, if ever one goes to
Hell, he will." [11] George Chalmers, a Tory historian, wrote
of Franklin that he was "trained in the hardy school of private
treachery, stained with the honourable blood of injured
friendship, he thought he was qualified to be a public traitor
—and he did not err. Unhappy man! His ambitious villainy is
stopt for want of space." [12]

These comments, however, should not be counted very heavily, for they were uttered by men with whom Franklin had only limited contacts. His colleagues, those with whom he worked closely while in France, should have known him better, and we should expect that their evaluations would be of more worth. John Adams worked side by side with Franklin for months. An admittedly testy person, Adams soon came to view Franklin darkly and held to this conviction all his days. He described Franklin as "secretive" and said that his "practical cunning united with his theoretick Ignorance render him one of the most curious Characters in History." [13] After Yorktown, as tentative peace negotiations with Britain began in earnest, Adams warned that in those delicate maneuverings, "Franklin's cunning will be to divide us; to this end he will provoke, he will insinuate, he will intrigue, he will manoeuvre." [14]

The opinion of Arthur Lee, who had known and worked under and with Franklin for years, is also interesting in this respect. Lee was a proud, cantankerous, difficult man at best, and later writers have sometimes described him as nearly paranoid in his relations with others. The charge originated with Franklin who felt that Lee had unwarrantedly crossed him, but it has remained to darken the worthwhile accomplishments of that cranky man from Virginia. For several years after their first acquaintance, Lee could speak of Franklin's "wisdom and industry" and his "firmness and equanimity which conscious integrity alone can inspire"; these were qualities which, Lee observed, "must endear him" to Americans.[15] Further association with Franklin and observation of him brought Lee to change his mind, however. By 1778 he was convinced that Franklin was "dangerous" and "capable of any wickedness." It would be necessary to watch Franklin circumspectly in order to gather information leading to his "detection and punishment." [16] On another occasion, Lee wrote that Franklin was "concerned in the plunder [of public money belonging to the Congress] and that in time we shall collect the proofs." [17]

In these ways was the Philadelphian assessed by two men —one of whom is dismissed as utterly unreliable by the bulk of historiography, while the other was destined to become the second President of the United States. Both were highly suspicious of Franklin, and their suspicions appear to have been abundantly true. But the full truth was even worse than anything these men even dared to suggest, although Arthur Lee seems to have hinted at the possibility. A cell of British Intelligence was located in Franklin's headquarters in France, and Benjamin Franklin—covertly perhaps, tacitly at least, possibly deliberately—cooperated with and protected this spy cell operating out of his home in France from shortly after his arrival in that country until the end of the war. Willingly or not, he made himself a party to treason toward his own country while serving as its representative abroad. British Intelligence referred to him in its codes as "72," "Moses," and perhaps in other ways.

One author has put the issue in a straightforward way. His words are so pungent that they bear reproducing in full.

. . . it was when Benjamin Franklin was at the American Embassy in Paris that the British Secret Service achieved its most conspicuous success. . . . Not only did Britain learn all the American secrets but many items of French intelligence as well, for the French trusted Franklin and gave him a great deal of information. The kindest deduction one could make from all this was that Franklin was duped by his assistant [Bancroft] and, from a security point of view, was utterly incompetent. But a close examination of the facts by no means suggests that this was the case. Franklin was widely travelled, an efficient administrator, a man of the world, fully cognisant of intrigues and highly intelligent. It is unthinkable that he did not know something of what was going on. And when Arthur Lee confronted him with the charge that Bancroft was a spy in the service of the British and actually gave proof of this, showing how Bancroft's links with the British Secret Service had been uncovered and how when he visited London he was in touch with the Privy Council, Franklin stubbornly refused to accept the evidence. Franklin countered by denouncing Lee and insisted that Bancroft's visits to London produced worthwhile intelligence for America. The truth was that all Bancroft brought back from these trips was false information provided by the British.[18]

If Benjamin Franklin was innocent of complicity in the British spying operations, then the information leakage from his embassy is incomprehensible. Those security leaks could be explained if Franklin was duped or himself somehow involved with the British Secret Service.

Consider other items regarding Franklin's career in France.

The French Foreign Ministry and other Americans in Paris complained that the British ambassador knew their every move.

Copies of many of Franklin's reports to the Congress as well as the reports of others ended up in the British archives.

Franklin vehemently rejected charges of espionage made against Bancroft, refusing to investigate these legitimate denunciations. Instead, he reviled those who had made the charges and continued to use Bancroft in positions of trust and responsibility. So employed, Bancroft had access to major American state secrets and all of the commission papers.

Manuscripts presently in the British Museum indicate that a great deal of shipping information (sailing dates, shipments of supplies, cargo details) passed on to Albion.

Intensively acquisitive, Franklin spent more time and energy in the pursuit of private gain for himself, his relations, and his cohorts than he did upon the mission which had brought him to Europe.

When relations with his fellow commissioners worsened, Franklin drew an even heavier veil of secrecy over his operations and reported to America that Adams and Lee were going insane.[19]

The following account of Franklin's activities in France has been pieced together using very few of his own manuscripts. His surviving papers have had to be supplemented in almost every case with material drawn from records of his contemporaries. Part of this difficulty has been caused by time's natural attrition of old manuscripts. Perhaps thousands of Benjamin Franklin's papers have been destroyed. His correspondence for a period of twenty years, including material which would have been helpful in reconstructing the early years covered in this study, were left in the hands of a long-time friend, Joseph Galloway, when Franklin sailed for France in the fall of 1776. Galloway's home was later ransacked and many of Franklin's records were destroyed. After Ben's death in 1790, others of his papers from the war years were stored in a barn and later given away to those interested in them. Of these many never have been recovered, and of those not dispersed in this way, many deteriorated badly from the conditions under which they had been stored. William Temple Franklin later took still others of his grandfather's manuscripts to London. He planned to use many of them for a printed edition of Benjamin Franklin's works. After he had used those which he wanted, the remaining ones were discarded, and after his death no one claimed those manuscripts still in his possession. Some years later a London tailor was found using those grand old quarto sheets for cutting dress patterns. Thus the years have taken their toll.

Other factors have reduced the total number of available documents. Caught up in clandestine diplomatic and political affairs, it is entirely possible that Franklin deliberately got rid of those papers which might compromise his position. We know that this was, upon occasion, the case. Franklin once wrote to Deane urging that a record be "buried in oblivion." "I earnestly desire," wrote Franklin, "that you would put that paper immediately in the fire on receipt of this, without taking or suffering to be taken any copy of it, or communicating its contents." [20] At another time his grandnephew, Jonathan Williams, Jr., who was deeply involved with Franklin in profiteering and, perhaps, spying, wrote his uncle to say that he had immediately destroyed the old doctor's letter after reading it.[21] What we have a record of in two cases after 190 years may be supposed to have happened on other occasions. We know that Franklin was an assiduous paper-saver and record keeper—a veritable "pack rat." He retained as many as possible of the documents that crossed his desk. Why would he frantically urge Deane to destroy a memorandum? Why should Williams have destroyed a message immediately after reading it? The most obvious answer is that those papers, held in the wrong hands, might well be used to hurt Franklin's career and the pursuits in which he was engaged.

What things were done on verbal orders only that were never committed to paper? This has always been the most common way in which intelligence agents have operated. Samuel Flagg Bemis has put the matter well. "It lies," he has written, "in the very nature of his trade that the international spy should, whenever he can, obliterate the traces of his work; nevertheless, despite his efforts, his story will sometimes leave material for the sober historian. . . ." [22] It is not only the spy who is interested in obliterating the record of his passing. From time to time involved governments also have suppressed or restricted public printing of such "traces." Such publications might damage future official policies or might picture past ones in unfavorable ways. If activities like these were publicly aired and the public at large learned about participation in clandestine programs, governmental office holders might find their reputations lessened.[23] Governments also have exerted themselves in efforts to protect agents who have been directly involved in the field, so long as hurt might come to the principals concerned or to their immediate relatives by such publications.[24]

Not too long after the close of the war, rumors appeared that the British government was indeed trying to keep some of Benjamin Franklin's writings from being published. In the introduction to an early collection of his printed papers, the editor charged that the English administration had bribed William Temple Franklin to keep him from issuing a long awaited edition of his grandfather's works. Temple, the editor wrote, "had found a bidder . . . in some emissary of government, whose object was to withhold the manuscripts from the world." Such charges had earlier been made in the *Edinburgh Review*, the *American Citizen*, and the *National Intelligencer*. One such story appeared in *The Argos or London Review in Paris*, 28 March 1807. Three days later Temple made a rebuttal in the paper in which he denied the allegation.[25] Whatever the reasons for Temple's delay in issuing his grandfather's papers (and a major factor may well have been his preoccupation with the very profitable land agency in which he was working), twenty-eight years passed between Benjamin Franklin's death and Temple's publication of his works in 1818.

The policies of Britain in those years have long since passed into dust. The archives of England and of France have for generations been open to the researcher. In these records, says Bemis, "may be found two principle classes of sources . . . : reports of operatives and spies to their superior officers, which in turn were digested and summarized for perusal by higher executives, and petitions and memorials for reward for past services rendered." [26] Such materials are available. Those two-hundred-year-old papers tell in their always archaic, often dry, sometimes quaint style the devious involvements of Franklin in Paris.

In addition, many of Franklin's papers have survived and have been used in this story. Of the records which he kept, many were retained simply because to him they did not seem compromising. He did not know that one day someone would lay them side-by-side with other records, fitting the whole into a revealing pattern. From such a procedure there emerges an unrecognized, or at least unexpressed, view that differs considerably from earlier descriptions of Franklin, his friends, his work. It can now be seen that many of the things Franklin said, used by earlier historians as evidence for his moderation, his industry, or his talents, were set forth to conceal himself from danger. Still other statements he made were camouflage for his real ambitions, desires, and activities.

The characters involved in this strange situation were numerous and varied. They included Benjamin Franklin (alias 72, Moses), Silas Deane (alias 51, Benson), Arthur Lee (Mary Johnston), Arthur's brother William Lee, Jacobus van Zandt (George Lupton), William Carmichael (alias P. Le Maître) from Maryland, Jonathan Williams, Jr., an ex-bakery clerk who had become commercial agent for Nantes, Paul Wentworth (who used so many aliases a listing of them would cover two pages), Edward Bancroft (Edward Edwards), the Reverend John Vardill from New York and Whitehall, 17 Downing Street, Ralph Izard from South Carolina, Joseph Hynson, a treacherous sea captain, Beaumarchais, and a host of other major and minor luminaries of English, French, and American society.

The story of their activities and of Franklin's part in them does not begin when their paths first crossed during the American Revolution. The roots are elsewhere, in the character of Benjamin Franklin and in his career during the prewar years.

CHAPTER TWO

———•◆•———

Great Affairs of the World

Benjamin Franklin was never the one-dimensional or even
the two-dimensional character his portrayers have so often
made of him. One of the most complicated, many-faceted,
and intelligent men in America's history, Ben had ready insights into the psychological flaws in human nature—his own
included. In August 1788 as he began once again to complete
his already twice interrupted autobiography. The first entry
he made contained the observation that "the great Affairs of
the World, the Wars, Revolutions, &c." are conducted by
men who, while pretending to act out of public or philan-
thropic motives, do so instead out of deep-seated selfishness,
"whatever they may pretend." [1] This thought, this idea, had
first come to Franklin more than fifty-five years earlier when,
as a young man, he had begun to read works on history. He
had jotted it down at the time, preserved it all those years,
and entered it as the beginning of part three of the story of
his life. In those lines it may be true that he spoke also for
himself, and as Benjamin Franklin had no hesitation in admit-
ting it, we need have none.

If every person is indeed the sum of all their experiences,
then we should begin our examination of Franklin with the
fact that he was the son of a poor candlemaker in Boston. He
attended school for only approximately two years and was ap-

prenticed twice early in his life. He loathed poverty and became intensely acquisitive, pursuing wealth until the day of his death. He learned quickly that he had a magnificent mind, and in later life, in the company of aristocrats and future presidents, he reveled in the fact that he was as accomplished as any of them.

With almost no schooling, using only his native talents, he taught himself to read and speak, albeit imperfectly, several foreign languages. He mastered science and mathematics. Some of the mathematical *games* he played still remain incomprehensible to later experts. His experiments in electricity put him on the cutting edge of scientific knowledge and brought him into contact with other men of world renown. Universities paid him homage and he was granted master's and doctorate degrees by William and Mary, Harvard, Yale, Edinburgh, and Oxford. "Thus without studying in any college I came to partake of their honors." [2] He was sought out and granted memberships by learned societies across the face of Europe. He was the intimate of such men as Edmund Burke, Voltaire, and Dr. Joseph Priestly.

Always practical, Ben Franklin capitalized on his apprenticeship as a printer and established or backed several colonial newspapers, the most famous of which was the semi-weekly *Pennsylvania Gazette*. Ben's roving eye often brought him into "intrigues with low women that fell in my way." Worrying about infection from venereal diseases, he married beneath him to a young widow who was useful primarily for releasing his sexual tensions and for helping him in his business.[3] Ben fathered an illegitimate son and daughter before his marriage and another boy and a girl within wedlock.[4] Only Sally, of his legal children, lived to maturity. The boy, Francis Folger, died in infancy from the ravages of smallpox. Ben was so grieved and felt his loss so deeply that even in old age his eyes welled with tears whenever he was reminded of his child.

At the beginning of his business career Franklin organized

a club, the Junto, among the tradesmen of Philadelphia. It was both a social organization and a chamber of commerce. Soon influential in both business and politics, the club under Franklin's management was able to steer business to its members and to blackball competitors. Franklin's fame as a printer spread and he was successively chosen by Delaware, New Jersey, and Maryland as the job printer for their public papers. Ben became clerk of the Pennsylvania Assembly, postmaster for Philadelphia, and Assistant Deputy Postmaster General for the American Colonies, the latter office a royal appointment.

Franklin had come far from his youthful poverty. He was now rich indeed. A housemaid of the time could expect to earn £10 annually; a store clerk, £25; an instructor at Franklin's Philadelphia Academy (now the University of Pennsylvania), from £60 to £70 each year. The chief justice of Pennsylvania made £200, the governor, £1,000. By 1748, the year Franklin retired at the age of forty-two, his income was slightly higher than that of the governor.[5] In his business life, he had never been averse to using a public appointment to aid his private income. When he became postmaster of his home town, he immediately began using the post riders to carry the *Gazette*, giving his newspaper an extensive circulation and a near monopoly in the area. This was one of the first instances of many where Franklin used public trusts and offices he held for private gain. So many such instances occurred that a century later one commentator, Charles Francis Adams, wrote: "The ethics of Franklin permitted of the enjoyment of advantages, obtained at the expense of others." This was done "by passively permitting them" or by "indirectly promoting them. Through the attractive benevolence which overspreads his writings, is visible a shade of thrift seldom insensible to the profit side of the account in even the best actions."[6]

Franklin's youthful bout with poverty long haunted him, constantly stirring his ambition. He was forever moving from one public job to another, each time climbing higher, as he sought to attain the top levels of his society. While still clerk for the Assembly, his support for a Philadelphia militia endangered his standing with the Quaker pacifists in control of the provincial government. There was some talk that Franklin might lose his clerkship. He wrote: "I shall never *ask*, never *refuse*, nor ever *resign* an office. If they will have my office . . . they shall take it from me. I will not, by giving it up, lose my right of sometime or other making reprisals on my adversaries." [7] This vengeful view toward those who threatened to thwart his will or who were in a position to do so is a side of Franklin's personality often forgotten. He could present a benevolent side at almost all times, but when crossed he was quite willing to use any tool available to destroy those who blocked his way. The humble chandler's son had come a long way and it is not surprising that he had picked up a thoroughgoing arrogance in the process. What does deserve to be noted, however, is that he was so well able to disguise his arrogance. In the years to come, when he felt stronger, Franklin would many times "make reprisals on his adversaries." At the moment, however, he was still busy forging the mask of his public visage.

  / Elected as a representative from Philadelphia, Franklin entered the Pennsylvania Assembly in 1751. He already had demonstrated himself to be a sharp businessman; now he was ready to develop his talents as a keen politician. He needed all his wits. Professedly neutral in the factional squabbles that characterized Pennsylvania politics, he worked with the proprietary party in urging military preparedness and defense for the colony while supporting the Quakers who desired the right to tax the proprietor's landholdings in Pennsylvania.\

  Franklin was convinced it was his destiny to lead men and gloried in his ability to deal with the political strife in his province. He neglected little that might advance his own position—doing favors, making friends, supporting other politi-

cians' measures, asking little and that seldom. He used the
right touch of deftness, subtlety, prudence, and, when necessary, boldness in forwarding his political career.

Troubles on the frontier presaged the opening of what is
known in European history as the Seven Years War and in
American history as the French and Indian War. This international conflict interrupted Franklin's provincial concerns,
creating questions and tensions with which Franklin could
not cope. In 1754 the English Board of Trade called a colonial congress to be held in New York. Franklin went as one
of the delegates to wrestle with the problem of how to deal in
a united way with common measures of defense. Talks were
held among the delegates and with chiefs of the Mohawk,
Cayuga, Seneca, Onandaga, Tuscarora, and Oneida nations.
These Indians were the members of the powerful Iroquois
confederation known as the League of Six Nations, founded
by the legendary Hiawatha.

On his way to the Albany Congress, Franklin drew up a
plan for intercolonial union "so far as might be necessary for
defense and other important general purposes." During the
conference, Franklin's plan and several others were referred
to a study committee. Ben's concept was reported from committee, debated on the floor, adopted by the delegates, and referred to the colonies and the Board of Trade for adoption. It
was not put into force. As Ben later recalled, "Its fate was
singular. The Assemblies did not adopt it, as they all thought
there was too much *prerogative* in it; and in England it was
judged too much of the *democratic.*" [8]

Back in Philadelphia, Franklin was caught up in the spirit
of the abortive campaign of the British general, Edward Brad-
dock. Like many others, he was surprised and demoralized to
discover that naked Indians could surprise and defeat a col-
umn of armed might. But legislative activities continued to
engross his attention.[9] Ben worked on paper money issues,
taxation of the Penn lands, defense, and Indian negotiations.
Such problems began to appear more and more insoluble and

Franklin sensed a weakening of his own leadership and support. He was by now an acknowledged leader of the legislature, and he worried that he might have to bear the burden of defeat if his programs and policies failed. What was best? Should he remain where he was and redouble efforts? Or were there other possibilities? Perhaps the old difficulties between the proprietor, the governor, and the Assembly held an answer for him. It would be difficult to be blamed in the Assembly for not finding solutions to problems if he were elsewhere. So Franklin finagled his own appointment as an agent for the colony to the official boards of Great Britain, to lobby there on behalf of the Pennsylvania Assembly. Appointed in 1756, Franklin did not reach London until 27 July 1757. His task was to secure royal permission for the colony to tax Penn lands.

Franklin had nothing personal against either the Penn proprietors or proprietorships in general. He hoped to become one himself on some future day. Franklin was still a young man when he first began to act on his interest in land. By 1753 he was involved in a project to buy land from the Six Nations. It was then that, angered by premature publicity on the matter, he set forth a rule he long followed: "Great Designs should not be made publick till they are ripe for Execution, lest Obstacles are thrown in the Way; and small Obstacles are sufficient to overset young Schemes, which when grown strong would force their Way over greater." [10] Nothing came of this first land effort but the next year he wrote a "Plan for Settling Two Western Colonies." [11] In 1756 Franklin wrote the evangelist George Whitefield of his dream of one day becoming a proprietor of a colony in the Ohio Valley region.[12] Then he was in England and his thoughts of the American West had to be kept in abeyance.

The office of colonial agent had become increasingly important in the eighteenth century.[13] Guided by instructions from home, an agent represented his colony's interests before the proper boards and agencies of the mother country: on

trade, Indian affairs, and legal matters. He was to promote in
every way possible the well-being of the colony that hired
him. As colonial agent for Pennsylvania, Ben passed on information from home to the British government and sent news
from the central government back to Pennsylvania. He was,
in effect, a personalized clearing house. He served, with only
a short break, as an agent for many years. Pennsylvania first
appointed him in 1757 and again in 1764. Georgia commissioned him in 1768, New Jersey in 1769, and Massachusetts'
lower house of legislature sought him out in 1770. To carry
out these duties, and because he was having the time of his
life, Franklin stayed in England from 1757 to 1762 and from
1764 to 1775. As spokesman for so many colonies, Ben came
to be regarded as the most important American in the mother
country.

Ben's actions, his striving for the main chance, soon caused
some observers on both sides of the water to reappraise him.
After a series of political quarrels with Franklin, John Dickinson of Pennsylvania concluded that Ben was erecting his career on the "Convulsions of his Country." [14] In England suspicion so mounted that Franklin was sneeringly called
(behind his back) "Old Treachery of Craven Street." [15]

Privately, Franklin enjoyed life in London. At home he always had lived frugally, at least in public, following (as a
proper bourgeois should) his own *Poor Richard* maxims. In
the imperial city, however, he chose to live more lavishly.
Money was no problem, for Franklin's income was around
£2,000 yearly. One of his first purchases after arriving in
London was the hiring of a handsome coach in which to ride
in splendor. He frequented the coffee houses and taverns, met
both highborn and low, made lasting friendships with men of
many kinds, and wrote for the public papers.

Franklin's dreams of land came again to the forefront in
1760 when he collaborated with Richard Jackson to write a
famous tract, *The Interest of Great Britain Considered with Regard to her Colonies and the Acquisitions of Canada and Guadel-*

oupe. The Seven Years War was winding down. Duquesne and Louisbourg had fallen to the British in 1758; Wolfe had captured Quebec in September 1759 and the French surrendered the rest of Canada in 1760; Guadeloupe, in the French West Indies, was also in British hands. Now an argument raged in England. Should the government, at the end of the war, retain the extremely valuable, but tiny, island of Guadeloupe or the large land mass and unexplored wilderness of Canada? In the tract, Franklin argued for the retention of Canada. Nor, he believed, should government be concerned that such removal of the French threat to the colonies in America might lead to the loosening of imperial bonds. A future union of those provinces "is not merely improbable; it is impossible; and if the union of the whole is impossible, the attempt of a part must be madness: as those colonies that did not join the rebellion, would join the mother country in suppressing it." [16] Although Franklin often is praised for his prescient looks at the future, this particular piece of prophecy indicates that he had not yet achieved the rank of an Elijah. Not on the mark on his predictions, Franklin still believed in later years that his tract had influenced the ministry to retain Canada.

By September 1759 Ben got government approval of the task which had brought him to London. On 2 September the Pennsylvania Assembly was authorized by the Crown to tax proprietary lands.[17] Nothing now kept Franklin in the mother country save his enjoyment of living there. Life in England was pleasant, more exciting and more cosmopolitan than in America. He was independently wealthy and there was much upon which he could spend his money in the empire's capital city. His home with the personable and attractive widow, Mrs. Margaret Stevenson, was comfortable, and he spent his leisure with Margaret and her daughter Polly. The thought of going back to rude, provincial Pennsylvania distressed him. Time after time he postponed his departure.

An unusual event occurred at this time. Ben's son William, himself illegitimate, brought home to his father in 1760 his own bastard child, born while William was enrolled at the Middle Temple for the study of law. Ben wanted to keep the little boy, named William Temple, and so the child was ensconced in the Stevenson home to be cared for there. Shortly thereafter, at Ben's instigation, his son was named governor for New Jersey by Lord Bute, head of the government.

At last there were no more excuses left to avoid going home. By 24 August 1762, Ben took ship on the *Carolina* for the return voyage to America.

Back in Philadelphia, Franklin resumed his place in Pennsylvania politics. His zeal for the Assembly did not usurp all his time. Touring the colonies to visit various post offices, Franklin met a charming young lady, Catherine Ray, of New York. He courted her extensively and futilely for a time before returning to his wife Debby.

₰ On 24 March 1764 the Pennsylvania Assembly, thanks to extensive logrolling by Franklin, passed a resolution calling for its government to be made a royal one. While still in England, Franklin had advised one of the political leaders of the Assembly on how to proceed. His words were carefully chosen; they suggested drastic action without seeming to do so; Franklin wrote in such a way that he could disclaim any responsibility should what he desired actually occur. "Tumults and Insurrections, that might prove the Proprietary Government insufficient to preserve Order, or show the People to be ungovernable, would do the Business immediately; but such I hope will never happen." [18] Now the Assembly had acted upon Franklin's advice. This change in charter was an extremely important matter and naturally became a key issue in the colony's elections of 1764. Franklin headed the pro-change group while John Dickinson spoke on behalf of the proprietorship. When the last ballot had been counted, Franklin learned to his dismay that he had lost his seat in the

Assembly. Even with his prestige damaged, Franklin still retained a degree of political influence. He lobbied with his
friends in the legislature to appoint him once more as a colonial agent. They did so. Franklin packed his bags and left
Philadelphia for England, 7 November 1764, arriving about a
month later.[19]

If Franklin hoped to accomplish a change in Pennsylvania's
charter while in England, he was destined to fail. New colonial policies of far greater importance pushed thoughts of the
charter out of the minds of Pennsylvanians. Even the former
supporters of the charter were now coming to fear that a
change in the colony's charter would simply increase British
power of which they were already becoming suspicious. The
English government, reasonably satisfied with the Penn proprietors and not wanting to further upset colonials, backed
away from such involvement. During the spring of 1766,
Franklin was rebuked by one Ministry spokesman for even
asking about progress on his petition for charter change. He
was ordered not to "attempt any further proceedings on
them, For if you did, you might depend, you wou'd meet
with such an Answer as wou'd be neither agreeable to you or
to the Assembly you represented." [20] Franklin reacted with
alacrity and there is no evidence that he supported the measure further. Besides, he was busy with other things.

Ben was again entangling himself in the snarl of American
land speculation. While in America in 1764 Franklin had
talked with John Baynton and Thomas and Samuel Wharton,
operators of the mercantile and trading firm Baynton and
Wharton, about the possibilities of successful speculation.
These men were Quakers, businessmen, speculators, and old
friends. The year before, speculation had been halted by
royal order. On 7 October 1763, George III issued a Proclamation which stated that, "untill our further Pleasure be
known," it was to be unlawful "to grant Warrants of Survey,
or pass Patents . . . upon any Lands whatever, which . . .

are reserved to the said Indians." Settlement west of a line
running from mountain top to mountain top along the Allegheny-Appalachian chain was henceforth forbidden.[21]

Baynton and Wharton was one of the earliest firms to spe-
cialize in the western trade. It established contracts with various traders as far inland as the Illinois River. Of the brothers
Wharton, the junior partners in the company, Sam was the
most single-minded of the two, spending most of his energies
(and money) for many years in efforts to capitalize on land
speculation.

In the course of their business dealings, Baynton and the
Whartons had discovered two large unowned tracts of land
in the province of Quebec. During a conversation with
Franklin they suggested to him that he join with them in purchasing the tracts for future development. Ben was only too
happy to do so.[22]

At about the same time, Richard Jackson, Franklin's old
collaborator on the Canada tract and resident colonial agent
for Pennsylvania, sought to involve Ben in a similar endeavor
in Nova Scotia. Franklin was pleased with the prospects of
northern speculation as an interim effort while the proclamation of 1763 barred the way west. He wrote Jackson that "I
have some Money to spare, I know not how better to dispose
of it for the Advantage of my Children." [23] This response
was and would continue to be characteristic of Franklin's eu-
phemistic references to his speculation throughout his career.
Committed to speculation and anxious to grow even
wealthier, he consistently couched his comments in altruistic
and dynastic language.

Acting on Jackson's suggestion, Franklin acquired over
200,000 acres in Nova Scotia. It was not as profitable as he
had hoped; Ben later complained that the weather was so cold
no one wanted to move there.[24] The same year, Ben joined
forces with another avid speculator, Colonel (later General)
Henry Bouquet of the British army. Bouquet had reveries of
future rewards when "you and I settle our Colony upon the

Scioto." [25] These dreams proved ephemeral; their plans did not materialize.

Although the projects in Nova Scotia did not work out well, the company of Baynton and Wharton in America was developing a project in the American West which quickened Ben's interest as a real possibility for profit. Both 1754 and 1763 had been hard years for Indian traders. Outbreaks of Indian wars forced many traders to abandon their goods and flee for protection to settled areas, and each time this happened the victims petitioned the home government for restitution for their lost goods and labors.[26] When peace was settled after Pontiac's Rebellion in 1763, the traders learned that no restitution was likely to be forthcoming. At this point, sensing possible future profit, some mercantile firms—including Baynton and Wharton—offered to buy up restitution claims from those furmen willing to sell them for a few pence on the shilling. Although this was only a pittance for their actual losses, the sum offered was real and immediate. Many men transferred their claims, and in the fall of 1763 the speculators who bought up these claims formed themselves into the "Suff'ring Traders" Company.

George Croghan—Irish immigrant, trader, furman, land speculator, Deputy Indian Agent for the Superintendent of the Northern Department of Indian Affairs since 1756, and member of the "Suff'ring Traders" Company—was selected by Samuel Wharton as agent for the speculators. He went to England and lobbied without success on behalf of claim compensations. Upon his return to America, the claim speculators decided to shelve the "Suff'ring Traders" Company for the time being. Croghan encouraged Baynton and Wharton to become government contractors and to enter the Indian trade where they could make "200 p'ct profitt." [27] For various reasons the firm failed to do well in this venture, nearly went bankrupt, and looked for a way to recoup its losses. They turned again to land speculation.

Croghan laid the base for the success of a new effort in

speculation when he secured the approval and participation of his superior, Sir William Johnson. Johnson had come to America in 1738 and had settled on the estate of his uncle in New York's Mohawk Valley. Johnson came to learn Indian ways, lived with them for a time, and married a squaw. He fought as commander of the colonial expeditionary force sent against Crown Point in 1755. Later he was rewarded with a baronetcy and in 1756 became Superintendent for Indian Affairs for the Northern District. In this office, he supervised forty-two tribes of Indians living in Nova Scotia, Canada, New England and the middle colonies, the Far West, and the Illinois country. As aides, he hired three deputy Indian agents of whom Croghan was one. His aide's persuasive words fanned Johnson's interest in land, overcoming his general objections to westward migration. That such settlements displaced Indians he was charged to safeguard was evidently of little importance to him.

Johnson called a meeting of Delaware and Shawnee sachems and convinced them to give up a portion of their lands in order to compensate the traders who had suffered losses during the earlier fighting. When told what Johnson had done, General Thomas Gage, commander-in-chief of British military forces in North America, forwarded a recommendation to Britain that Johnson's scheme be implemented. On 29 March 1766 some of those who had been members of the now defunct "Suff'ring Traders" Company met in Philadelphia and formed a new land firm to take advantage of the land Johnson had weaseled out of the Indians. With Samuel Wharton heading the meeting, the men made Franklin a partner, without expense on his part, because he was "forever with one Member of Parliament or other." He was also given a few shares of stock to give to influential Englishmen who might be able to help the project.

The speculators planned to ask for a complete new colony to be established between the Illinois and Mississippi rivers.[28] If successful, these men would become proprietors rather than simply sellers of real estate. As such they would continue to receive the various benefits due proprietors. They would gain social status and they would have political power. Franklin was thoroughly pleased when he learned what had happened. "I like the project of a colony," he wrote to his partners, "and will forward it to my utmost here." [29] Knowing that their methods might not be looked upon with favor in all quarters, the partners kept the names of some of their members secret: Ben Franklin, his son William Franklin, and Sir William Johnson all were silent participants.[30] Recommendations made by these officials carried more value so long as British officeholders believed them to be disinterested spectators rather than avaricious participants.

The partners made the most of their project. They claimed that many scarce and desirable products could be had from the region. If Britain settled a government there it would go far toward counteracting whatever French influence remained in the region, calming the actions of rancorous settlers toward one another, and smoothing the path of Indian traders. Further, they claimed, the area could produce almost anything: medical drugs, saltpeter, iron, potash, cotton, copper, flax, silk, furs and skins, hemp, and tobacco.[31]

Of course Franklin's cohorts could not know as a certainty that these products would come from the American West. But they did know that such a list would be received in Whitehall with great favor, helping to implement the chartering of a new colony. When such a province had been settled there would be time enough to find out what products could really be harvested.

At this time the big government buildings at Whitehall were witnessing a constant flux of officeholders. Entire ministries had appeared and passed into history in quick succession. Bute, Grenville, Rockingham, and Pitt (now elevated to the peerage as Lord Chatham) all had stood at government's helm since George III had acceded to the throne in 1760. Administration heads hardly had time to become acquainted

with some of the problems facing them before they found
themselves out of office. Personnel changes were also the rule
for other Cabinet offices. Lord Shelburne, for example, was
President of the Board of Trade for a few months in 1763
under Grenville. He reappeared as Secretary of State for the
Southern Department in 1766 in the Chatham administration. Leaving office in 1768, he bided his time until 1782
when he joined the Rockingham ministry. For nearly seven
months in 1782 and 1783 he was head of the government.

When Shelburne, who was extremely interested in American affairs, became one of the secretaries of state under Chatham, Franklin and his speculator friends found in him a sympathetic listener to their problems. They worked through him
whenever possible and put one of his aides, Lauchlin Macleane, in their pocket through judicious bribes. For a promise
of £400 sterling annually, Macleane promptly recommended
"a settlement at the Illinois." [32] Securing Shelburne as an ally
was an important step inasmuch as any plan for a new American colony eventually would have to be authorized by the
Secretary of State for the Southern Department.

Thomas Gage, who had recently approved Sir William
Johnson's land deal with the Indians, had changed his mind.
He sent Shelburne full reports in which he lamented "abuses
in the Grants of Lands," "fraudulent purchases," "usurpa-
tions," and how Indians were "defrauded of their Lands." [33]
Franklin countered Gage's arguments so well that he convinced Shelburne that he was one of the "best authorities for
any thing that related to America." [34] Franklin might well
have known conditions around Philadelphia or London, but
there is little evidence to indicate that he was an expert on the
North American West.

While Shelburne may have favored aiding the speculators
in their efforts, his successor at the Board of Trade, Lord
Hillsborough, looked with trepidation upon settling a new,
interior colony. He worried that such a venture might drain

needed population from Ireland and could diminish American exports to England. Far from the settled areas in America it would make imperial rule more difficult to administer. Even with Shelburne's approval, Franklin and his partners had other barriers to cross. Hillsborough and the Board of Trade would next review the plan. Should it pass that agency, and Hillsborough hoped it would not, it first would be surveyed by the Treasury, and then would be reviewed by the solicitor general and attorney general of England. After that it would be put on the calendar of the Privy Council for their consideration. Should it clear through all these stages, the King-in-Council would create a patent granting the colony to Franklin and his cohorts.

Franklin was not at all happy with the progress of the scheme. By early 1767 little really had been accomplished. He helped to work out new approaches that might jolt the British official boards into acting more quickly. The plan which he adopted with great hope was actually conceived by Samuel Wharton in America. Letters would soon arrive from America for Ben, Lord Shelburne, and Lord Hillsborough. They would tell a story of great unrest in the West. The Indians there had promised to grant their lands to the speculators and, because of bureaucratic slowness, they had not yet been allowed to do so. Now they were angry. They threatened to go on the warpath unless the way was opened for them to give away some of their best hunting lands.

Franklin received one letter which read, in part, "it will be but a very short Time, before we are engaged in a most bloody and expensive War with all the Western Nations." [35] Sam Wharton wrote of "the absolute necessity, of the King's Ministers giving Directions to Sir William Johnson for the purchase of the Boundary." Wharton insisted that "Future Peace . . . depends on [this] being expeditiously transmitted." The Six Nations, Mingoes, Delawares, Shawnees, and other tribes were all readying themselves for war. We would soon see, wrote Wharton, "all the Horrors of an immediate Indian War." [36] These letters were shown by Franklin to those he thought might be persuaded by them.

Many prominent Americans sent similar letters: William Franklin, Sir William Johnson, George Croghan, John Baynton, Thomas Wharton, and William Trent. Even the Pennsylvania Assembly was spooked into sending a petition for action to England. Shelburne was convinced. He gave the matter his approval and turned it over to the Board of Trade. On 23 December 1767 the Board recommended creation of a new line extending from Lake Erie to the Mississippi, replacing the old line of 1763. This would open vast areas for settlement and would "prevent the fatal consequences of an Indian war that seems at present to threaten the Middle Colonies." [37] The Board of Trade had been convinced by Franklin and the others. No war was pending. No Indians were painting their faces and reaching for tomahawks. The letter campaign had, however, accomplished its purpose. The settlement line separating Indian lands from white areas would be moved. Now a new colony could be planted. The tactics used might not have been aboveboard, but they were effective.

Ben wrote to his son of the role he had played in the affair. "I pressed the importance of dispatching orders immediately to Sir William to complete the affair." [38] It looked as if Ben's efforts had been fruitful ones and he boasted that he would soon be a "*Considerable* Proprietor of Terra Firma." [39]

At about this time, the British government created a new office: Secretary of State for the American Department. Its first head was the Earl of Hillsborough. The Earl's power over American affairs was substantial, for he was not only chief of the new bureau but retained the presidency of the Board of Trade. He ordered a new boundary line to be negotiated with the Indians. The new line would open the area around Pittsburgh for settlement. This gave the speculators of the Illinois Company the opening for which they had been looking since they realized that the earlier target at which they had aimed was too distant for convenience; settlement would be much easier near Pittsburgh. The partners also believed that getting grants directly from the Indians at an upcoming Indian conference would be a far easier task than appealing through the bureaucratic channels of the government for a Crown-authorized settlement.

At this point the speculators sought to cash in their claims for trading damages by a grant of Indian lands in what was known as the Indiana country. They reactivated the earlier name of "Suff'ring Traders" and quietly laid the name of the Illinois Company to rest. As early as May 1768, long before the Indian conference at which they hoped to gain their prize, they began to advertise lands for sale. Some such ads appeared in Franklin's old paper, the *Pennsylvania Gazette*.

News traveled slowly. Franklin did not hear for some time of this new plan of his American associates. Samuel Wharton told Franklin's son to "urge your Father, rather to drop the Illenoise affair, Than miss succeeding in the Restitution; for be assured, the Latter would be an immediate very great Thing & is of infinitely more consequence to . . . us, than the former." [40]

Sir William Johnson told Wharton, Croghan, and William Trent, during the summer of 1768, that he was ready to deliberately violate Hillsborough's instructions. He would instead ratify an earlier line arranged in 1765 with the Indians. Hillsborough had been specific on the point that no changes from the line sought by the Ministry would be allowed, but this would still leave some choice lands in Indian hands, and this the speculators thought would be an ugly situation.

The Indian conference was held at Fort Stanwix, New York, in November 1768. After it was over, so many private deals had been made by William Franklin, Wharton, and Croghan for the Indiana Company that Johnson had to admit that "I know of no good place [left] vested in the Crown." [41] Wharton wrote with glee to Franklin of the recent develop-

ments. He enclosed a copy of the Deed of Cession to the
King and the Indian deed to the Indiana Company. He had
seen to it that the wording was iron-clad. If the private deal
with the Indians were not approved, the cession of lands to
the Crown would be invalidated and title for the whole
would revert to the Indians. Sadly, the lands ceded were the
hunting territory of the Delawares, Shawnees, and Cherokees
but it had been the Six Nations of the Iroquois who had tra-
ded them away.

Wharton indicated to Franklin that if there were any delay
in ratification by the Crown, the Indians might resent being
treated as children, not capable of being allowed to do what
they wanted, and might even begin war preparations again.
Here was a hint that the hoax of Indian war was to be used
for a second effort.[42]

Hillsborough was furious when he learned of Johnson's duplicity. He told General Gage: "I never had the least doubt
but that the accounts received from the Indian Country, of
the intrigues and machinations . . . were greatly exaggerated, and that many idle stories were propagated with the
view and for the purposes" of certain greedy men in America.[43] The Board of Trade shortly reprimanded Sir William
Johnson for his part in the treaty. Hillsborough wrote the Indian Superintendent that the "Grant of Land made to the Indian Traders" was so patently illegal that "His Majesty does
not think fit at present to confirm those Grants." [44]

Aware that the group's plan was being uncovered for the
sham that it was, Samuel Wharton realized that the time had
come for an all-out effort to save his company's investment in
time and capital. He packed his bags and left to join Ben
Franklin in England. The two men would defend jointly
their case for western speculation.

CHAPTER THREE

———◆◆◆———

This Old Rotten State

Benjamin Franklin was an extremely troubled man by the time Samuel Wharton arrived in England early in 1769. The government intercepted his letters and copied them. Worried about what might be revealed to these censors, Ben often sent messages by courier rather than through the mails. Occasional hints came to him that he should either resign his position as Deputy Assistant Postmaster General or go to America where he could actually perform his duties. At such times he recalled the policy he had followed in Pennsylvania when his job as clerk of the Assembly had been threatened. He would "never ask for [jobs], and never refuse them, [and] never resign them." [1] This may have soothed his feelings but did not provide solutions for his difficulties. In letters to America, Franklin urged the colonists to continue steadfastly to support nonimportation and nonconsumption in the continuing fight for relief from the Townshend duties. This advice infuriated the British government. At the same time, as a speculator, Ben had to ask the Ministry for favors which it was increasingly reluctant to grant. More and more often, Ben learned that others called him "Dr. Doubleface," "the old dotard," "Old Traitor Franklin," "The Judas of Craven Street." [2]

Franklin found ways to circumvent the growing suspicion and the increasing government surveillance of his actions. He used feigned handwriting in letters, sent messengers in roundabout ways. Letters intended for one man, Ben sent to another with instructions to forward them to the proper person. Ciphers were occasionally used. As another protective device, Franklin adopted a code name. "Moses." [3]

Over the years since 1765, Franklin had become acquainted with many prominent and influential Englishmen. With all hope for the Indiana Company gone, Franklin suggested to Wharton that they shift their focus once more. Practice had made this an easy prospect. They had first formed the "Suff'ring Traders" Company which had become the Illinois Company. Some of the original partners had been left behind and others enrolled. The Illinois Company had changed to the Indiana Company. Again, some who had been partners were dropped while new men had been enlisted for whatever influence they might be able to contribute. Now the Indiana Company carried a stigma. There was nothing sacred about the name or its membership. Why not, asked Franklin, organize a new firm using primarily English partners? It would be a completely new image and the government might not be so reluctant to grant lands to influential Englishmen as to powerless provincials. Wharton liked the idea, and they soon found the man to hear their latest venture. He was Thomas Walpole, nephew of the late head of government from 1721 to 1742, Sir Robert Walpole. Thomas was an important banker with status and connections that made him influential with those who counted in the British government. Walpole was enthusiastic about a plunge in American land speculation and eagerly brought the matter to the attention of prospective partners. His own brother Richard was one of those who joined the new land partnership.

The rolls of the Indiana Company were purged thoroughly. Only Franklin and Wharton remained. With their two new partners, Thomas and Richard Walpole, they enlisted others in the next weeks and were for a time known only as the "Walpole Associates." They extended membership to some because of family ties. Most of those asked to become partners in the new enterprise, however, were sought out solely because they could wield power and prestige.

Samuel Wharton brought in his two brothers, Thomas and Charles. George Croghan and Sir William Johnson, from the old company, were given shares because they were needed. Ben saw to it that his son William and his long time associate Joseph Galloway got into the enterprise. William Trent got a share. With the rest, however, Franklin and Wharton were ruthless; many former associates who had sunk much time and money into earlier schemes were simply abandoned because they had too little potency with those whose favor was sought.

Franklin, Wharton, and Walpole surveyed each possible candidate carefully. Only after careful consideration did they act. Anthony Todd, the Secretary of the Post Office, and John Maddison, Todd's brother-in-law, were allowed to buy shares. So also was Robert Trevor, receiver-general of the Post, and John Foxcroft, joint Deputy Postmaster General for North America. Henry Dagge, the group's attorney, and his brother John bought into the enterprise. Thomas Pownall, ex-colonial governor and now a Member of Parliament, John Sargent, director of the Bank of England and a Member of Parliament for Midhurst, became members. Lord Hertford, born Francis Seymour Conway, came into the Walpole Associates. Hertford was Lord Chamberlain, a relative of Walpole's, a privy councillor, and an intimate of George III.

Ben Franklin brought in Charles Pratt, Lord Camden, who was Attorney General and later a Lord Chancellor. Richard Temple Grenville, or Earl Temple, a brother of

George Grenville, also joined, as did Granville Leveson-Gower or Earl Gower, the Marquis of Stafford. Another new member was William Henry Zuylestein, Lord Rochford. Gower served as Lord President of the Privy Council and Rochford for some time acted as Secretary of State for the Northern Department. The Earl of Grafton, now head of the government, was approached but did not participate. His private secretary, Richard Stonehewer, did. Thomas Bradshaw and Grey Cooper, secretaries of the Treasury, also joined the speculators.

The whole spectrum of English society and politics had been drawn from in setting up the Walpole Associates. Bankers, lawyers, jurists, commoners and lords, the rich and the respected, the famous and their relatives, supporters of the ministry and members of the opposition, those familiar with the colonies and others equally versed in the intricacies of the homeland, Grenvillites, Townshendites, Rockinghamites, the Post Office, the Privy Council, the Treasury—all were represented in this bewigged parade of English land speculators. In this way the Walpole Associates took shape in the spring of 1769. What could go wrong this time?

It was time for a vacation, his second in France. When Franklin had returned from his first visit to that land in 1767, François-Marie Durand, the French chargé d'affaires, invited him to return whenever he could. In July 1769 that time came. Old Ben Franklin, it seems, felt at home in France. He was welcomed by those he had met in 1767. He met again with his physiocrat friends and was entertained at dinners by Du Pont, Barbeu-Dubourg, and the compte de Maurepas and his wife. What they talked of, we do not know. We have only the vague hint that many conversations centered on politics and on France's hopes of severing the American colonies from England. Franklin revealed this much when he wrote the Boston radical, Samuel Cooper, that "all Europe" sided with North America in its contest with Britain.[4]

According to some accounts, Franklin's trip was cut short

by a letter he supposedly received from his English friend Joseph Priestly. The Englishman purportedly wrote that "I strongly advise you to return at once to London. Letters, without signatures, have been printed which do you harm in the public, and your stay in Paris is commented as a visit to the enemy." [5] Franklin did not want trouble at this point, with the Walpole Associates on the brink of success, and so he left France—not to return until the last month of 1776 when he would come as an agent for the Continental Congress.

When he got back to England Ben learned that the past 24 July, Wharton, acting for the company, had petitioned the Privy Council for 2,400,000 acres of land within the area of the Fort Stanwix grant. For that grant, the British Treasury had spent £10,460, 7s 3d, sterling. The Walpole Associates promised to pay that sum in return for the land they sought. The Privy Council in August turned the matter over to the Committee of Council for Plantation Affairs. It reached the Board of Trade in mid-November.

The Board of Trade put the petition on its agenda for early December. When the item was brought up for discussion, a committee of the Walpole Associates—Franklin, Thomas Walpole, Thomas Pownall, Samuel Wharton, and John Sargent—was present. The speculators were dumfounded to hear the *bête noire* of new colonies, Lord Hillsborough, encourage them to increase their request to twenty million acres, allowing for the establishment of a new colony. The earl even said he felt the Treasury would look favorably upon such a change and that he would himself present it to them.

There is no evidence that Hillsborough had changed his mind. Perhaps he believed that if the request were enlarged, the cost also would be proportionately raised, beyond what the men could afford to spend. What is more, by handling the case himself he could do it irreparable harm by the way he presented it. What he perhaps did not know was the extent to which the Treasury was ridden with Walpole Associates. This had been kept relatively quiet.

Franklin presided at the next meeting of the speculators, held on a Wednesday evening, 27 December 1769. The agenda consisted solely of how to best take advantage of this new opportunity. First the men decided to drop the name they had been using and to call themselves the Grand Ohio Company. It sounded better and was more in keeping with the land for which they aimed. Secondly, they approved the earl's suggestion of asking for the much larger tract of land. Now they might soon have a whole colony in their hands. Visions of empire, power, and great wealth flooded their imaginations as they gloried in all the possibilities.

Hillsborough did indeed forward their request to the Treasury. It took Thomas Bradshaw and Grey Cooper at the Treasury just eight days to report favorably on the plan that would make them wealthier than they had ever hoped. When he learned of the decision, Hillsborough realized his mistake and began a tireless struggle to get the decision reversed. In late April 1770 the Treasury retreated under the onslaught of Hillsborough's anger at their precipitate judgment. Bradshaw and Cooper had to tell their partners that their earlier report dealt only with such matters as the purchase price and qui-trents. It was not a recommendation that the grant should actually be made. So on 8 May 1770 Franklin and the others again had to petition the Privy Council for the land grant. On the 25th the Council referred the issue to the Board of Trade.

While waiting for the Board of Trade to act, Franklin and Wharton turned their attention to possible competitors for the grant lands who might spoil their scheme. Their chief rival was the Ohio Company of Virginia. It sought lands in the same area and based its stake on old charter grants of Virginia. Franklin got rid of this danger by extending membership in his own company to George Mercer, the London agent for the Ohio Company of Virginia. No one in the imperial city would now press the Old Dominion's land claims.

Another competitive firm was the Mississippi Company. Arthur Lee, a young doctor who had studied medicine at Edinburgh and one of the Virginia Lees, was its agent. Politically ambitious and radically inclined, Lee wrote polemic pieces defending American interests for the London newspapers under the signature of *Junius Americanus.* He was an intimate of the English radical John Wilkes, and Arthur and his brother William were often guests at Wilkes' home, Mansion House, the residence of the Lord Mayor of London. Fiery, often suspicious of the motives of others, Arthur Lee was totally dedicated to the cause of America and the vindication of its rights in the current struggle with Britain.

The Mississippi Company, which Lee represented, had been organized in 1763 by the Lees, Washingtons, Fitzhughs, and others to exploit the American northwest. It originally had sought five million acres at the juncture of the Ohio and Mississippi rivers. Thwarted in this, it redirected itself toward a 2.5 million-acre grant at the confluence of the Ohio and Allegheny, near present-day Pittsburgh. Then Arthur Lee learned of the Grand Ohio Company and its petition for twenty million acres embracing all of present-day West Virginia, the eastern half of Kentucky, and parts of Ohio and western Pennsylvania. It covered all the area hoped for by the Mississippi Company.

Lee admired Franklin's attitudes toward the imperial conflict and his private advice to America. He wrote later of Ben's "wisdom," his "firmness," his "integrity," which "must endear him" to those in the colonies who struggled on behalf of America.[6] Lee also knew the other side of Franklin's character, his strong desire for advancement, his desire for profits, his willingness to bend principles in order to advance his speculative goals. Instructed by the Mississippi Company to block the Grand Ohio application in any way he could, Lee found that Franklin's cabal thwarted him at every turn. Lee described the Walpole Associates in a letter to his brother in America. "Take my word for it," Lee wrote, "there are not a set of greater knaves under the sun. As their Scheme originated in a most villainous fraud, it has been carried on in expence [and] corruption." [7]

Objections by Lee and curious letters from the Ohio Company of Virginia inquiring about the faithlessness of George Mercer gave Hillsborough the opening he needed. He informed Benjamin Franklin that before any grant could be made, competing claims would have to be studied carefully.

Franklin now told Wharton that there was no legal justification for waiting further for the slow bureaucracy of Britain to finish its deliberations. The Six Nations had an "inherent and undoubted" right to do what it had done. "He would not seek for any other title" but that of the Indians. They should go ahead to "sell or settle" the lands of their grant. If any believed they should "pay" England for the lands, it should be by token only, perhaps "a Beaver Skin or small Quit Belt." [8] He was persuasive. By the middle of 1771 Wharton could write George Croghan that "Every man of Understanding and publick character . . . laughs at the Idea of coming to England to get a Title to lands in the Indian Country, when the rightful independant & natural Owners of those Lands, are living, and are willing to sell a Part of their Country." [9]

Slowly, however, judgment prevailed again. The partners decided to wait for governmental approval before beginning their great adventure. This was a hard decision for they had incurred heavy debts in their effort to get favorable action on their project. Trent was impoverished; Wharton had drawn on his mercantile firm for nearly £10,000; Franklin often complained of the interminable bills he had to pay and warned his family of straitened circumstances.

Money was not the only problem for the speculators anxiously awaiting a decision. To make matters worse, they had a rather severe falling out among themselves. At the bottom of the troubles this time was Franklin's multi-faceted career. The agent for Massachusetts, Dennys DeBerdt, had died and the House of Assembly there searched for a successor. Sam Adams favored Arthur Lee, whose radical stance harmonized well with Adams' own views. Some recent letters of Franklin's to Thomas Cushing and Samuel Cooper were read to the legislature and these influential men persuaded their colleagues to choose Franklin as agent. Lee had been hoping to be selected and was deeply disappointed when he learned that the job had gone to his rival and that he would have to be content with the position of sub-agent, or deputy, under Franklin.[10]

Ben had been chosen agent by the lower house of the legislature only; the upper house and the governor had not concurred in a joint commission. When Hillsborough learned of Ben's appointment he used this technical point to refuse to recognize Franklin as a properly credentialed agent and publicly scolded him for trying to serve without the governor's assent. Ben responded acidly in a way which helped him neither as a politician for the colonies nor as a speculator. Moreover he aggravated his already nervous partners, and both Wharton and William Strahan, Franklin's newspaper friend who had recently joined the land enterprise, grew angry with him over the incident. They complained of Franklin's growing ineffectiveness, as in Wharton's letter to Croghan in which he complained that Ben "has had no more Interest, Trouble or Concern on reflecting the Negociation about the Ohio Colony, than the smallest Farmer in Cumberland County." [11] For six months Franklin and Wharton were so angry they would not speak to each other.

Franklin's comments to friends in America became increasingly radicalized. Continued relations with England "seems like Mezentius' coupling and binding together the dead and the living." [12] Or, again, " 'tis time to submit to ab-

solute Power when we can no longer resist it, when those
who chuse rather to die in Defense of their Liberty . . . are
accordingly dead: when those who chuse to spend all their
Property in defending it . . . have spent it." [13]

The angrier Franklin's comments about the government
became, the less hope there seemed to be for speculative success. At one point he "proposed to Mr. Wharton to strike his
own name out of the list [of members] as it might be of prejudice to the undertaking." [14] The suggestion was vetoed for
the moment but the idea was held in abeyance should the
need for it arise in the future. Whatever else happened, the
grant must succeed. Before he left London that summer of
1771, Ben, Wharton, and Trent resurrected the old scheme
of a threatened Indian war and decided to use it again. Croghan was told that "Nothing will so soon make the great L—s
[Lords,] immediately agree, to the Policy of settling the
Country over the Allegany Mountains, as the Fear of a general Indian War. . . . I need not say much on these Points to
a Person of your Penetration. . . . act as you and I did about
the Boundary Line [in 1768] . . . for Mens Passions must be
alarmed and awakened." Croghan was to send petitions purportedly from frontiersmen asking a government to be settled
upon them because of current Indian unrest. The signatures
of westerners were not essential; anyone could sign, although
Croghan was to be careful not to allow too many names to be
signed in "*One* Mans Hand Writing." The trick was to make
this appear that it was a spontaneous movement by American
settlers. Croghan was to do absolutely nothing to provoke "a
Counter Petition from the Settlers, *against a new Government.*" [15] Croghan shortly began sending his handiwork to
England.

Thomas Gage, hearing of what was happening, wrote
Hillsborough that "it is not easy to get a true and perfect
Knowledge of those distant Countrys. Some are deceived by
Reports, believe too lightly without examining into Things

and . . . Others are warped by Interest or Inclination, and Magnify or detract, as it suits them." [16] Thus armed, Hillsborough continued his delaying tactics. By February 1772, Franklin wrote in a disgusted mood to Galloway to say that "The Ohio Grant is not yet compleated." [17]

Then in April 1772 came the long awaited report of the Board of Trade. It was unfavorable. Written largely by Hillsborough, the message to the Committee of Council stated that the Lords of Trade were unable to "recommend to your Lordships . . . to comply with . . . this Memorial, either as to the . . . separate government, or the making a grant of them to the Memorialists." [18] The Grand Ohio Company, however, had not been idle. Its membership sat in offices throughout Whitehall, and their influence was pervasive. In spite of this adverse report, Franklin and other leaders of the speculators were authorized to appear at a hearing of the Committee of Council in June. The Committee gave them an opportunity to rebut Hillsborough's report. Wharton was the chief spokesman although Franklin had worked out beforehand the approach he would take.

Wharton spoke of the need for government in the lawless area of the West. He reminded his listeners of the need to quell Indian unrest and brazenly announced that there were no valid competing claims from other speculators or companies. He insisted that the land was owned by the Six Nations who had granted it and were anxious for transaction to be completed. He handed to the waiting lords lists of products supposedly raised in that country, including the cultivation of silkworms. Wharton argued that this vast interior area was, contrary to report, indeed readily accessible both by land and water routes. When he had finished his presentation Wharton had spoken of many things but had barely touched upon the truth. The settlers were no more lawless in that region than elsewhere. There was little Indian unrest save that stirred up by speculators. There were valid competing claims for the region. The Six Nations had not owned the area. No one in his right mind would have tried to cultivate silkworms in those lands. And access to it at that time was extremely difficult by land and almost impossible by water.

The Privy Council heard all this, knew at least some of the objections, and approved the speculators' petition. By so doing, several of the lords, partners of Franklin, hoped to enrich themselves measurably when the grant finally received the King's patent. A disenchanted Hillsborough resigned the seals of office on 1 August 1772. Franklin was clearly gleeful. In a moment of candor, he wrote William Franklin that we "got rid of Lord Hillsborough." [19]

William Legge, Lord Dartmouth, became the new Secretary of State for the American Department. He notified Sir William Johnson to forward any necessary information so that the grant could be settled. Meanwhile, the speculators decided to name their proposed colony "Vandalia," in honor of George III's queen, Charlotte, whom some thought to be a descendant of the early Vandals.[20]

Within six months of taking office, Dartmouth was already worried about the suitability of the grant. He continually received warnings of dire consequences from the Indians should the colony be formed. Still he allowed matters to proceed. On 6 May 1773 the Board of Trade submitted a first draft of the new province's proposed charter. Thirteen days later they sent it to the Privy Council. By early July, the Councillors ordered the Attorney General and the Solicitor General, Edward Thurlow and Alexander Wedderburn, to complete the necessary papers.

The two law officers found some information lacking. The boundary was vague and there was insufficient data regarding quitrents and tenancy rights. After receiving more material on these points they continued their work. Anxious day followed day for Franklin and the others as their long-sought dream began to take shape. Then Benjamin Franklin committed one of the biggest *faux pas* of his career.

Although originally known to the radical group in Massachusetts only by reputation, Franklin's correspondence with them in the years since he had been appointed as agent for the lower house had given them a firm knowledge of his views. Each party found the political persuasions of the other contagious. Certainly Franklin did nothing to calm the ruffled feelings of those to whom he wrote. He advised that "there was never an instance of a colony so much and so long persecuted with vehement and malicious abuse." [21] In another letter Ben reflected: "I think one may clearly see, in the system of customs to be enacted in America by act of Parliament, the seeds sown of a total disunion of the two countries." Franklin was bluffing here, for no new tax levies were under consideration; he had simply made up the story out of whole cloth. It did, however, make exciting reading for those in the colonies, as did his words, "The bloody struggle will end in absolute slavery to America." [22]

The radical leaders in Massachusetts included such men as Sam Adams, Speaker of the House Thomas Cushing, and Samuel Cooper, a prominent preacher. Familiar with Franklin's radical rhetoric, they believed him to be a man who could be trusted and they shared with him their desire to rid the colony of its governor, Thomas Hutchinson. The governor, a descendant of the Anne Hutchinson who had been prominent in the early days of the colony's history, was a respected man who loved his native New England. As a royal governor, however, he believed it was his duty to administer the laws. The Massachusetts radicals sought a way to diminish or destroy his influence. Adams hoped to get hold of Hutchinson's letters. He had used letters of Frances Bernard, the governor's predecessor, to get rid of that man, and the tactic seemed worth trying again. Correspondence, after suitable editing, could be printed in the public newspapers with damaging effect.

The opportunity came in 1772 when Franklin gained possession of ten of Hutchinson's letters written between 1767 and 1769 when Hutchinson had been Chief Justice for the colony. On 2 December, Franklin sent them to Speaker Cushing with a cover message of his own. The most damaging statement Adams could wrench from Hutchinson's purloined letters were the words, "There must be an abridgement of what are called English liberties." Hutchinson was to complain for years that they had been taken completely out of context. Indeed, read as part of the whole they were not indicative of tyranny or oppression. They were, however, sufficiently suggestive of coercion for them to be printed in the colonial papers.

At about the same time, the Tea Act was being discussed in Parliament. By this act, designed to save the East India Company from bankruptcy, the Company was to be given the right to send tea directly to consignees throughout the empire rather than selling it to the highest bidder at auctions in England. In effect it would mean that tea drinkers in America would find their favorite bohea blend cheaper than it had been under the earlier arrangement. But the monopolistic flavor of the act, the stockpiles of smuggled tea which some American merchants had on hand, and the fact that Parliament had again passed a law directly affecting America caused revolutionary fires to flare once again. On the night of 16 December 1773, the Sons of Liberty in Boston, dressed like Mohawk Indians, worked through the dark hours to throw 342 chests of tea overboard from three ships. "If the late Proceedings dont alarm the Country nothing can do it," Governor Hutchinson complained irately. "There never was greater tyranny in Constantinople than has been lately in Boston." [23]

The Boston Tea Party had come at the worst possible time for Franklin. The plans to destroy Hutchinson through publication of the governor's letters had backfired. Franklin had hoped to keep quiet his part in sending the letters but people somehow whispered that Franklin was the culprit. Before his role was widely known in England, however, a man named

William Whately accused one John Temple of having stolen Hutchinson's letters from him. They fought an inconclusive duel on 11 December 1773 in Hyde Park and scheduled another confrontation for later. Only at that point did Franklin come forward to admit his own guilt.

When he learned what Franklin had done, Whately instituted a suit in chancery against the American. Then, while Franklin was trying to present a petition from Massachusetts calling for Hutchinson's removal, he was publicly scolded for his radicalism, for his role in the affair, and for a general lack of ethics. Alexander Wedderburn, Solicitor General for the Crown and one of the law officers completing the papers for the Vandalia colony, made the speech against Franklin. A few days later Ben was fired from his job as Deputy Assistant Postmaster General for the colonies. To make matters worse, the Council of Georgia concluded shortly thereafter that he had not properly represented them and failed to reappoint him as agent.[24]

Wedderburn and Thurlow, the law officers, announced that they could not complete the application for Vandalia while Franklin was a part of it, for he was "unworthy the Favors of the Crown." [25] Franklin believed he might shortly be arrested. "Hints were given me that there was some thoughts of apprehending me, seizing my papers, and sending me to Newgate." [26] Perhaps nothing could be done to forestall arrest, but at least Franklin could do something to safeguard the nearly completed Vandalia enterprise. Remembering that he had offered before to resign his partnership in the Grand Ohio Company, Franklin figured that this was the time when such a ploy might be extremely useful. In concert with Thomas Walpole, Ben composed a public letter of resignation, dated 12 January 1774; at the same time a private agreement drawn up by Franklin and Walpole made certain that Ben would actually retain his shares of stock. He simply became another of the many undercover members. This cleared the way for the government to proceed with the grant inasmuch as its major objection was now seemingly removed.

In spite of Franklin's resignation, Thurlow and Wedderburn refused to complete the papers for the Vandalia grant.
The delays infuriated Ben. He wrote Cushing that "It may
be supposed that I am very angry on this occasion." [27] Franklin may have been angry, but not remorseful. He maintained
that sending Hutchinson's letters had been "one of the best
actions of my life." [28] In still further efforts to gain revenge,
and ruin Hutchinson, he continued to look for other letters of
the governor which he could use. In June 1774 he wrote
Cushing that "At present, I only send copies of two more letters of Mr. Hutchinson's." [29]

It was obvious to the investors in the Grand Ohio Company that gaining Vandalia depended on their maintaining a
low profile until the grant was completed. In this situation
Franklin's inability to hold his temper, his continuing efforts
to malign Hutchinson, and his angry letters which were certain to be read by the censors in the Post all boded ill for him
personally. Neither his proprietary hopes nor his relations
with his partners was improved by his conduct at this
time.

The British Ministry worsened matters for the speculators
in the early part of 1774 when it acted against the rebellious
province of Massachusetts. Its moves aroused the emotions
and fears of nearly all America. The bills came from the parliamentary hopper like the slow roll of military drums: 30
March, the Boston Port Bill; 20 May, the Administration of
Justice Act and the Massachusetts Government Act; 22 May,
the Quebec Act; 2 June, the Quartering Act. Britons understood the laws to be proper attempts to secure the colonists'
obedience to both law and justice, but the Americans believed
that by those measures Parliament sought to utterly abase
them.

Franklin's coterie of speculators saw the Quebec Act as the
most dangerous bill in the lot. They still harbored hopes that
Vandalia could somehow be rescued from oblivion, Wharton

looking forward to "many chearful and pleasurable Hours"
when he might "ride, or strole on the verdant Banks of
Ohio." He longed for the time when he might look out over
vast acres of his lands while sipping "Coffee or Tea," as
"painful Twinges of the Gout,—will, I fear, hereafter forbid
. . . quaffing the generous Grape." But such hopes were
threatened by the passage of the Quebec Act, as a result of
which, Wharton wrote, "Niagar, Detroit, Mihilimachinaik,
the Illinois, Wabash &c—will be governed by Justices of the
Peace, appointed by the *Governor of Quebeck.*" [30] Thus if the
speculators were to secure a Crown grant for the lands, they
would have to begin the process of petitions and writs and ap-
pearances at official meetings all over again. The prospect
was not a happy one. With all the built-in influence exercised
by the partners of the Grand Ohio Company, it had taken
them five long years to shepherd their request through
officialdom's maze, and the patent was not yet drawn.

A mixture of reasons brought together the First Continental Congress to protest the late acts of England. On 5 September 1774, twelve of the thirteen colonies—Georgia alone
not present—met in Philadelphia to discuss common measures of redress. Franklin, who was definitely not a calming
influence, poured coals on a burning fire, and part of the reason for his actions might well have been the consideration
that separation from the mother country might well be the
key to the development of the Vandalia tract. Unwilling to
suggest pacifying measures, Franklin, calmly and dispassion-
ately, told his allies to fight, if necessary, for their rights. He
wrote Cushing that the colonists might soon "be worse than
Eastern slaves." [31] When Joseph Galloway, Franklin's friend
and political ally of many decades, introduced a resolution intended to heal the rupture between mother country and colony while still protecting America's interests, Franklin voiced
firm objections. Ben wrote that "When I consider the ex-
tream Corruption prevalent among all orders of Men in this
old rotten State . . . I cannot but apprehend more Mischief

than Benefit from a closer Union. . . . Here Numberless and needless Places, enormous Salaries, Pensions, Perquisites, Bribes, groundless Quarrels, foolish Expenditures, false Accounts or no Accounts, Contracts and Jobbs, devour all Revenue, and produce continual Necessity in the Midst of natural Plenty. I apprehend, therefore, that to unite us intimately will only be to corrupt and poison us also. It seems like Mezentius's coupling and binding together the dead and the living." [32] The fervor of Franklin's animosity toward Britain at this point may well have had something to do with the needs of the Grand Ohio Company. Of course he did not mention the fact that Galloway's plan of union was almost a carbon copy of his own Albany plan submitted in 1754, but the connection did not escape Sam Wharton, who told his brother he hoped Galloway "did not present it to the Congress *as his Own;*—for it is . . . Dr. Franklin's Plan as presented to the Congress at Albany in 1754." [33] Joseph Galloway's plan was defeated.

Before adjournment, the First Congress adopted the revolutionary Suffolk Resolves, established the Continental Union, and drew up a list of grievances from which, by petition, they asked redress. It then dissolved, to meet a year later.

The speculators grew more agitated as the weeks passed and no patent was issued for them. Thomas Walpole produced a new memorial urging that the grant be made. Franklin told his son that the great "Event [was] still uncertain." [34] Thomas Wharton growled that "it is truly disagreeable to find with what determined obstinacy the crown lawyers have delayed their report on the papers establishing the Government of Vandalia." [35] George Croghan was more cutting in his remark that "Men laugh when they hear that Vandalia is likely to take place." [36] Then Sir William Johnson had the temerity to die during the summer of 1774. Franklin and his partners were at the point where they could resent even death if it might in any way further delay their plans. They waited restlessly as the months passed.

In America, 19 April 1775, the opening shot of the Revolutionary War was fired. For most men in the colonies that first volley meant a radical upheaval of their lives. To Franklin and his speculative partrers it was also an opportunity they had been looking for, a chance for their plans for Vandalia to bear fruit. William Trent left for his home in America, there to further the scheme in any way he could. Croghan was told that "No Time should . . . be lost" in purchasing more Indian lands.[37] Franklin knew that he should not stay longer in England and so at last sailed for America, 21 March 1775. Wharton and Walpole would continue to push in England for the completion of the patent while Franklin would explore new avenues of approach in the colonies with the Second Continental Congress.

Both Franklin and Wharton firmly believed the latest crisis between America and England might be used to further their speculations. Early in 1775, Sam had written his brother Thomas in Philadelphia to tell him of their latest plans. His words sounded apologetic for waiting so long. "I always proposed interesting you in this Purchase, And you may rest fully assured, I shall do it, in a handsome Manner." What he really meant was that the associates now needed more American partners. The Vandalia machine had started a major change of direction. What had begun as an effort by American speculators had become, in 1769, more English than colonial. With all the political clout its British partners had given it, the company still had not achieved its purpose six years later. Now in 1775, the original movers of the effort began a shift back to American preponderance. They knew how helpful British officials had been to the organization once they were made partners. The same methods might be used to sweeten the attitudes of Congressmen. Through carefully awarded partnerships, the Congress might well be persuaded to adopt proper resolutions, hastening the day when Franklin, Wharton, and the others could settle Vandalia.

Sam reminded Thomas: "Lord Camden & all the able Lawyers of this Country, are decided in their Opinions, That a Grant from the Native proprietors . . . vests the Grantees, with . . . [a] perfect Title, for the Lands granted." He told of the "very respectable Company [which was] determined to make a large Purchase for their Familys, On the Western Side of the Ohio." Sam suggested a way that this "respectable" firm might more quickly achieve its aim. "I would have you strengthen your Interest, as much as possible, with Mr [Patrick] Henry (Whose Sentiments . . . coincide with These, of the ablest Lawyers here) and the other principal Delagates from Virginia [chosen to the Second Continental Congress] As . . . It may be politick, to *interest* some of them in the Plan." [38]

Two problems could be solved in this way. The Mississippi Company would be caught off guard before it could act if Wharton could involve several Virginians in the Vandalia scheme. Secondly, Virginia delegates at the Congress could help steer the Ship Ohio around some of the rocky shoals it had foundered upon in England.

While Franklin was still at sea, journeying for home aboard the Pennsylvania *Packet*, Wharton wrote him a letter telling how he and his British fellows were trying to marshall forces in Parliament for repeal of the Quebec Act. At the same time he wanted Franklin to work on the delegates to the Congress. "I have obtained a very full and satisfactory Opinion . . . Upon the Title to our Indian Land." William Trent would contact Ben with this legal opinion and the two would do what they could to get "*concurrent* Opinions from Mr Galloway,—Mr Dickinson, and the Lawyers from Virginia etc, who may be at the Congress; as *this* is certainly, the favorable Crises, to establish Titles for Lands fairly obtained from the native Proprietors." [39]

What is especially interesting in this letter is its description of what were apparently Wharton's and Franklin's shared sentiments about the outbreak of war. For them it was "the favorable crisis." This is as good an indication of their attitudes and methods as any that could be cited: move quickly while the Congress was still forming; subvert any who could be approached; use a public crisis as a personal opportunity.

Wharton shared their plans with his father. "I see very little Prospect of true harmony being speedily, if Ever, restored between this Kingdom and America," he wrote, adding that "When the General Congress . . . are stating all the Rights of America . . . no Time ought to be lost . . . to procure a Resolve or Declaration (To be entered on the Minutes) of that Body, expressive of the Validity and Sufficiency of a Title to Lands, fairly bought of the Aborigines, And held under Grants (Only) from Them." To insure such a congressional decision, which "would forever render our Title a safe, and Popular One," Wharton thought they should "take into the Partnership, *Eight* of the Members of the Congress . . . and assign to each of Them, *half* a Share." This sort of move would create a "Thousand political Reasons" urging that body to move.[40]

Franklin liked the new thrust and thought it stood a good chance of success. Besides, it would not cost him anything. As George Morgan explained to Thomas Wharton, "our Agreement" had been that the old doctor was to pay no money for his shares of stock as "Your Influence was all we asked." [41]

Thomas Walpole, a faithful partner for years, joined in this new enterprise also, although he seems to have had some trepidation about doing so, for he wrote Ben Franklin that his service must be "kept *as private as possible* for should it be known" in England "it might rather prejudice us than do us any service." [42] Speculation seemed to be a great builder of flexible ethics: Walpole, to the disservice of his own nation, was seeking favors from the American Congress.

William Franklin saw Walpole's letter to his father and

warned Ben that it hardly seemed likely that the Englishman's role could be kept quiet. If it were discovered, the
reaction of the Congressmen might jeopardize the chances of
the rest. William told his father that he should be prepared
for such an eventuality. "You ought," he wrote, "to weigh
well the Consequences before you adopt the Measure." [43]
Ben thought the matter over and wrote out a memo to show
to other delegates to the Congress. His resolution called for
"all the lands in America claimed by the Crown" to be ap-
propriated. All individuals "who have purchased Lands from
the Crown, and have not yet paid the Purchase money, are
advised to withhold the Same; and all Persons wanting Lands
are advised to forbear Purchasing of the Crown." [44] The
more proper agency to approach now was the Congress.

CHAPTER FOUR

———•◆•———

Mr. Bancroft at Turnham Green

Benjamin Franklin returned from England to his home city of Philadelphia. The next day the Assembly chose him as a delegate to the Second Continental Congress. New doors had once more opened for him. Through his congressional position, he would be able to continue to push his personal projects while simultaneously serving the interests of his state and America. So long as there was no conflict between his selfish goals and his patriotism, Ben was free to pursue both with an appropriate highmindedness. But as far as he was concerned, politics were one thing, profits another. Thus Franklin wrote out the following letter to his partner in land speculation, William Strahan:

Philadelphia, July 5, 1775
Mr. Strahan: You are a Member of Parliament, and one of that Majority which has doomed my Country to Destruction.—You have begun to burn our Towns, and murder our People.—Look upon your Hands! They are stained with the Blood of your Relations!—You and I were long Friends:—You are now my Enemy,—and I am

Yours,—
B. Franklin.

The sentiments were admirably patriotic, but they didn't keep Ben from plunging into other land ventures with Strahan. Indeed, the letter had been created purely as a propaganda device: although it was published both in America and Europe it was never sent, and Franklin probably did not intend for it to be sent when he wrote it.

The Congress may not have been ready for independence, but the days of every delegate were still filled with activity. The period between Ben's return home on 8 May 1775 and his departure for France on 25 October 1776 was probably the busiest of Franklin's public life. One of his first tasks was to sit on a committee of five which was directed to send a petition to England explaining the nature of the colonial cause. The group included John Jay of New York, whom Ben met for the first time on this committee but with whom he was later to be closely associated in Europe.

Other committee appointments for Ben came in quick succession. He served on a committee charged with procuring saltpeter to use in making gunpowder. He worked on another to arrange for the printing of paper money. Ben saw to it that his son-in-law Richard Bache was approved as one of three men chosen to supervise the printing of that currency.

Early in July Franklin was chosen as chief of the Pennsylvania Committee of Safety. On the twelfth, he began work with a committee charged with devising ways and means to protect colonial trade. On the last day of that month Franklin was appointed to a committee to locate lead ore deposits in the colonies. The group also was supposed to determine an easy method of making salt in areas where natural deposits were rare. During August Franklin was asked to establish an American Post Office to replace the increasingly inoperative English system. Later, never one to shy from nepotism, he got Bache the job of heading this new American Post.

On the last day of September, Ben Franklin became a member of a committee instructed to determine, in collaboration with George Washington, how the Congress might best maintain and regulate the new army. It was necessary for the members of the committee to go to Cambridge, Massachusetts, to carry out their charge, and it was early winter before Franklin started back to Philadelphia. On his way home he visited Warwick, Rhode Island, to see the Greene family there. During the short time Ben spent in Warwick he became enamored of a young girl in the family, Betty Greene. She was a younger cousin of Catherine Ray Greene, with whom Franklin had once flirted in the early 1760s. Attracted to Betty, he was astonished when she rudely rebuffed him. So was her father, who thought perhaps she had been too abrupt and ordered her to go horseback riding with Ben in order to placate him. Afterward Betty sought out her father, told him of a pass Franklin had made, and insisted, "Don't you ever ask me to ride with that old fool again." [1]

When Franklin returned to Philadelphia, he began work on a new committee to which he had been named the past September. This was the Secret Committee, later called the Committee of Commerce. The group's initial charge was to procure munitions, paying for them by exporting produce.[2] Still more positions came to Franklin. On 29 November 1775 he, John Jay, Thomas Johnson, Benjamin Harrison, and John Dickinson began work as the Committee of Secret Correspondence. This was the first group designated by Congress to deal strictly with foreign affairs. On 30 January 1776 Robert Morris was added and on 11 October 1776 Richard Henry Lee, John Witherspoon, and William Hooper became members.[3]

On 30 November 1775, the day after its formation, the Committee of Secret Correspondence chose its first European agent. The members sent a letter to Arthur Lee in London. "An intercourse should be kept up," the committee wrote, "for it is considered as of the utmost consequence to the cause of Liberty" that the committee be kept informed of developments in Europe.[4] On 12 December 1775, the committee forwarded Lee £200 for his use in finding out the "disposition of foreign powers towards us." At all times, Lee was to use "great circumspection and impenetrable secrecy" in his actions.[5] Arthur took his charge seriously and spent a great deal of time in efforts to forward the American cause.

In November and December 1775, three French agents came to Philadelphia. They were only the latest in a long series of official and semi-official French agents sent to America to spy out the land. Etienne François, duc de Choiseul, the French Foreign Minister at the close of the Seven Years War, was incensed at the results of the Peace of Paris, 1763, which stripped France of her North American possessions. At that time Choiseul began a policy of sending "travelers" to the colonies to observe and to send home periodic reports. In 1764 he sent M. de Pontleroy to tour America.[6] The next year an anonymous French tourist heard Patrick Henry's famous "if this be treason" speech before the Virginia House of Burgesses and relayed an account of it to his government.[7] In 1768 Choiseul sent Jean de Kalb to the colonies; his mission was to determine whether the colonists would need engineers, artillerists, and munitions if war broke out between America and England. Kalb wrote home in February of that year that "All classes of people here are imbued with such a spirit of independence and freedom from control, that if the provinces can be united under a common representation, an independent state will soon be formed. At all events it will certainly come forth in time." [8] Kalb knew what he was talking about, but by the time the events he foresaw came to pass, neither he nor his boss, Choiseul, were around to see them. Choiseul's policies endured, however. When Louis XVI came to the throne in 1774, his Foreign Minister, Charles Gravier, compte de Vergennes, continued Choiseul's program of sounding out the American colonies. He sent Bonvouloir, the first of the three French agents to arrive in November 1775, to the rebellious provinces of Britain to estimate their strength and determination. Bonvouloir was instructed only to hint that France would be willing to help

America. He was admonished to make it understood by his listeners that his mission was both secret and unofficial. The French Ministry did not want to awaken American fears that it would use a colonial rebellion as an opportunity to regain lost lands in the New World. Bonvouloir was to assure the colonists with whom he spoke that France had no desire to regain Canada. He was also instructed that under no circumstances was he to reveal any direct ties between himself and his government.

Bonvouloir sailed 8 September 1775. Upon his arrival in America he posed as a Flemish merchant. Francis Daymon, a French bookseller and librarian of Philadelphia, put him in contact with Franklin's Committee of Secret Correspondence. The agent and the committeemen met three times during December under cover of dark, arriving separately at the appointed place. Franklin led in the discussions, trying to get Bonvouloir to answer his questions clearly. He failed. Bonvouloir refused to talk in any other than general terms to "le conseil privé," as he called the Committee.

Franklin had questions he wanted the Frenchman to answer. What was the disposition of the French toward the colonies? Officially, Bonvouloir replied, he could say nothing. Unofficially, he could assure the committee of France's kindly intent. Could the colonies get two good engineers from France? Bonvouloir did not know but he promised to forward a request to friends at home and he thought perhaps the request might be carefully considered. Would it be possible to get arms directly from France in exchange for colonial products, and could American vessels enter and clear French ports without interference from the government? Sales of munitions, the Frenchman maintained, were private matters between merchants for them to work out as they saw fit. Ship clearances were another thing. France would not, Bonvouloir thought, wish to do anything that might openly antagonize Britain. Would not French authorization for American ships to use its harbors be a breach of neutrality? And so went the talks. Little as he told Franklin and the other committeemen, Bonvouloir's attitude was sufficiently encouraging for them to consider sending agents to Europe's royal courts to sound out their willingness to aid the Congress.

Bonvouloir's report, written 28 December 1775, reached Paris 27 February 1776.

> Everybody here is a soldier [he wrote]; the troops are well dressed, well paid, and well commanded. They have 50,000 men under pay and a large number of volunteers who desire none. . . . They are stronger than others thought. It surpasses one's imagination, and you would be surprised at it. Nothing frightens them. Take your measures accordingly.[9]

It is extremely difficult to understand where he got this information unless it had been spoon fed him by Franklin and the others. Regardless of the inaccuracy of the report, however, France already had begun surreptitious aid, and the Foreign Minister's continued interest in supplying America with secret aid might be accounted for in part by reports like this one from Bonvouloir.

Of the three Frenchmen who came that winter to America, the second and third were Emanuel de Pliarne and Pierre Penet. Pliarne was a small businessman in Nantes and Penet was a gunsmith from Alsace, but sometime before November 1775 they established a trading partnership. The two men were supported in this new venture by Jacques Barbeu-Dubourg, who, in addition to being Franklin's French editor, also occasionally served his government on clandestine operations.[10]

The new firm formed by Pliarne and Penet planned to open trade in war matériel with the United Colonies. On 10 December 1775, the two partners arrived in the New World to seek a contract from the Congress. Landing at Providence, they sought out Governor Nicholas Cooke of Rhode Island, who informed General Washington that the Frenchmen had come supplied with excellent recommendations. Washington listened to their offer to supply arms and ammunition and sent them on to Philadelphia to talk with the Congress. Between January and March 1776 they met several times with Franklin and his Secret Committee and were finally awarded a contract. They would provide war supplies in return for indigo, tobacco, and other American produce.[11] In May 1776, Pliarne and his partner returned to Nantes. Penet traveled through France collecting cannon and other firearms for shipment to the Congress and on 10 June 1776 Dubourg was able to write Franklin that he had recently presented Penet to Vergennes.[12] If the two men had no direct connections with the French government, they at least had its tacit backing.

Unfortunately for the struggling colonies, the cost of dealing with this French firm would be very high. Sometime after their return to France, the partners began working with a leading French commercial firm at Nantes, J. Gruel, and for a time the company was known as Pliarne, Penet, and Gruel. Their interest in war profiteering soon became evident. At one point in the war Lambert Wickes, captain of the American ship *Reprisal* and a favorite of Benjamin Franklin, captured a prize ship loaded with a cargo of indigo. He turned the cargo over to Pliarne, Penet, and Gruel. The French firm sold the indigo but remitted only a fraction of the proceeds to Congress' agents.[13] The rest of the profits were funneled into their own and other private accounts. Pliarne, Penet, and Gruel also were involved in sending substandard weapons, old and rusty flintlocks and matchlocks, to Virginia, making huge profits on the transactions.[14] One of Congress' agents in Europe, whose own official duties were hampered by the firm's activities, complained that they deliberately obscured their finances so that no one could call them to account. Sometimes, he said, their operations were in the name of Penet, sometimes of the Congress, sometimes of Robert Morris, a Congressional leader involved in profit racketeering.

The agent recommended that Congress not settle any accounts with the firm until it had given an explicit reckoning of its finances.[15] John Schweighausser, officially appointed to supervise American business at Nantes, complained that he was totally ignored by Pliarne, Penet, and Gruel in the conduct of their business.[16] In short, Franklin and his Secret Committee had made an appointment that proved to be a troublesome one to the Congress.

In March 1776, while Pliarne and Penet were still in America, the Committee of Secret Correspondence decided to send an envoy to Paris to negotiate with the government there. America desperately needed more help from Europe than it was getting in its struggle with the mother country. Silas Deane was eager to be the Connecticut yankee at King Louis' court. The previous year, 18 September 1775, Deane had been chosen by the Congress as a member of the Secret Committee, but by the time the Committee of Secret Correspondence was formed, 29 November 1775, Deane's home state of Connecticut had turned him out as a delegate to Congress. During his waning days in office it is certain that he used what influence he had trying to secure a new job for himself. Indeed, John Adams was later to suggest that the provision for an overseas agent in the original resolution forming the Committee of Secret Correspondence was included especially to take care of Silas Deane.[17] Describing Deane's appointment by the Committee of Secret Correspondence, Adams wrote that from the very start "He possessed not [Connecticut's] esteem or confidence. He procured his first appointment in 1774 to Congress by an intrigue. . . . [H]e got a committee appointed with some discretionary powers, under which they undertook to appoint the members to Congress." As a member of that group, Deane still was "obliged to vote for himself to obtain a majority" vote sufficient to send him to Congress. The next year, "on the second Thursday of October, 1775 [the voters of Connecticut] left him out. . . . Instead of returning home

. . . he remained in Philadelphia soliciting an appointment
. . . first in the West Indies and then in France." [18] As a
member of the Secret Committee, Deane worked hard to advance his own candidacy.

The Committee of Secret Correspondence officially chose
Deane on 2 March 1776. His instructions were written the
next day by Benjamin Franklin, whose signature headed that
of the other committee members. In this letter Ben ordered
Deane to seek out Edward Bancroft upon his arrival in
France. This was the gambit that allowed Bancroft to become
an integral part of the American overseas mission. Franklin
directed Deane "to procure a meeting with Mr. Bancroft by
writing a letter to him, under cover to Mr. Griffiths at Turn-
ham Green, near London, and desiring him to come over to
you, in France or Holland, on the score of old acquaintance."
In other words, Bancroft would cross over to see Deane because of his acquaintance with Franklin. The letter continued: "From him you may obtain a good deal of information of what is now going forward in England, and settle a
mode of continuing a correspondence." It was not to be a single meeting, but a continuing relationship. Concerned about
his partner in speculation, Franklin suggested to Deane that
"It may be well to remit him a small bill to defray his expenses in coming to you, and avoid all political matters in
your letter to him." [19]

Hardly had Franklin finished writing Deane's instructions
when he turned to another phase of his own personal affairs.
Ben was still actively concerned with his long-standing hopes
for a proprietorship of a western colony. On 20 March 1776,
nearly one year to the day since he had sailed from England
leaving Sam Wharton in charge there, Ben called a meeting
of the American partners of the Grand Ohio Company.
They met at the Indian Queen tavern in Philadelphia.

Franklin still believed there was a chance for success in
western speculation. Those present that March Wednesday
agreed with him. They were unwilling to give up the chance

for eventual profit from trans-Allegheny lands simply because
a war was intervening. If the Crown would not act, perhaps
an American branch of the Grand Ohio Company could succeed in wresting a charter from the Continental Congress.
Once again this small band of indefatigable men thought it
convenient to try a new tack. Temporarily putting aside their
plans for developing the Vandalia area, they shifted to the
resurrection of the earlier claims to Indiana lands granted to
them by the Indians at the Fort Stanwix treaty conference.
Although far less than the twenty million acres of Vandalia,
there were, after all, about one and a half million acres involved in the project. This new effort, in short, was to be part
Grand Ohio and part Indiana Company.

Franklin had been maintaining for years that Indians had
an "inherent and undoubted Power to grant the Lands" to
whomsoever they chose, and that if it were entirely up to
him, "He would not seek for any other title" than that conveyed by the Indians at the time of transfer.[20] After Franklin
left England, Wharton had sounded out several lawyers, including Sergeant Glynn, and had received affirmative opinions about Franklin's thesis. In 1775, while writing View to
Indiana, a history of speculative dealings with the Indians,
Wharton and Bancroft shaped their evidence in such a way
as to emphasize the sufficiency of Indian titles. Franklin took
up their cudgels and aided in the American edition of that
work in 1776.

In seeking congressional approval for the claims of the
company, Franklin and his fellows actively sought to enlist
members of Congress in the enterprise. They looked for
"leading men" of the Congress to join the enterprise. Franklin and his partners were most hopeful that this approach
would work to their benefit. They had, they thought,
planned for every contingency. Should the Congress successfully defend its right to speak for the United Colonies, the
land grant might be furthered through the efforts of the partners within that body. If Britain put down the rebellion, the

speculators could then revert to their earlier Vandalia claim, which had been nearly completed at the outbreak of fighting. Franklin was a member of Congress. So was his fellow speculator, Joseph Galloway. They found allies among such men in Congress as James Wilson, Patrick Henry, William Grayson, and Edmund Pendleton. Ben hoped that Congress would be empowered not only to settle boundary disputes between states, but also to "plant . . . new colonies, when proper." He had suggested this in an earlier draft manuscript of a constitution, and when John Dickinson headed a committee to draft a constitution for the new government, he included among the powers delegated to the central government that of administering western lands.

Ben Franklin presided at that 20 March 1776 meeting of the speculators. Those present elected Joseph Galloway as president of their new project and Thomas Wharton as vice president. George Mercer, once the agent for the Ohio Company of Virginia and then a member of the Grand Ohio Company, became secretary for the group. In that capacity he was to open a land office and immediately begin advertising and selling four-hundred-acre tracts within the Indiana claim. As long as they could find buyers interested in parting with their money, the speculators could afford to ignore the fact that they had no legal title to those lands and no right to sell even one acre of them.

William Franklin was not present that day. Discredited politically because of his Tory views, he was at his home in Perth Amboy, New Jersey, forbidden to move about freely under pain of arrest. Although Ben was politically divorced from his son, he still looked out for William's economic interests. Thus he voted not only his own but also his son's shares of stock on those items which came up for consideration. Indeed, Ben provided both for his natural kin and for his in-laws. At the same meeting Franklin also arranged for his son-in-law, Richard Bache, to be one of the three trustees needed for the firm. All in all, it had been a good and promising day.

For a time, however, Franklin had to turn his attention away from his own affairs. Shortly after that meeting at the Indian Queen tavern, he left for Canada. The preceding 17 January, Congress had learned that General Richard Montgomery had been killed in the American attack on Quebec. Benedict Arnold had been wounded also, and the Continentals were retreating. The news was a blow to the ambitious plans of Congress, which had hoped to interest Canada in joining the revolution, thus showing Britain that all of her North American colonies were against her. Militarily such a union would have made it impossible for the British to use a northern invasion route. American attacks on the Quebec Bill of 1774 and the general anti-Catholicism of the colonies had, however, alienated the Canadians and ruined the chances of a Canadian-colonial alliance.

When news of the military disaster came to Philadelphia, Congress decided to try diplomacy. Perhaps reasoned argument might work with the Canadians where armed force had failed. Franklin, Samuel Chase, and Charles Carroll were selected by Congress to travel to Canada, there to convince those in authority of the benefits of cooperation with the Continental cause. Carroll was a Catholic and both he and Chase were from Maryland, which had been organized as a haven for those convicted of papish superstitions. It was hoped that their association with Maryland and with Catholicism might prove useful in persuading the Canadians to change their minds. To make the group even more attractive to their northern neighbors, John Carroll, Charles' brother and a Jesuit priest, decided to make the journey.

John Adams recorded the reasons for Franklin's inclusion in the group. His "masterly Acquaintance with the French Language, his extensive Correspondence in France, his great Experience in Life, his Wisdom, Prudence, Caution; his engaging Address," wrote John, made him "the fittest Character for this momentous Undertaking." [21]

The four men set out for Canada on 25 March 1776. They

traveled up the Hudson River and across Lake George and Lake Champlain. On 29 April, cold and exhausted, they arrived in Montreal. There they were welcomed by Arnold, who told them of the state of affairs in Canada and made it plain they had come in vain. The French there, encouraged by their religious leaders and angered by the American military effort to coerce them, saw little advantage to be gained by cooperation with the United Colonies. Twelve days later, accompanied by John Carroll, Ben began the long trek home, leaving the other congressional agents to expostulate in vain with the Canadians.

Franklin got back to Philadelphia early in June, worn, tired, and sick. He arrived just in time to hear Richard Henry Lee's motion of 7 June 1776, made to the members of the Congress: "We hold that these United Colonies are, and of right ought to be, free and independent states." The delegates were finally ready to declare the colonies independent. Lee's motion was approved. Congress, on 11 June, chose Thomas Jefferson, Benjamin Franklin, John Adams, Robert R. Livingston, and Roger Sherman as a committee to draw up a declaration of independence. Their work, done primarily by Jefferson with some aid from Franklin and Adams, was completed by 28 June. That day they reported their efforts back to the Congress. A few days later the United Colonies became the United States of America as Jefferson's Declaration of Independence was proclaimed to the world.

Franklin's days were long, busy with work and detail. He had sat on committees almost without number, as state and national public affairs consumed almost all his waking hours. He was seventy and tired. On the trip to Canada he had spent himself nearly to death. Yet no sooner had he returned than he once again plunged into still other efforts. Weariness nestled deep in his bones.

For most men, the years between 1775 and 1783 were a time of revolutionary and patriotic passions, and Franklin has been described as *primus inter pares* among those seized with

such emotions. Yet we should not be surprised that many
then foresaw the collapse of the revolution as inevitable. As
we look back from the vantage point of two hundred years,
we see not only the events of 1776—not only Valley Forge,
the retreat from New York, and Arnold's treason at West
Point—we see also the crossing of the Delaware River, the
Battle of Trenton, the French Alliance of 1778; we see Saratoga and Yorktown. We know the outcome of the war and so
those events are, for us, part of a pattern that had a foregone
conclusion. This view was not possible then. There were no
prophets occupying commanding general slots in the American army or holding committee chairmanships in the United
States Congress.

   In 1775 and 1776 those involved could take pleasure only
from a few incidents: the capture of Ticonderoga by Ethan
Allen and Benedict Arnold for one, the pyrrhic victory of the
British at Bunker's Hill for another. American leaders saw a
multiplicity of problems, all damning to their cause. There
was little money available. Governing organization was weak
and mainly ineffective. Conflicting factions, military rout,
and armed disaster all piled upon one another. Small, squab-
bling colonies were trying to fight the greatest power on
earth. It is not odd that those involved often suffered from
acute depression. Franklin may or may not really have made
the famous quip that it was necessary "to hang together lest
we all hang separately," but hanging, he knew, was a distinct
possibility for all the leaders concerned in what was then
often perceptible only as a debacle.

   All these thoughts must occasionally have run through
Ben's mind. We know that, at least by midsummer 1776,
Franklin was considering possible ways to remove himself
from the difficulties both he and the new nation faced. His
life was in danger should the rebellion fail. He was terribly
overburdened with work. Residence in America seemed dull
and simple after his years abroad. More European than
American by this time, having spent nearly all the years since

27 July 1757 abroad, Ben naturally gave some thought to living overseas. There he would be back in his milieu. Perhaps he also thought of that time twenty years earlier when, pressed by Pennsylvania politics, it had seemed wise for him to leave for England and a new field of endeavor rather than to stay and perhaps suffer irreparable personal damage in factional infighting.

A new committee to which he was appointed gave him further opportunity to think about these things. Besides Franklin, it consisted of John Dickinson, John Adams, Benjamin Harrison, and Robert Morris. Authorized by Congress on 12 July 1776, the committee was instructed to draw up tentative treaties of alliance with foreign nations. The committee first met on the 18th of July and its report was adopted 17 September. This report formed the basis of the Plan of 1776. During the committee's deliberations, Franklin wrote a memorandum which was not used in which he let slip the fact that he was already thinking of leaving America. In suggesting that credentialed peace negotiators be sent to Britain, Franklin wrote:

> . . . having . . . powers to treat of peace, *will furnish a pretence for B. F.'s going to England,* where he has many friends and acquaintance, particularly among the best writers and ablest speakers in both Houses of Parliament, he thinks he shall be able *when there,* if the terms are not accepted, to work up such a division of sentiments in the nation, as greatly to weaken its exertions against the United States, and lessen its credit in foreign countries.[22]

His words are clear enough. Franklin was considering possible reasons to use for leaving America while still keeping his reputation intact. He was most eager to be sent to Europe in the dual role of peace negotiator and political agitator. There is an interesting contrast between Ben's desire to play the

role of peace negotiator in England and the belligerent attitude he publicly presented to a recently arrived British peace
commission. Admiral Richard Howe and his brother, Major
General William Howe, had come to New York carrying a
royal commission allowing them to treat for peace with the
Americans. Franklin had been in contact with them since
early July when he had received a letter from Richard, an old
friend from his days in England.

Although Ben had written in his memo that if he were furnished by Congress with powers to treat of peace it would
provide him with a pretence for going to England, in his correspondence and talks with the Howes in July, August, and
September he spoke in a different tone. In a letter to Richard
Howe, dated 30 July, Franklin spoke of the "wanton Barbar-
ity and Cruelty" of the British which caused them to burn
"defenceless Towns" and had excited Indians to "massacre
our Peaceful Farmers and our Slaves to murder their Masters,
and is even now bringing foreign Mercenaries to deluge our
Settlements with Blood." He spoke of "atrocious Injuries"
given America by Britain.[23] All in all, it seemed a rather ill-
tempered letter to send to peace negotiators.

Nor was Franklin's tone more gentle when he came face to
face with the Howes in September at a meeting authorized
by Congress. The conference, after some three hours, came
to an end when Franklin complained that it seemed "America
is to expect nothing but upon unconditional submission—"

Howe interrupted to explain that this was not at all the
case. He said "that Great Britain did not require unconditional submission; that he thought what he had already said to
them proved the contrary; and desired the gentlemen would
not go away with such an idea." [24] The meeting ended at this
point. England would not again offer terms of peace until
early in 1778.

Whatever it was that had made this option come to seem
unfeasible, Ben did not continue to seek congressional selec-
tion as a peace negotiator to Britain. His only move in that di-

rection seems to have been the unused memo he drafted, while serving on the July committee, before his meeting with the Howes. It may be that he realized, upon reflection, that even though he was acquainted with good writers and able speakers in both Houses of Parliament, it might be difficult, singlehandedly, to "divide the nation's sentiments and weaken its foreign credit." It is possible that he considered that such a course of action, once launched, would hurt his reputation in America if it did not end in success.

There was another possibility. Congress had been laboring frantically for some time to achieve trade agreements with foreign nations and had been hoping desperately for open alliance with some royal power against Britain. For some reason, Ben had opposed such moves. He told the Congress "that a virgin state should preserve the virgin character, and not go about suitoring for alliances." [25] In 1777 he repeated those sentiments to Arthur Lee; he was, he said, still "clearly of opinion, that we could maintain the contest, and successfully too, without any European assistance; he was satisfied, as he had said formerly, that the less commerce or dependence we had upon Europe the better, for that we should do better without any connexion with it." [26] At least Franklin was consistent. What he felt in 1775 and 1776 he continued to feel in 1777 while serving abroad as ambassador. Yet it was not a case of "doing better" without aid from the Old World; it was either getting it or not going on. Congress realized this, as Franklin seems not to have. The delegates determined to send men to the courts of Europe specifically charged with borrowing money, arranging for trade agreements, and arguing for open alliances.

In spite of his personal views, Franklin thought about his own difficulties and his desire for a change of pace. The men chosen by Congress would be headquartered in Paris. The idea of being one of them came to Ben as a warming thought. Should France come into the war as our ally, he would receive much of the credit for this, insuring his reputation and reward at home. If the American cause failed, he would be safer from British retribution in Paris than he could ever be if he remained in the United States. And if England should offer sufficient enticements, perhaps he might still go back, as he had indicated in his July memo, but this time as a diplomatic representative of the United States of America rather than as a simple colonial agent. From whatever angle he looked at the situation, an ambassadorship in Paris seemed the best solution to all contingencies. France, he concluded, might well provide a proper field of endeavor for one sent there as an American commissioner. It was cosmopolitan and cultured. There he could return to the leisurely life he had lived in England in former days.

It was September and Congress was then deliberating over its choices of those to go. Franklin solicited the appointment among his colleagues on the Committee of Secret Correspondence. The names of Benjamin Franklin, Silas Deane, and Thomas Jefferson were placed in nomination before the Congress by Franklin's committee.

Congress selected those three men. Deane was chosen because he was already in France. Jefferson was widely respected as a man of vigor and honor. Franklin was approved because he was a man with important friends in Europe and had previous experience in the royal courts there. This was surely to be preferred to sending someone without those assets. When the vote was announced, Franklin turned to Benjamin Rush, seated beside him, and said: "I am old and good for nothing; but, as the storekeepers say of their remnants of cloth, 'I am but a fag end, and you may have me for what you please,' just so my country may command my services in any way they choose." [27] The vote was taken 26 September. When, a few days later, Jefferson pleaded his inability to go because of his wife's ill health, a special election was called in October, at which time Arthur Lee was selected to replace him.[28] Lee was a natural choice. Already an operative for the

United States, he had been active in its service since 1775 when he was first contacted by the Secret Committee.

Ben's rhetoric now became strangely muted. His expressed sentiments were hardly those of one likely to give all he had for the cause of the mission on which he was to be sent—the arrangement, if at all possible, of an alliance with the monarchy of Louis XVI. While perhaps not completely dedicated to his assigned task, he took on new vigor as he prepared to leave for France. He turned over his postal duties to Bache, making certain that this lucrative office remained within the family. He arranged for his two grandsons, Temple, aged sixteen, and Benjamin Franklin Bache, seven, to go with him. He busied himself packing, writing letters, completing unfinished committee business, and saying goodbye to friends.

The news of his planned departure soon spread, and comments rained upon his shoulders for weeks. An American newspaper writer claimed that Franklin had disunited kingdoms, rendering men of the same empire "strangers and enemies to each other." [29] Lord Stormont, British ambassador to France, thought Franklin had secured his appointment as a clever way of escaping from the inevitable collapse of the rebellion.[30] So also did Ambrose Serle, a New York Loyalist. Writing in early December to the Earl of Dartmouth, he said: "There is a strong Party forming in Philadelphia; and it will be no Matter of Wonder, if some of the remaining Members of the Congress should be taken proper Care of. Dr. Franklin, however, has had the Address to get off, on Pretence of negotiating a Treaty with the Court of France." [31]

Such views could be dismissed as slanders from Franklin's enemies, were it not for the fact they were shared by his friends. Edmund Burke was a Member of Parliament, a Rockinghamite, and had been close to Franklin since 1765 when the two had worked together toward repeal of the Stamp Act. They had grown so fond of one another that

Franklin felt it impossible to leave England without seeing
him. Two days before his departure from Britain in March
1775, Franklin had spent several hours with his old, dear
friend. Burke could not now bring himself to credit the news
he heard about Ben's mission to France. "I never will believe," he wrote, "that he is going to conclude a long life
which has brightened every hour it continued, with so foul
and dishonourable a flight."³²

Benjamin Franklin left America 25 October 1776, not to
return again until 14 September 1785. He sailed on board the
Reprisal, Lambert Wickes commanding. On 29 November—
a year to the day after Congress formed the Committee of
Secret Correspondence—the ship arrived in Quiberon Bay.
It was not until 3 December, however, that Franklin de-
barked at the little village of Auray. From there it was a two-
day carriage trip to Nantes, his first stop. Recuperating at
Nantes from the ardors of his winter voyage, Franklin met
again with Penet and Pliarne, his visitors in Philadelphia the
previous year. They introduced him to Gruel, their new associate, and gave him assurances of their devotion to his cause.
Franklin finally arrived in Paris 21 December.

As if waiting for his arrival, the British Secret Service was
thoroughly prepared to mesh him into its network. Franklin's
middle passage had ended. Now he would be plunged into
the deepest waters of secrecy and espionage.

CHAPTER FIVE

———•——

The Eyes of Argus

The British Secret Service was one of the most ruthlessly powerful, efficient, and feared agencies in the world. Early in the war, the English ambassador asked the French Foreign Ministry to release prize ships taken into its ports by American privateers. Vergennes coldly replied, "You cannot expect us to take upon our shoulders the burden of your war; every wise nation places its chief security in its own vigilance." The ambassador, Lord Stormont, sharply responded that "The eyes of Argus would not be too much for us." [1] If it was necessary to develop, like the Greek mythological giant, one hundred watchful eyes, so be it: England would position a network of spies across the countries of Europe and North America. Soon, from Gibraltar to the River Elbe, foreign ministries knew that their every move might be observed and quickly reported by British agents to London.

There were three primary control centers: Paris, New York City, and Amsterdam. The Dutch office, under the supervision of Frouw Marguerite Wolters, a widow whose husband had once held the same job, sent streams of reports on shipping news to the silent service and the British Admiralty. Philip Stevens, Secretary of the Admiralty, synthesized this mass of information and passed it on to his own chief and to the Secret Service. [2] The Paris bureau was run by Paul

Wentworth, a New Hampshireman. His string of agents was probably as productive as any group then operating.

The bureau for each target nation was staffed by a chief and his own crew of undercover agents. Whenever possible, these men were nationals of the country in which they worked, or so thoroughly trained in the language and culture of the area that they could pass for natives. The argus-eyed service also used casual agents recruited from many sources. Some were "tourists" who happened to be passing through various European countries and the Americas. Others were ship captains, tradesmen, mistresses, gamblers, whorehouse madams, and professional people. Whenever possible, the service favored using "blind" agents—that is, agents working side by side on the same task, none aware that others were also laboring on the assignment. The records sometimes show one spy suspecting another agent of spying! In this way, London was able to get independent corroboration of information, melding the whole into a cohesive pattern. The amount of raw data gathered by these agents was so amazing that Ralph Izard, an American in Europe, complained in 1777 to Henry Laurens, President of the Congress, that "There is another thing respecting the Public which I have to recommend to you . . . that I believe the British Ministry—have been better informed of our affairs—from authority—than the Commissioners themselves." [3]

The Secret Service spent money freely in gathering its information. In 1775, it spent £119,560 sterling; by 1778 the figure had risen to over £200,000.[4] These figures do not include nearly unlimited contingency funds available when needed. The amount of information gathered and the money available to finance its activities compare favorably to the clandestine warfare systems developed by modern nations in the twentieth century.

Other arms of the British government cooperated freely when requested to do so by the silent service. For a time in early 1777, Lord Sandwich, First Lord of the Admiralty, kept

seven armed naval vessels patrolling in coastal waters outside
the port of Le Havre in order to seize an American ship
which the Secret Service expected momentarily to clear port.
For eight days those ships waited, ready to pounce, before the
project was canceled. The cost of just that one action must
have been staggering.[5]

The table of organization of the Secret Service was a
tightly knit one. George III was nominal head of the service,
but actual operational officers deliberately let him know no
more than essential, for the king was a very moral and up-
right person whereas spies have never been known for their
morality, and indeed might be unable to function if they paid
too much attention to the ethics that normally operate among
men. Therefore George did not know many of the operatives
and only was told of those projects that needed his authorization. Even the little George III did know of the work of the
Secret Service upset him. He was continually offended by the
base character and methods of many agents. Although Americans, ironically, have been taught to think contemptuously of
George III, he was in fact a highly principled man whose
view of personal morality was such that he could not always
bring himself to credit information from men whose lives
were corrupt. The king thus distrusted some of the reports
which came to his attention, and as a result he more than
once forestalled preventive British action until it was too late.

For this reason, the number of reports and recommendations of the silent service that were brought to the monarch's
attention was kept to a minimum. Whenever possible, authorization of programs and policies was made "in-house" at
lower levels. Thus Lord North, the king's prime minister,
knew more about the operations of the Service than did his
master. Even North, however, preferred to be bothered only
by the more crucial decisions that had to be made, leaving
most matters to be handled by the man within whose department the Secret Service was actually housed. This was Lord
Suffolk, Secretary of State for the Northern Department,

who managed to be in charge of Secret Service operations even though the service operated in areas which, strictly speaking, were within the sphere of the southern, rather than the northern, Secretary of State.[6]

It was Suffolk who chose the actual head of the Secret Service. His choice was William Eden, later Lord Auckland. He was to direct the force for four years, until early 1778, when as a member of the Carlisle Commission he sailed for America in a vain effort to negotiate peace. Eden was an ambitious, keen, intelligent man, with piercing eyes and a face like a clenched fist. Eden originally had been recommended to Lord Suffolk by a relative, Alexander Wedderburn, the Solicitor General. Suffolk liked the young man and Eden became an Undersecretary of State in June 1772, in which post he served as the confidential secretary to Suffolk. He soon was trusted with information about secret policies and was charged with reorganizing the defunct spy network. Eden proved adept at his work. Although correspondence regarding the force does not appear in his records prior to November 1776, it is probable that he had been involved in this work for some time. He gathered his lieutenants and bureau chiefs and scattered the web of his field agents through the nations of the continent.[7]

Perhaps from reports received from his operatives, perhaps because he was a perceptive man, Eden felt that America's abilities had been greatly underestimated. He did not rejoice, as did his countrymen, when news of the British victory at Bunker's Hill arrived in London. "If we have eight more such victories," he wrote acidly to North, "there will be nobody left to bring news of them." [8]

Eden chose his operatives carefully. He knew he was but one part of the system he was erecting and his choices of agents had to be good ones if the new force was to function with efficiency. In Paul Wentworth, Eden acquired his best operative. The agent proved so valuable that he became chief of the French bureau. A former councilman of New Hampshire, Wentworth was a cousin or brother—the record is not clear—of that colony's governor, John Wentworth, and a distant relative of Rockingham. Having speculated in and acquired properties both in his home colony and in Surinam, Wentworth had lived for a time on his sugar plantation in the West Indies before he made up his mind to move to England. After 1770, thanks to the influence of Governor Wentworth, Paul served in England as resident colonial agent for New Hampshire and he and Ben Franklin knew each other well. Wentworth was a confirmed speculator and "stock-jobber," but was well thought of, mainly because he always paid his gambling debts promptly.

Eden recruited Wentworth because of the shrewdness, real talents, and the "respectability" under which the man could operate.

Wentworth was entirely capable of turning any occurrence to his own advantage. Once, in Paris, he called upon William Lee, only to discover that Lee was out. Wentworth pocketed Lee's calling card and personal correspondence seal so that the home office could make forged copies. Eden was interested in the use of forged materials. The chief once had asked Anthony Todd of the British Post if his staff could produce false seals and spurious letters. Todd, a little taken aback, replied that this could be done easily. There might be other and better forgers elsewhere, Eden knew, but his own were skilled for he had trained them himself.[9]

Wentworth served the spy system well throughout the war. He occasionally engaged in hazardous missions, but more often he lived with tension one moment and tedium the next. He bristled at being thought a spy, preferring to regard his activities as those of an honorable man fighting for his country's welfare. He was enthusiastic in his work and believed his clandestine and dangerous duties were helpful to his nation. Eden's confidence in him was not misplaced and Wentworth, who could have bargained well with the chief for his services, chose not to. He received only £200 per year, although when necessary he could also use the liberal funds of the Secret Service. William Eden promised him what he seemed really to want most: a future baronetcy, a seat in Parliament, and a job with a government office if he accomplished something really spectacular.[10]

Perhaps Wentworth's greatest achievement was to suggest to Eden that he recruit Edward Bancroft into the silent service. For that alone he should have gotten his government sinecure. Wentworth and Bancroft had long known one another—in fact, since Wentworth's days in Surinam when Bancroft had lived for a time on his plantation.

Bancroft was born in 1744 in Westfield, Massachusetts. He was an unhappy youth who ran away from two apprenticeships. At one period he lived in Hartford, where he was tutored by Silas Deane, who had recently graduated from Yale.[11] As a young man, Bancroft traveled to Surinam and there became interested in science. He experimented with Tyrian dyes for cloth and wrote a work on tropical flora and the natural history of Guiana.[12] By 1767 he sailed to London to study medicine. There, while perfecting his studies, he met Ben Franklin, who helped him with his writing style and used his influence to get Bancroft's works published.

By 1772 Franklin had introduced Bancroft into his own circle of speculators. In 1773 Franklin sponsored Bancroft's election to the British Royal Society. Afterward Bancroft wrote occasional papers in defense of American positions. When Franklin sailed for America in March 1775, he left Bancroft and Wharton in England to do what they could to secure the Vandalia charter from the recalcitrant government.[13]

By 1776, perhaps by 1775, Bancroft had been initiated into Eden's secret force of agents. So well did those involved with Bancroft hide his duplicity that he was regarded for nearly a century after the Revolution as a patriot to America's cause.

Arthur Lee quickly learned, however, that Bancroft was a British spy. Bancroft, he found out, took frequent trips across the channel and used them to meet with the Privy Council and various members of government. For many years, historians of this period used Lee's charges as proof of the Virginian's irresponsibility and instability. After all, as Francis Wharton, grandnephew of Samuel Wharton, wrote, to admit Lee's charge that Bancroft was a spy "would involve grave imputations on *at least* the sagacity and the vigilance of Franklin." [14] Thus Wharton, writing a century after the Revolution, came to the conclusion that Bancroft was a solid American patriot.

> It may hereafter appear, on the unearthing of the secret service papers of the British foreign office, that this was really Bancroft's position. But if it be so, he presents a case of which history affords no parallel. To believe him guilty of such atrocious and yet exquisitely subtle perfidy we must believe that, ingenuous, simple-hearted, and credulous as he appeared to the general observer . . . he was, nevertheless, a dissembler so artful as to defy the scrutiny of Franklin, with whom he was in constant intercourse; an intriguer so skillful as, without money or power, to deceive Vergennes and the multitudinous police with which Vergennes encircled him; a villain so profoundly wary as to win the confidence of Paul Jones, professedly aiding him in desperate secret raids on the British coast, and yet, by an art almost unfathomable, reserving the disclosure of these secrets to British officials until a future day which never came; a double traitor, whose duplicity was so masterly as to be unsuspected by the British court, which held him to be a rebel; and by such men as La Fayette, as John Adams, as Jefferson, who regarded him as a true friend. This amusing combination of apparently absolutely inconsistent characteristics may exist in bewildering harmony in the character of Edward Bancroft; but such a phenomenon should not be believed to exist without strong proof. [15]

Further than this Wharton could not bring himself to go. He

labored mightily to show that Lee's charges were false, and dredged up every possible bit of evidence to prove that Bancroft was a loyal patriot. Unfortunately, in 1889, Benjamin Franklin Stevens published his *Facsimiles* which showed beyond dispute that Bancroft was a spy and that from 1776 to 1783 the British knew more about the affairs in Passy than did the American Congress. Stevens' work, and other material, revealed that Franklin's home in Passy was a foreign branch of the British Secret Service.[16]

The extent of Bancroft's involvement with the Secret Service stands out in his own words. In 1784, protesting because his salary from the force was in arrears, Bancroft pointed out how valuable he had been. He wrote:

> . . . in 1776 I went to Paris, and during the first year, resided in the same House with Dr. Franklin, Mr. Deane etc., and regularly informed the [British] Government of every transaction of the American Commissioners; of every Step and Vessel taken to supply the revolted Colonies, with Artillery, Arms etc., of every part of their intercourse with the French and other European Courts; of the Powers and instructions given by Congress to the Commissioners, and of their correspondence with the Secret Committees etc. and when the Government of France at length determined *openly* to support the Revolted Colonies, I gave notice of this determination, and of the progress made in forming the two Treaties of Alliance and Commerce, and when these were signed, on the Evening of the 6th of Feb'y, I . . . conveyed this intelligence to this City [London], and to the King's Ministers, within 42 hours, from the instant of their Signature. . . . Afterwards, when that decisive measure, of sending Count D'Estaign with the fleet from Toulon, to Commence Hostilities at the Delaware and New York, was adopted, I sent intelligence of the direct object and Plan of the Expedition.[17]

Bancroft, it seems clear, believed in faithful performance of his duties. His instructions from the silent force ordered him to forward to London the names of American agents in Europe and the Indies, copies and original reports of all kinds that he could get his hands on, information about treaty negotiations with France, Spain, and other continental countries, commercial and banking details of America and its European agents, and anything else that seemed important to him.[18]

To perfect Bancroft's cover, the Secret Service arranged for him to spend some time in prison for aiding and abetting rebel plots. Released, he "fled" to France with a contract in his pocket for £500 immediately, £500 annually during his period of service, and a life pension afterward. He was referred to by the force by several aliases, the chief of which was "Edward Edwards," a thin disguise but perhaps better than none at all. Bancroft's reports were written between the lines of "love letters" addressed to one "Mr. Richardson," in "white" or invisible ink, "the wash to make which appear is to be given to Lord Stormont." Bancroft placed his letters in a bottle tied to a string and lowered it into a hole under the trunk of a box tree in the Garden of the Tuileries. Each Tuesday, Thomas Jeans, secretary to Lord Stormont, removed the messages and left instructions which Bancroft later retrieved.[19]

Upon his arrival in Paris, Bancroft went to work quickly. The files of the Secret Service show that within a few weeks he had forwarded to Eden copies of several important letters. Eden read a letter from Robert Morris to Silas Deane written 20 December 1776 which contained a lengthy description of war news, campaigns, depreciation of continental currency, shipping news, and the benefits to France from trade with the United States.[20] Bancroft also sent to London a copy of a memo from Charles Thomson noting the appointment of Franklin, Deane, and Jefferson to the Court of France. Eden learned that they were to keep "an account of their Expenses," to have an immediate sum of £10,000 and to hire a secretary with a yearly salary of £1,000.[21] Bancroft soon had the job of secretary.

It was not long before Eden also received copies of further instructions sent by Congress to its agents in France urging them to make early contact with other European courts for treaties and aid.[22] Bancroft also buried in his bottle a message from Congress, dated 22 October 1776, telling of Jefferson's unavailability to act as envoy and Lee's election in his stead.[23] He sent to London a copy of a proposed "Plan of a Treaty of Alliance and Commerce," a list of French officers who had sailed to fight for America, dozens of extracts from Congressional messages to the commissioners and their replies, including orders to borrow on the faith of the United States, to send agents to Spain, Portugal, Berlin, and Tuscany, and to buy arms, ammunition, ships, blankets, and other types of military supplies.[24]

In order to keep in touch with headquarters, Bancroft made frequent trips across the channel. In order to justify his travels, he generally returned with information to be passed to America. Those trips should have been sufficient warning to any embassy interested in security, but Franklin and Deane fully accepted Bancroft's excuses for his journeys. The information he brought back, they said, was invaluable to the American war effort. His news consisted of English ship movements, troop assignments, ministerial plans, and so forth. Congress was so impressed with reports of his work that it paid him a salary also. All of the news that Bancroft reported, however, had been fed to him by Eden and Wentworth; it was either inconsequential and of no help or false and damaging if acted upon.

William Eden had done his work well. He, Wentworth, Bancroft, and a host of lesser spies worked hard for the defeat of America. They had the money, the machinery, the numbers, the power. Against them initially stood only Arthur Lee, the first American recruited by the Congress as a secretive, if not a secret, agent.

Arthur Lee had been recruited by the Secret Committee of Congress when it sought someone living abroad to act on behalf of the colonies. Ben Franklin, the committee's chairman, contacted him and wrote his instructions on 12 December 1775: "It would be agreeable to Congress to know the disposition of foreign powers toward us and we hope this object will engage your attention. We need not hint that *great circumspection and impenetrable secrecy* are necessary." [25] Lee believed his assignment to be both a real responsibility and an opportunity for which he had long looked.

Lee had not waited for an official appointment to use his influence on behalf of America. Since Franklin had left England in March 1775, Lee had been resident colonial agent for the Colony and Province of Massachusetts Bay. He was one of the few prominent Americans still living in England. His brother William was another. William and another colonist, Stephen Sayre, had done what no Americans had ever before accomplished: They were elected aldermen for London in May 1775.

Arthur and William Lee had long been acquaintances and supporters of the prominent radical John Wilkes. As frequent guests at Wilkes' home, Mansion House, the Lord Mayor's official residence, Lee met a French visitor there sometime around May 1775: Pierre-Augustin Caron de Beaumarchais, who had just written *Le Barbier de Seville*, and was later to write *Le Mariage de Figaro*. In addition to being a musician and playwright, Beaumarchais was also an adventurer, watchmaker to the king, social climber, and a suspected murderer against whom nothing was ever proved. Sometimes he was employed as a special agent by the monarch of France. Beaumarchais readily complied with such requests because of the valuable contacts they gave him; his primary goal in life was to amass as large a fortune as possible, and to this end he would do many things.

Louis XVI used Beaumarchais for a sensitive mission in London. The city was familiar to him, for he had but recently been there while involved in a blackmail scheme with Théveneau de Morande, whose former mistress had been Madame du Barry, the favorite of Louis XV. Now Beaumarchais rode the streets of the foggy city in search of one Chevalier D'Eon, a transvestite, duellist, dandy, and ex-secret agent of France to the Court of Russia. D'Eon had fled France, taking with him government papers which could severely compromise his country. Beaumarchais was to retrieve them.[26]

D'Eon had gravitated toward the Wilkes coterie upon his arrival in England and so did Beaumarchais. At Wilkes' home, the playwright met Arthur Lee. Beaumarchais spoke little English save "Goddam," and was happy to be cultivated by the American, who spoke fluent French. Lee intrigued him with stories of the wealth to be had from the American West—wealth which, so long as America remained a colony, lay locked into the commerce of the English empire. The Frenchman also renewed an earlier acquaintance with Lord Rochford, a music lover he had met in Spain. From Rochford, Beaumarchais learned that Britain was determined to keep its colonies, just as from Lee he had learned that Americans were certain to continue their resistance to British authority.

Beaumarchais knew of his government's policy of watchful waiting toward England. In 1763 France had been stripped of Canada, Isle Royale, Senegal, and Louisiana. England controlled Dunquerque on the French coastline and stopped and searched shipping at will.[27] Now, with France's traditional enemy in open conflict with her colony, the thought of aid to America among the French was popular indeed. The comte d'Artois, the duc d'Orléans, the comte St. Germain, Chevalier d'Anemours, the duc de Noailles, the duc de Broglie, and the young marquis de La Fayette—all important men—favored aid to the English colonies. Under the tutelage of Lee, Beaumarchais added his name to this impressive list.[28]

Alive to the possibilities which this conflict opened up for France, Beaumarchais, on 23 September 1775, sent his king a wildly inaccurate letter.[29] He described England as on the edge of catastrophic revolution. The cabinet was soon to be dissolved and the monarch was to be deposed and exiled. Beaumarchais' reckoning of America's armed strength was even more inaccurate than the one sent to Paris later that year by Bonvouloir, who reported colonial military might at around fifty thousand men. Beaumarchais spoke of eighty thousand men besieging the British garrison at Boston, slowly starving it into submission. He asserted that Britain had lost her colonies and that internal reaction to this fact was such that the homeland was facing imminent civil war.

Beaumarchais wrote again, 7 December 1775, urging his king to act. A third message, 29 February 1776, began with the words, "Sire—The famous quarrel between America and England, soon to divide the world and change the European system, makes it necessary for each power carefully to examine in what way this event of separation can effect it and either be an advantage or a destructive influence." [30]

Modern writers have perpetuated the myth that aid to America came through the efforts of Benjamin Franklin or, if not Franklin, then Silas Deane. Both France and Spain, however, already had started giving aid through Beaumarchais six weeks before Deane's and six months before Franklin's arrival in Europe.[31] One author has written:

> . . . that even if Deane had succeeded in sending a ship-load of munitions within a few weeks after his arrival in Paris, July 7, 1776, it could not possibly have docked on this side until very late that year. But by that time nearly 9/10ths of the imports [of guns in America] had reached our ports, the larger part of them unloading at Philadelphia, where Congress took them in charge. It is possible that Arthur Lee deserves more credit for his part in procuring supplies from France during the early months of the war than he has yet been accorded.[32]

Yet even here, not much credit can be given to American

effort. France wanted desperately to hurt Britain and would have done so without any encouragement from Lee, Franklin, or Deane. Those men could have slept throughout the war and in all probability France still would have moved with measured speed toward aiding the United States.

When Beaumarchais had completed his mission in London by retrieving the secret papers from D'Eon and delivering them once more into the safekeeping of his government in Paris, he used the opportunity to urge aid for the American colonies. A few weeks later he was back in England, where he continued to meet with Arthur Lee. Lee now spoke with more authority on behalf of Congress, for he had by now received Franklin's letter commissioning him as an undercover agent and urging him to learn the disposition of foreign nations toward the colonial cause.

Lee lost no time in promoting French efforts on behalf of the colonies.[33] And his efforts bore fruit. At first France sent arms to one of its islands in the West Indies for covert transshipment to the American coastline. This tactic, however, was too open for the French government, which wanted to preserve a show of neutrality. With the knowledge and consent of Louis XVI, Vergennes decided to support America more fully but to shroud French participation as much as possible from the British. Vergennes ordered Beaumarchais to establish a dummy trading firm, under cover of which military supplies would be shipped to America. In his study of Beaumarchais, Loménie has suggested the terms Vergennes may have used in his instructions to the playwright:

> The operation must essentially in the eyes of the English government . . . have the appearance of an individual speculation, to which the French ministers are strangers. . . . We will give a million secretly, we will try to induce the court of Spain to . . . supply . . . an equal sum; with the cooperation of individuals who will be willing to take part in your enterprise you will be able to

found a large house of commerce, and . . . can supply
America with arms, ammunition, articles of equipment,
and all other articles necessary. . . . You shall ask for no
money from the Americans, as they have none. . . .[34]

Thus it is clear that the French sent aid to the colonies because they felt it was to their own interests to do so. What is
more, this aid began too early to have been significantly influenced by anything done by Franklin or Deane, who did
not reach France until later.

After the French government gave Beaumarchais his initial
million livres for America, Spain followed suit with the same
amount in September 1776. France contributed a third million the next year and additional money was given by French
businessmen who saw aid to America as a way to make handsome profits for themselves and their firms. For several
months Beaumarchais and Lee corresponded about the details
of the aid program, Lee writing under the code name of
Mary Johnston.[35] The distance between the ideas of the two
men was, unfortunately, great. As Beaumarchais flitted about
France gathering ships and supplies, his mind turned from id-
eological concern for a struggling people to thoughts of possible self-enrichment through his new trading firm, Roderique
Hortalez et Cie.

Silas Deane came to Paris in the first days of July 1776.
Deane was to serve several masters. Officially, he was agent
for the Committee of Secret Correspondence. Privately, he
was to act for Robert Morris as a commercial agent, helping
Morris' brother Thomas, who was already living at Nantes.
Upon his arrival, the ex-school teacher, ex-Connecticut merchant, and ex-member of Congress posed as a trade merchant
from Bermuda. This cover was partly valid inasmuch as he
was involved with the firm of Willing and Morris, Philadelphia, which did in fact operate in the West Indian trade.
Moreover, it had been Robert Morris of that company and
Benjamin Franklin who had pushed Deane's appointment to
his new post. Deane thus combined diplomatic and commer-

cial, public and private matters in one mission. From the start, those several tasks proved unharmonious.

Deane spoke no French and thus was totally dependent upon those who transacted his business or who spoke "macaroni" English. He soon demonstrated an aptness for intrigue, double-dealing, and covert activities. As *Poor Richard* had once lamented: "Poor plain dealing! Dead without issue."

Deane's instructions ordered him upon arrival to contact both Lee and Bancroft. He quickly wrote to Bancroft and got in touch with Franklin's friends, Jacques Barbeu-Dubourg and Donatien le Ray de Chaumont. Bancroft replied that "Nothing can give me greater pleasure than to renew and improve 'our old acquaintance.' " Before he could make the trip to Paris, however, Bancroft explained, he would have to spend three days at the home of Thomas Walpole; while there, he expected to dine with Lord Camden. Both Camden and Walpole were friends of Franklin and fellow partners with him in land speculation. For Bancroft to see them now indicated to Deane that speculative possibilities still existed even in time of war.[36]

Despite his instructions, Deane made no effort whatsoever to contact Lee. Indeed, when Lee made the first overture, Deane actively resented the interference. Lee had the temerity to warn Deane against several persons, one of whom was Edward Bancroft, and Deane criticized Lee for this act and made no use of the information sent him.[37] Lee also warned the new agent to have no dealings with Paul Wentworth, whom he described as a dangerous man. This too Deane saw fit to ignore.[38] Receiving little response from his letters, Lee determined to go to Paris to visit Deane. When Silas learned of the trip, he wrote Vergennes that Lee's presence was neither needed nor wanted and that he hoped Lee would soon return to London.[39] To Vergennes' secretary Deane spoke even more pointedly; he told Gérard that "I could have wished . . . that he [Lee] had suspended his Visit, as I know not otherways, how he can serve me, or my affairs, now . . .

in as favorable a Course as the situation of the times will admit." [40]

Griping against another official agent of one's own government in this way was unprecedented. The reason for it, however, is simple. Deane and Bancroft, who duly arrived in Paris after having paid his visit to Walpole, had already come to terms. Using various inducements, Bancroft had recruited Deane into the service of the British silent force. The two men soon involved themselves in a number of activities—some on behalf of Eden, some for their own profit. They cooperated in ventures promising speculative success in the American West. They bought supplies for America and inflated the prices they asked the Congress to pay. They found privateering enterprises extremely profitable, and shared in the plunder to be found there. Naturally Deane was displeased to learn that Lee was coming to town. He was already deep in the mire and wanted no outsider—especially an outsider who was already suspicious of Bancroft—peering into the relationship he had established with Bancroft on Franklin's advice. [41]

Of Deane's first weeks in France we have two records. One is Deane's own, which he sent to the Committee of Secret Correspondence. The other is by Bancroft, which he forwarded to the Secret Service. [42] Deane's report is the poorer of the two and he wasted more time before writing it than did Bancroft. Thus Eden knew of Deane's arrival before the American Congress did.

Unused to diplomacy, unfamiliar with the French language, unable to keep in close contact with America, and enmeshed in the intricacies of intrigue, Deane quickly slipped away from loyalty to America. His own personal interests became paramount to him. Bancroft's style and personality quickly won him the upper hand over the weaker and inexperienced Deane.

After he had secured the services of Deane in Paris, Bancroft returned to England to work out details with the Secret

Service. From that country he wrote Deane urging him to correspond extensively about the American's activities. Thus Bancroft would be filled in on secret material as often as possible while he was absent from Paris. Deane wrote John Jay that the Surinam doctor was giving good service, "but it costs something." [43] The files of the British Secret Service no longer make it necessary to wonder what the cost was. It was treason. Nor do we need to speculate as to what Deane would pay. His association with Bancroft ultimately cost him his opportunity for service to a new nation, his reputation, and eventually his life.

The nature of their offices meant that Deane and Beaumarchais would soon meet. They conferred, tested each other's morals, and promptly began a program of profiteering at the expense of both France and America. Months earlier, when Beaumarchais had approached Arthur Lee in London to tell what he had been commissioned to do, he stated that French aid would be freely granted, although some cargoes might be shipped back from America to avoid having his vessels run in ballast. Now, with the aid of Deane and his connections with Willing and Morris, Beaumarchais concocted a fantastic scheme to ship to America second-hand French goods for which the Congress would have to pay handsome prices. First the cargoes were procured with money provided free to Beaumarchais by the Bourbon governments and by French businessmen. One of these entrepreneurs was Donatien le Ray de Chaumont, who was Ben Franklin's landlord and partner in land speculation. Chaumont soon joined forces with Deane and Beaumarchais.

Chaumont was a wealthy merchant of Blois, a government contractor supplying clothing for the army, and a member of the Farmers General. Le compte de Maurepas, a principal member of Louis' cabinet, was a relative of his, and the minister of Marine, Emanuel Sartine, was a close friend. Chaumont liked the plans of Beaumarchais and Deane enough to advance a credit to them of around a million livres. He also

promised to supply a great many uniforms for the American
forces. Through Chaumont and Sartine, Deane arranged for
the early efforts of American ship captains at privateering. In
time, Deane and Chaumont were to have their own privateering navy. When John Paul Jones later pitted his *Bonhomme Richard* against the British *Serapis,* he did so not as an
officer of the United States Navy but as a privateer; both he
and his ship had been chartered by Chaumont and Deane as a
private force.[44] Learning of these things, Lee protested to
Congress that Jones was not acting for his country, but was
"kept upon a cruising job of Chaumont and Dr. Franklin." [45]

Deane and Beaumarchais operated out of L'Hôtel d'Holland, a large building in Paris which had once been the site of
the Dutch embassy but was now the headquarters for Roderique Hortalez et Cie. Their private navy consisted of eight
ships: *L'Amphitrite, Le Mercure, Marie Catherine, Flammand,
Amelia, Seine, Thérèse,* and *Mère Bobie.* Of these, the *Seine*
was captured by the British before her first cargo could be
unloaded in America. The first two shipments, carried by *Le
Mercure* and *L'Amphitrite,* reached America in April 1777.
At Portsmouth they unloaded clothing and blankets, about
sixty cannon, many kegs of gunpowder, and approximately
twelve thousand muskets. The muskets were a good illustra-
tion of the business practices of Deane and Beaumarchais.
They had been sorted from French armories and were out-
moded and unworkable. Bought for pennies, they were "refurbished" and sold dearly to the American Congress.

When this was discovered, the finger of derision pointed at
both Deane and Franklin and their reputations suffered. As
late as 1783, William Lee noted that it had been necessary for
Franklin to give "a Certificate in vindication of Silas Deane,
relative to the charge against him about the Magazine of Old
Firelocks." [46] In 1787, when Jefferson was in Paris, he saw
some three thousand of those old arms still rusting in ware-
houses at Nantes. He wrote of them as "firearms of various
kinds taken from the peasantry of Bordeaux when they were

deprived of the droit de chasse [hunting rights], and purchased by Mr. Deane." They were, said Jefferson, "broken,
eaten up with rust, and worth nothing." In addition, he discovered various chests of gun parts mixed together randomly,
presumably bought for shipment to America eleven years
earlier. To his government he explained that the "muskets of
which they belonged were so bad that they never were found
worth mending or cleaning and it was a long time questioned
whether they should be sent over to America or not. But as it
would have been difficult to sell them, Dr. Franklin ordered
that the stocks which were mostly broke or worm-eaten,
should be taken off to save freight, and that the barrels and
furnitures should be packed as they are." [47] These guns had
been bought initially, even though worthless at the time of
purchase, for three livres each. Deane and Beaumarchais then
charged Congress a Louis d'or—that is, twenty francs—
apiece for them.[48]

Deane and Beaumarchais quickly accumulated a large as-
sortment of goods with the money they had acquired. Within
three months they had bolts of material for the making of uniforms, shoe buckles, handkerchiefs, neck scarves, pocket
knives, buttons, needles, and thread. They claimed to have
blankets, shoes, and stockings enough to equip thirty thousand men. They also procured about two hundred cannon,
three hundred thousand fusils, one hundred tons of gun powder, three thousand tents, plus bullets, mortars, and cannon-
balls. For all this Beaumarchais claimed to have spent 5.6 million livres: 2.5 million for clothing, 2.5 million for munitions
and ships, and 600,000 for renovating and equipping his eight
vessels.[49] The finances of this operation were deliberately
made as complicated as possible. Few records were kept and
those that were retained were often unsigned statements that
simply declared that a particular sum had been disbursed.
Later auditors felt it was hopeless to try to untangle the purposefully snarled expenditures.[50]

Deane's correspondence with Morris during this period

partially reveals the extent of profiteering in which he in-
dulged. Robert Morris wrote Deane, 16 August 1776, to say
"It seems to me that the present oppert'y of improving our
fortunes ought not to be lost. . . . All sorts of . . . goods
[sent here] fit for Winter wear must bring any price. . . .
These goods may . . . come out 2/3rds on account of Willing, Morris & Co., 1/3d on your account." Or again, "There
has never been so fair an opportunity of making so large a
fortune since I have been conversant in the world." [51]

Not too long after his arrival, although the actual date is
not known, Deane established his own enterprise separate
from his profiteering partnership with Beaumarchais. On behalf of himself and Willing and Morris, Deane created a giant
international land speculation and trading firm. The people of
America had English, not French, tastes and buying habits;
they were hungry for the kinds of goods they always had
used. Deane's new enterprise catered to this appetite. Some
of those involved included Thomas Walpole, a London
banker and land speculator, Ferdinand Grand, the French
banker for the American Commissioners, the Delaps of Bordeaux, Donatien le Ray de Chaumont, the Montaudoins of
Nantes, Bordieu of London, Friginux of Amsterdam, the
Crommelins and Hornica of Amsterdam, and of course Willing and Morris of America. These men capitalized their enterprise at £400,000 sterling. Their efforts were described by
a contemporary observer:

> The articles besides others—are Cloathing of all denom-
> inations—Sail Cloth—Cordage—Osnabrigs & Linnen
> —Shoes—Hose—Blankets—Drugs etc etc Great quan-
> tities are shipped by various means to Dunkirk & Os-
> tend & then in Coasters to Havre, Nantes & Bordeaux
> etc where they are reshipped in armed Ships provided
> with American papers besides the necessary papers as
> French Ships sailing on french acct—by which means
> they assure themselves of Safe Conduct to the very Har-
> bours of No America. [52]

These goods were purchased in England. Thus, in the midst
of war, the American Commissioner to France had established a firm to trade with Britain. The goods thus purchased
filled some of the available convoys with private goods for
private profit while the army of America strangled for lack of
equipment.

Deane's contribution to the firm was the arrangement and
coordination of its operations. Chaumont wrote to Morris, 7
January 1777, that "Upon the friendship which I have for
Mr. Deane I have accorded him 100,000 livres in the ship
Union . . . the half of which is upon your account." [53] On 11
January, Morris wrote Deane that "Should you obtain a
French Fleet to come out here, then will be the time to speculate." On 6 January 1777, Deane wrote to Morris that
"Herewith I send you invoice of cargo of goods shipped by
M. Chaumont. . . . The money was advanced for the goods
by M. Chaumont and every advantage taken for our joint interest . . . you will see I engage for one third." On 18 December 1777 he wrote, "I hope you will be able to procure a
freight for my brother's goods in Montieu's vessels, if there is
room over the goods of the public." [54] With goods coming
from America, another ploy was used. Five ships with
cargoes of salted fish arrived in a French port. Beaumarchais
had them restrained from unloading until their cargoes had
been assigned to Deane. Then they were unloaded. [55]

Morris also urged Deane to insure cargoes with British
firms. In February 1777 he chided Deane for falling down on
opportunities for profit. No cargoes had been received at
Philadelphia or the West Indian base of Willing and Morris
from either Deane or Morris' brother Thomas, who was in
charge of operations at Nantes. Shipping was often slow,
which might account for the matter, but if they had not actually shipped any cargoes "you may have leisure to repent
hereafter that you missed so fine an opportunity of making a
Fortune. The prices of all imported articles have been enormously high. I cou'd have sold any quantity of European

Manufactures for 500 to 700 pr Ct." He added that "there is plenty of room to make as much money as you please." [56]

The *Union*, referred to above, finally arrived in Charleston. Although its goods were sold "at a considerable advance," the publicity given the sales embarrassed Morris, who wrote Deane requesting him to exercise more care in the future in choosing consignees. The consignee of the *Union* shipment "has told to everybody the concern you and I had in the *Union*'s cargo, [and] . . . the people in that country are acquainted with the whole concern, and from hence it is not improbable that they may conjecture by and by that Private gain is more our pursuit than Public Good." [57]

Brissot de Warville, a French traveler through America, commented that it was "scarcely to be credited that amidst the disaster of America, Mr. Morris, the inhabitant of a town just emancipated from the English, should possess a fortune of eight millions." He added that it was "in the most critical times that great fortunes are acquired . . . commerce bears everywhere the same character . . . it excludes alike the virtues and the prejudices that stand in the way of its interest." [58] Morris has often fondly been called in American histories "The Financier of the Revolution." On this point, one author, Thomas Perkins Abernethy, has acidly commented: "The idea that Morris financed the Revolution out of his own pocket is purely mythological. The truth is that the Revolution financed Robert Morris." [59] It also financed Silas Deane.

Deane channeled many cargoes and part of his profits to his brother Barnabas in Connecticut. Shortly after the arrival of Silas in France, Barnabas began a land office trading business which he called Barnabas Deane & Company. He was involved in marine business, congressional contracts, privateering, and trade with the West Indies. Backed by Silas in France, he may or may not have been aware that Silas was supported by funds from the British Secret Service. That Silas' own trading enterprise was in part funded by the British Treasury is seen in a state paper of Britain, dated 30 January 1778. On that day George III received from his chief minister, Lord North, a letter drafted by John R. Robinson, Secretary of the Treasury. If the king approved it, it was to be sent to Paul Wentworth. North told the king that "Mr. Wentworth must be the purchaser and the shipper of the goods and must fix upon the consignee at New York, who will continue either to send the profits or the goods themselves to Mr. D. in Connecticut." North included in the packet to the king some memoranda from Wentworth. Of them he commented that "The most important are Mr. D's proposals, to which are added some pieces of information Mr. W. received from him" on a trip to France from which Wentworth had just returned.[60]

"[Wentworth's] consignee . . . will continue . . . to send the profits or the goods themselves to Mr. D. in Connecticut." This can only refer to an existing arrangement between Silas Deane and the British Secret Service to funnel such things to his brother Barnabas. Such payoffs could only have been for "pieces of information" Deane supplied to his masters. Deane, in this role, used the cover name of "Benson," [61] and British records are filled with letters from "Benson." Deane was deeply involved in stock-jobbing and insurances. Insurance could be played like a form of gambling by putting so much money down against fairly high odds that some agreed upon event would actually occur within a given time. For those without inside information, the odds made it a fair game of chance. But if one had inside knowledge, as did Deane/Benson, and then placed bets, he could clean up heavily. He carried on this gaming through Samuel Wharton, who wrote him often.[62] For example, on 13 March 1778, Wharton wrote of the fluctuations of the London stock market. He had not heard from Deane/Benson recently and hoped to receive a letter soon with information to use, for "War Was [is] the only thing that can serve & save Us." [63] Again, 21 April, Wharton wrote to speak of "wars," "profits," and the "commissioners," and seven days later he told Deane/Benson that "I thank you for [the news?] about the Toulon fleet: it [will be?] a perfect secret with me." [64]

With one hand, Deane/Benson wrote to Wharton for one sort of personal advantage. With the other, he sent information through the channels of the Secret Service for use by the British in their war effort against America. The King himself attested to Benson's value. He told how information from Benson through Wentworth was "certainly of great importance," and added that "Undoubtedly, if the intelligence sent by Benson is founded, France has taken her part and a War with G. Britain must soon follow." [65]

Bancroft and Deane. Two men whom Franklin knew and trusted. Two men whose positions had come to them largely through the efforts of Franklin. Two men who were thoroughly involved in spying and personal profiteering. These were the men with whom Benjamin Franklin would work after his arrival in Paris at mid-December 1776.

CHAPTER SIX

———— • ◆ • ————

Surrounded by Spies

The British Secret Service spread its net. Its field agents were in place. Already those agents had subverted a large number of people. "The King, North, Eden, Wentworth; no one of them would have been astonished if they had found even Franklin corruptible." [1] They had no cause for surprise. Franklin, with eyes open, walked into the nest of spies operating in France.

At the American mission in Paris spying was so common at so many levels that it almost might appear those involved thought it was some kind of game. In certain ways it may have been. To those who became agents such intrigue promised adventure and excitement. For some there may have come the thrill resulting from dangerous devotion to a cause. Others saw the money they were paid as the chief value. All knew they were in deadly danger. Penalties for treason or spying were vicious; a captured spy inevitably faced death.

America's attitude was plain enough. Major John André, personal aide to Sir Henry Clinton, was captured in civilian clothing after he had met with General Benedict Arnold, 21 September 1780. While searching him, his captors found plans and other papers in Arnold's handwriting hidden in André's boots. Tried by military court, André was hanged on 2 October.

Four years earlier, a spy acting for General George Washington had met a like fate. Nathan Hale was teaching school in New London, Connecticut, when conflict began in 1775. He joined a Connecticut regiment and became a first lieutenant. By 1776 he was a captain. Assigned to the New York City area, he volunteered to slip behind enemy lines and obtain information. On 21 September 1776, the British captured him and found on him notes and sketches of their fortifications. The next morning, the British major in command, Cunningham, refused Hale's request for a Bible and destroyed the letters he had written to friends. Cunningham asked if Hale had any last words. "I regret," said Hale, "that I have but one life to give for my country." Cunningham snarled, "String the rebel up." Seconds later, Hale choked away his life, twisting slowly at the end of a length of hemp.

Both André and Hale acted as spies on only one mission, yet they were hanged. Those in the American Paris mission passed information week after week, in some cases for years. Should they be trapped and caught, much more tender mercies awaited them. An example of what they might expect if arrested occurred in January 1781. In the first week of that year a man named Henry Francis de La Motte was arrested and charged by the British with spying. The jury found him guilty. He was hanged by the neck until he was almost dead. Then his executioners cut him down, took out a portion of his bowels, and burned them before La Motte's agonized and dimming gaze. Before life flickered from his body, an axeman decapitated him. They then chopped the Frenchman's corpse into four quarters.[2]

Those who engaged in this ancient profession had, in their own minds, to come to terms with their possible fate. They weighed the risks and continued their activities. Dedication did not diminish fear. Paul Wentworth worried on every trip to the continent that he would be unmasked for what he was and arrested. Bancroft kept a spare passport available so he might flee at any time if it became necessary. Spy work

might be valuable to the employers who paid for it, but those
involved seldom could afford to relax. If their lives and activities were games, they were deadly serious ones!

Ben Franklin had long experience with security problems.
In 1773 while acting as colonial agent in London, Ben wrote
Thomas Cushing that he had sent some letters to America,
"which I hope got safe to hand." [3] To his sister, Jane Mecom,
Franklin complained that "the letters between us, though
very innocent ones, are intercepted." [4] On another occasion
he said to a correspondent that he was "glad to hear from you
what letters of mine came to your hands, as I suspect they are
often intercepted." [5] These comments, written prior to
Franklin's return to America in 1775, show that Ben was no
stranger to surveillance; he felt it daily and did what he could
to guard against it. At that time Ben may well have been involved only in domestic intrigues, but he knew also of the intrigue that went on at the international level.

When Ben prepared to leave England in the spring of
1775, Garnier, the chargé d'affaires for France, called on him
and told him plainly that the colonies could count on aid of
some kind from the government of Louis XVI. Since 1774
Garnier had been gathering information regarding colonial
administration. He bribed a clerk in the Colonial Office with
five hundred guineas a year to give him secret information.
He had an informer in the House of Commons who told him
the gist of secret debates there.[6] Franklin's long association
with Garnier may have given him some insights into the reality of international intrigue.

His knowledge had to be heightened during his service in
the Congress between May 1775 and October 1776. His
work on the Secret Committee and the Committee of Secret
Correspondence brought him into contact with intelligence
activities of several kinds. He appointed Arthur Lee as an
agent. He met with Bonvouloir and other French agents. He
discussed with his colleagues various procedures to follow in
gathering intelligence data. There can be no doubt of his

thoroughgoing knowledge of clandestine methods. Nor can there be any real question of Franklin's intimate acquaintance with the need to use constant security measures to forestall intelligence leaks to the enemy. Even in his own personal affairs he had long practice in the use of mail drops, cyphers, pen names and aliases, letter interception, deliberate use of false information to mislead others, and all the rest of the clandestine paraphernalia. Indeed, his experience in such matters fitted him as well as any living American for the task he was sent to Paris to fulfill. Yet the story of his life in France is an account of one disaster after another, debacle piled upon calamity. Most biographers, however, tend to be too shocked by any allegations against Franklin to view the record carefully or to consider the evidence calmly.

In all his relations with friends in Europe, Franklin acted in a naive way, covering up for them, apologizing for their weaknesses, reacting in anger at allegations against them, refusing to consider evidence of wrongdoing. As he said to Ralph Izard, in a scathing letter dated 29 January 1778, it was better "Always to *suppose* one's friends *may be right,* till one *finds* them wrong, rather than *to suppose them wrong* till one *finds* them right." [7] Such sentiments are appropriate for someone in private life, but for someone trusted with state secrets they are unwise, especially if one persisted in such views when so much evidence to the contrary was available. There are simply no records to indicate that Franklin ever reacted in any positive way when he was confronted by those who faulted him for his security measures.

Upon his arrival in France, Franklin wrote to Silas Deane informing him of his own new commission and telling him that Arthur Lee had been named as Jefferson's replacement.[8] Reaching Paris, Franklin was taken in tow by Deane and settled in rooms at Deane's quarters, L'Hôtel d'Hambourg.[9] Juliana Ritchie, the wife of a Philadelphia businessman who lived in France during the war, visited him there. On 12 January 1777, after having seen the cluttered condition of state papers in Franklin's offices, available to anyone's hands, Mrs. Ritchie wrote Ben reminding him that he was "surrounded by spies." [10] Franklin's response is revealing. Laconically, Ben replied:

> I have long observ'd one Rule which prevents any Inconvenience from such Practices. It is simply this, to be concern'd in no Affairs that I should blush to have made publick, and to do nothing but what Spies may see & welcome. When a Man's Actions are just and honourable, the more they are known, the more his Reputation is increas'd and establish'd. If I was sure, therefore that my Valet de Place was a Spy, as probably he is, I think I should not discharge him for that, if in other Respects I lik'd him. [11]

This answer was incredibly naive. By the very nature of the task to which Congress assigned him, Franklin's work had to be done with some regard for secrecy. If he actually performed his tasks, he could not help but work at some jobs which by their nature could not be made public knowledge or allowed wide dissemination. No matter how just and honorable the man, in governmental work some tasks call for secrecy, just as do some in private life. Franklin's concern at such times for increased personal reputation demonstrates misplaced arrogance. Or perhaps he sought to use misdirection in his answer to Mrs. Ritchie. For his answer was typical "franklinese"—it replied without directing itself to her concerns.

Bancroft was already employed by Deane as secretary, and Franklin continued to use him in this capacity. Arthur Lee, now on the scene, quickly determined that Bancroft was a British spy. He told Ben of this and submitted his evidence. Bancroft, said Lee, on his frequent trips across the channel, met with the Privy Council and other members of the enemy government. This was obvious grounds for his dismissal from the American embassy. Franklin did not listen kindly to this news. He reacted with hostile alacrity in defense of Bancroft. Thereafter his attitude toward Lee was venomous. Franklin continued to use Bancroft as "adviser" throughout the war and even in the peace negotiations of 1781 and 1782.

Lee and Mrs. Ritchie were not the only ones concerned about Ben's lackadaisical attitude. He was soon visited by another friend, William Alexander. The two men had known each other since Franklin's trip to Edinburgh in 1774. By 1776, the Scotsman had moved to Dijon, France. It was only natural that he look up Ben when he learned Franklin was in Paris. Alexander enjoyed his visit with Franklin but was troubled by the disarray of public papers evident everywhere. After returning to Dijon, Alexander wrote to warn against this practice. Wording his caution softly, the Scotsman said:

> Will you Forgive me, dear Doctor, for noticing, that your Papers seem to me to lye a little loosely about your house. You ought to consider yourself as surrounded by spies and amongst people who can make a cable from a thread; would not a spare half-hour per day enable your son [actually Temple, his grandson] to arrange all your papers, useless or not, so that you could come at them sooner, and not one be visible to a prying eye? [12]

This was written 1 March, weeks after Mrs. Ritchie had noticed the same state of affairs. When Juliana had visited Ben, he had just arrived in the country. Perhaps there was some excuse for lack of security measures. In the interim, however, Ben became the guest of Jacques Donatien le Ray de Chaumont, the French intendant, land speculator, and cohort of Deane. Chaumont offered Ben use of a large and elaborate wing of his palace, L'Hôtel de Valentinois, in the little village of Passy, just outside Paris. The offer was rent free, and Ben accepted. This was Franklin's home from early in 1777 until his departure from France in 1785. It was here at Passy that

William Alexander called on him. It is evident that Ben had still seen fit to do absolutely nothing about the disorder surrounding him.

In a youthful creed he had set forth, Franklin ranked "Order" as the third of the virtues he sought to acquire. "Let all your Things have their Places," he stated.[13] This quality was judged to be just less important than temperance and silence, among the thirteen desirable attributes. Of the first three, taciturnity seems to have been the only one Ben mastered. Either he failed to acquire the characteristic of order, or his state papers at Passy were deliberately left available for anyone to consult. Alexander's warning, like those of the others, went unheeded.

Benjamin Franklin's attitude toward security procedures so deteriorated that even the Paris police became concerned. The following item appeared on 20 August 1777 in the newspaper, *Nouvelles de Divers Endroits*:

> Certain sinister-looking persons, seen lurking around Dr. Franklin's lodgings at Passy, and others no less suspected, who have even penetrated to his presence upon different pretexts, have led the government to give positive orders to the Lieutenant General of Police to watch over the safety of this respectable old man, and take all the precautions to this end that prudence could suggest.[14]

Neutral observers like Mrs. Ritchie, colleagues like Arthur Lee, friends like William Alexander, and even the police of the host country all marveled at Franklin's disinterest in precautionary measures. Franklin continued his unmodified ways. His ways were an affront to normal intelligence operations, yet he was quick to criticize Arthur Lee's one fall from grace when, on a mission to Berlin in 1777, the British Secret Service stole, copied, and returned his papers.

The table of organization at Passy continued to be staffed

with spies. More and more men who associated with Franklin or who served his household were members of Eden's silent service. Shortly after his arrival in Paris, Deane hired William Carmichael, who suddenly and mysteriously appeared on the scene offering help. Young Carmichael continued to work as a secretary after legation headquarters was moved from L'Hôtel d'Hambourg to L'Hôtel de Valentinois at Passy. An earlier author, Samuel Flagg Bemis, has written that Carmichael "went to the verge, if not over the edge, of treason." [15] Carmichael was more dedicated than Bemis allowed for. A young rake, witty, fond of intrigue, and quite intelligent, Carmichael served both the American embassy and the Secret Service during the war years.[16] Franklin used him often on diplomatic missions to Germany, Holland, and elsewhere. Like Bancroft, Carmichael successfully hid his duplicity from the Congress if not from the Paris embassy. When Arthur Lee and Vergennes came to suspect him, Franklin and Deane sent him back to America as an honored servant of the nation. He served in Congress from Maryland in 1779. In the same year he went with John Jay on a diplomatic mission to Spain as Jay's secretary. He served in this position until Jay left for the peace negotiations in Paris. In 1783 Carmichael was appointed the first official representative of the United States to Spain. He served there until his recall, under suspicion, in 1794, but died in Madrid, 9 February 1795, before he could sail for America.

Bancroft. Deane. Carmichael. There were others. Early in 1777 a young man from New York, Jacobus van Zandt, came to Franklin's home and knocked on the door. Calling himself George Lupton, van Zandt stayed on and on at Passy. Of all the spies who reported to Eden, Lupton could boast the finest handwriting. Many of his messages told little, but at least they had the advantage of being easily read. Fearful that his cover might be blown and aware that Eden doubtlessly saved and filed the reports sent him, Lupton wrote his boss asking him to destroy all the letters he had forwarded so they could not accidentally be used to compromise him. That letter, too, was saved.[17]

Lupton became jealous of Bancroft and reported to Eden that he was trying to get the job of secretary that Bancroft held. If he became secretary, he would be in a much better position to spy. (This was a good example of Eden's use of "blind" agents, for Lupton did not know that both he and Bancroft served the same master.) Lupton also complained that his salary from the British was too low and sought an increase. On one occasion, after having received a payment from England, he wrote Eden that "I wish it had been more, as I am obliged to entertain sometimes—in order to keep in with them." [18] Keep in with the Franklin entourage Lupton did, and Eden received a steady stream of information from him.

Franklin continued to associate with spies and men of curious character throughout the war. One was John Thornton, a British army major. Thornton was, like the others, welcomed into the Passy legation and introduced to Arthur Lee, who was momentarily without a secretary. Franklin and Deane urged the Virginian to hire Thornton and Lee did so. His two colleagues then told Vergennes they could have no confidence in Arthur because he consorted with suspicious Englishmen!

Another Franklin associate known to be a spy was a ship captain, Joseph Hynson, from Maryland, who had wondrous adventures stealing embassy dispatches to the Congress. Still one more spy may well have been Franklin's old friend Samuel Wharton. On a trip to Paris, Paul Wentworth wrote Eden that a "Williams" was to be the contact between John Vardill, a henchman of the Secret Service, and "Wharton." The "Williams" referred to was probably John Williams, Franklin's cousin and, like Ben, an uncle of the American naval agent at Nantes, Jonathan Williams, Jr. There were two Whartons in England at the time. Samuel lived there, as did his brother Joseph. A little later Samuel Wharton moved to France and became a member of Franklin's inner coterie at Passy. The contact was probably thus John Williams, who carried information from Samuel Wharton to John Vardill of the Secret Service.[19]

As astute as Franklin was, as aware as he has been reputed to have been, warned that spies surrounded him—was there any way he could not have known of the dual character of Bancroft, Deane, Carmichael, Lupton, Thornton, Hynson, Williams, and Wharton?

Arthur Lee arrived in France from England at about the same time that Ben Franklin reached Paris. Lee was probably not overjoyed when he reached the city. He had been rebuffed earlier when he tried to help Deane. Now another man with whom he had never had good relations had been appointed and was to work with him. Lee knew from reading his congressional appointment that he, Franklin, and Deane had been chosen as co-equal commissioners. From the start, however, Lee saw that the old doctor was acting as though he were head of the mission. Ben seemed to believe that the position of *primus inter pares* was his by natural right.

Lee saw Franklin living at Passy with Chaumont, an old partner in the Vandalia enterprise. Edward Bancroft, already suspected by Lee on other grounds and also known to be a Vandalia speculator, lived in residence with Franklin. Deane seemed to resent Lee's presence. It was natural for Lee to assume that these men were up to no public good. He watched his companions carefully, although he took pains to avoid open trouble with any of them. From the beginning Arthur willingly took upon himself more than his share of the duties that faced the three men.

At Lee's first meeting with Franklin, Ben tried to dampen the ardor of his associate. He told him he was making a great sacrifice: his employment in France was only a temporary matter, and when the war was over Lee would be left without place or resources. He would be proscribed in England. If all this conversation was an attempt to sound Lee out, Arthur refused to take the bait. He spoke enthusiastically of his appointment and of the opportunities it presented to help the United States. About three months later, Ben returned to the topic of their earlier talk and of the reason that had brought them to France. He told Lee that "I have never yet chang'd the Opinion I gave in Congress, that a Virgin State should preserve the Virgin Character, and not go about suitoring for Alliances, but wait with decent Dignity for the Applications of others." In his usual disclaiming style, Franklin added the words, "I was overrul'd; perhaps for the best." [20] That he did not really believe it to be "for the best" is seen in a conversation with Arthur's brother William, which Franklin had almost exactly two years later. Speaking about that talk, William said, "The Doctor replyed that it was a matter to be considered whether it was worth our while to ask any of the Courts of Europe to acknowledge our Independence." William was shocked that Ben could say such a thing at that juncture of the war, occupying the position he did. "This, I confess," wrote William Lee, "astonished me greatly." [21] Neither of the Lees appreciated Franklin's attitude at a time when America was so beset with troubles and when its only salvation lay in aid and recognition from Europe.

Arthur Lee possibly wondered if Franklin's laissez-faire approach was the reason that nothing had yet been officially accomplished. On 23 December 1776, the American commissioners composed a letter to Vergennes asking for an open treaty of commerce.[22] No reply came until 6 January 1777. Vergennes' secretary, Conrad Alexandre Gérard de Rayneval, answered for the French government. He sent a note requesting the Commissioners to "postpone the communication of the memorial containing particular requests." [23] That postponement of action, in which Franklin seemed to concur, would last eleven long months while America agonized.

Upon hearing this news Franklin wasted no time turning to his own affairs. One of the first letters he received in France was from Bernard, Frères and Company. The firm

proposed a business deal for the purchase of American tobacco which it believed Franklin had at his disposal. The
company would offer him "the best of terms and will engage
to take any quantity he may import in the future." [24] From
the very start, the records give the impression that Ambassador Franklin was busy with private commercial ventures in
France when he should have been exerting his utmost effort
in diplomatic duties.

Bernard, Frères and Company were but one of Ben's correspondents. Anthony Todd, at his desk in the British Post
Office, learned of others. First warned by Lord Stormont,
Todd soon confirmed that Franklin often wrote to various
politicians in England, both in the Cabinet and of the opposition, as well as to men with whom he had associated in business for years. Included among the latter were some of
Franklin's partners in the Vandalia effort; Franklin used
cover names to address them, so that Lord Shelburne was
Jones, Lord Camden was Jackson, Thomas Walpole was
Johnson, Samuel Wharton was Watson, and John Williams
was Nicholson.[25]

Ben may have written these men only because they were
old friends. His motives may have been as varied as the men
to whom he wrote. One thing, however, they all, save Shelburne, had in common was an interest in the Vandalia enterprise. It may be that Franklin believed they could in some
way aid America's cause, yet with the exception of Shelburne, who later became Prime Minister, there is no evidence
that any were in a position to do so. Of the others, some had
very curious and suspicious, if not outright execrable, back-
grounds and careers.

Lee may not have known at this early date of Franklin's
letter writing, but he learned of it later. He did know, for it
was no secret at Passy, that Deane already had shown interest
in joint development by American and European speculators
of some twenty-five million acres of land between the Ohio
and Mississippi rivers.[26] He also found out that Franklin

knew of and participated in some of these speculative activities.[27]   The days trickled away. By early January 1777, Ben Franklin, Arthur Lee, and Silas Deane had worked out the handling of the assignments Congress had given them.[28] When assigning Franklin to Europe, Congress suggested that he proceed to Spain for talks with officials there. On 1 January 1777 Congress officially resolved "That Benjamin Franklin be directed to proceed to the court of Spain. . . ."[29] Communications were slow, and it was weeks before Franklin received these orders. By that time Ben had made other arrangements. He knew he was expected to go to Spain, but it was winter and he was seventy and feeble. He had been very sick on his passage across the Atlantic only a few weeks before. The ardors of a midwinter trip across France, over the Pyrenees, and into Spain were more than he could face. He asked Lee to go in his place. Arthur replied that he had no authority to treat with the Spanish; only Franklin had that power. Ben persisted, telling of his physical weakness. Lee probably was not overjoyed about the prospects of a carriage trip over rough roads in winter snow and ice, but he agreed to make the trip. Franklin wrote to Congress resigning his commission to Madrid and asking them to appoint Lee in his stead. Weeks later, after Lee's return, a commission came from America appointing the young Virginian to do the job he had by that time completed.[30]

In conversations with Franklin before he left, Lee was assured that "either Mr. Deane or Dr. Franklin [would go] to the Hague" to begin proceedings there on behalf of the United States. Only Lee acted on the informal arrangements made in those talks. As soon as he was safely out of Paris, Franklin and Deane forgot about their share of the diplomatic workload and settled in comfortably for the winter to pursue their own, more private, aims.

Arthur Lee faced real dangers in his Spanish trip. In addition to the normal hazards of roads and weather, Eden's force presented an even more important threat. The British Secret

Service was so thorough that European governments knew they were constantly watched and their activities quickly reported back to Britain. During times of crisis, they often made certain that their actions could not be misinterpreted by the English. The whole picture was immensely complicated by the fact that Spain was at war with Portugal over a boundary dispute in La Plata, South America, while England, an old ally of Portugal, followed the conflict closely. Spain feared that any interest she showed in the American rebels might well bring the British navy to her coasts. The presence in Madrid of an emissary from the American rebels could give Albion the excuse to open hostilities. Spies were endemic and would report his arrival at the first opportunity. In order to obviate some of these difficulties, Lee disguised himself as a British merchant for his trip to Spain. Nevertheless, the government was frightened and ordered him held at the border. Although he was refused entry to the country, Lee refused to give up his mission. He would wait until he got satisfaction. To get out of its difficulties with this stubborn man, the Spanish government pressed into service an agent who journeyed all the way from Madrid to the border town of Vitoria to meet with Lee. Spain agreed to supply secret aid. Arms, blankets, and clothing would be sent to New Orleans and Havana where the Congress might transship them. The Americans were urged to attempt to seize the British stronghold of Pensacola. Charles III, the Spanish king, ended up sending (hard upon the heels of the misspent million livres already supplied to Beaumarchais) nearly 400,000 livres for American use. Additionally, the Spanish Treasury would pay for the supplies shipped to Havana and New Orleans.

With these promises in his pocket, Lee returned to Paris having achieved the first major American diplomatic breakthrough of the war. Arthur graciously thanked the Spanish government for its aid in a glowing letter to the Foreign Minister, Floridablanca.[31]

Sometime during his stay in the Pyrenees, Lee learned to

his surprise some bitter news about a former acquaintance. As an American colonial agent in England before the outbreak of war, Lee had known and occasionally worked with the New Hampshire agent, Paul Wentworth. Now he found through some source that Wentworth was playing a dual role in the war and that his allegiance rested with the British rather than the country of his birth. Remembering that Deane and Franklin had told him that one or the other of them would be going to The Hague for negotiations, Lee wrote them on 12 March 1777, advising whoever should go to Amsterdam to be on guard against Wentworth.[32]

When Lee returned from Spain he was surprised at the state of matters in Paris. Franklin and Deane, his two co-equal colleagues, seemed not at all glad to see him. Before many days passed, Franklin began to sound him out about the prospects of taking on another mission to a foreign court. It may have been the Joseph Hynson affair that caused Franklin and Deane to want to send Lee on another mission, since that affair had not been completed when Lee returned from Spain.

This strange episode began only a few weeks after Ben Franklin arrived in France on Captain Lambert Wickes' ship, the *Reprisal*. Sometime after Ben disembarked, Wickes quite accidentally met a cousin, Samuel Nicholson. Both men were from Maryland. As they visited with each other, Lambert learned that Samuel was out of work. He suggested to his cousin that he go to Franklin and ask for employment. Toward the end of January 1777 Nicholson made the trip to Paris carrying Wickes' recommendation that he be given command of a ship. Samuel was an experienced shipmaster and two of his brothers were already officers in the American navy. When William Carmichael saw Nicholson ushered into Franklin's quarters he must have been pleased, for the two were great companions who had junketed about London together in 1776. During those weeks they had made their home in a London whorehouse at 13 Stepney Causeway. The bordello was operated by Mrs. Elizabeth Jamp under the guise of a boardinghouse. In fact, while the boardinghouse was a front for the whorehouse, the whorehouse was a front for Mrs. Jamp's activities as an agent of Eden's Secret Service. It may even have been at her home that Carmichael originally had been recruited to the Service.

As they renewed their friendship, Carmichael and Nicholson thought of another friend who surely deserved employment out of the American mission. This was Joseph Hynson, Lambert Wickes' stepbrother and a fellow Marylander. He too was a devotée of Mrs. Jamp's boardinghouse. Just as he had recommended his cousin, Nicholson, to Franklin, now Wickes supported his stepbrother, Joe Hynson, who at the moment was in England living at Jamp's, for employment as "a reliable man to carry the dispatches to America in the first cutter procured." [33] Thus Maryland contributed quite a motley delegation to the American war effort.

Franklin quickly agreed to hire Hynson. He instructed Sam Nicholson to go to England to contact him. Nicholson wrote Hynson about the nature of his assignment and Hynson in turn boastfully told of it to Mrs. Jamp and her son Robert. Elizabeth Jamp promptly took her news to her contact, John Vardill. The Reverend John Vardill was only twenty-five years old, yet he was important enough in the ranks of Eden's service to warrant a strategically located office at 17 Downing Street and to report directly to the chief. He was a New York Tory chosen by Eden to work primarily with resident Americans in England, to keep watch over them, and to draft them freely or otherwise into the silent network. Vardill hoped his faithful service to his country might some day be rewarded by appointment as Regius Professor of Divinity at King's College, New York (now Columbia University). In the meantime, he was content to carry out his duties meticulously.

Early in February Mrs. Jamp appeared at Vardill's office to acquaint him with the activities of Joe Hynson.[34] She had learned that Sam Nicholson was coming to England and that

he and Hynson were to purchase a cutter suitable for
carrying dispatches to America. Vardill was elated to get this
news. On 7 February he drove his coach to the Jamp house
and parked in the street. He called Hynson to him and the
two men sat in the carriage for some time. When Hynson
emerged, Vardill immediately drove away. A transformation
had occurred. As Hynson got out of the coach he ceased
being a patriotic Marylander and became an agent for Eden.
The price had been cheap enough—a small pension enabling
him to live comfortably in England. Vardill cautioned Hynson not to tell anyone, even the Jamps, that he was now an
agent.[35]

That same day, Hynson traveled to the little coastal town
of Deal, there to await the arrival of Sam Nicholson. Nicholson had quickly come to England, pausing in London briefly
enough to pick up his girlfriend Elizabeth Carter, and had set
out for Deal. To Hynson he wrote that "My Business are of
such a Nature, won't bare putting to Paper." [36] When they
met on 9 February he urged Hynson to hire a coach and
come at once to a prearranged location for a meeting. After
they talked, Nicholson and Elizabeth set out for Dover,
leaving Hynson to come later. That same day, 9 February,
John Vardill, Lt. Col. Edward Smith, and William Eden conferred over the recent course of events. After the meeting,
Eden briefed Lord North and Lord Suffolk, his own superiors. They ordered Vardill and Smith to travel to Dover to
meet again with Hynson and to work out with him a detailed
plan.

Two days later Vardill and Colonel Smith met with Hynson in Dover at his lodgings in Harvey's Ship Tavern. Hynson was told to buy an old discarded customs ship, the *Dolphin*, which Nicholson later described as able to "neither
fight nor run away." Hynson was to pick up the Congressional dispatches in Paris, then take them to Le Havre. There
he would contact his control, supply his sailing date, and then
slip anchor for America. The British navy would take care of

the rest. Smith remained with Hynson until 18 March, going over the details of the plan again and again so there would be no slip-up. Hynson was also ordered to keep his eyes open while in Paris and report to Vardill any pertinent information he might pick up there.[37]

As a cover for his journey to Dover, Hynson wrote his friends in London of the lazy vacation he was spending with Nicholson. Hynson wrote his lady friend at Jamps', Isabella Cleghorn, that "We have a fine time of it nothing to do but Drive from one place to another." Not pleased at having been left behind on such an enjoyable trip, she scrawled on the back of his letter: "I have not slept one hour since you left. For God's sake write to me . . . I am wreatched."[38]

Elizabeth Jamp wrote Hynson telling him that Vardill had called on her to question her about Hynson. "Make a Friend of him for God sake, I think he is of the right Side of the Question."[39] Obeying his instructions about secrecy, Hynson replied that ". . . it is too late to make offers now, as I am engaged in a manner very agreeable to myself . . . exerting myself in my Country's Cause . . . I still say, I want no favour of him [Vardill] nor his Masters. I bid them all defiance."[40] This letter, too, quickly became a part of the Secret Service files. Although Hynson had passed his test, Eden still did not trust him. He assigned John Walcot, the postal clerk in Dover and an agent for British packet boats, to keep a "cautious and unsuspected watch" on the Marylander.[41]

Soon Colonel Smith left for Calais with £800 of Secret Service money to use in France.[42] On 17 February, after Hynson and Nicholson had purchased the *Dolphin*, Sam left Dover for France and Hynson, unable to stay away any longer from Isabella, headed for London.[43] Perhaps he had been touched by her Valentine letter in which she told how she had chosen him "out among the rest, the reason is I love you best."[44] They were with each other from Thursday, 20 February, to Saturday, 22 February, at which time they parted and Hynson sailed for Calais to meet Colonel Smith.[45] Smith had already had misgivings. He had planned to wait for Hynson in Calais but left for Dover on 20 February to check on him. There he conferred with John Walcot, the postal clerk, and returned to Calais on 21 February.[46]

Hynson was anxious to go to Paris and wanted to begin his mission, but Franklin and Deane told him to wait at the coast.[47] On 28 February Hynson began outfitting the *Dolphin* at Havre de Grace.[48] While at Havre, Hynson maintained contact with "a sort of an English man who hath been here ever since april or may, 1777. God knows what he does; he dwells with his Wife in a little Country house a quarter of a mile out of the Town. I suspect him very much to be pay'd by the Court of St. James to look what one is doing here." So wrote a friend, Andrew Limozin, to Arthur Lee in 1778 as he recalled Hynson's visit at Havre.[49] By that time Lee was quietly making enquiries in an attempt to piece together the treachery of Hynson.

Colonel Smith reported to William Eden that Hynson would sail on 10 March carrying diplomatic pouches and a cargo of dry goods. Now the plan earlier concerted among Smith, Eden, North, and Lord Sandwich, First Lord of the Admiralty, went into operation.[50] Sandwich ordered two vessels to stand by as watchers, while five others coasted the port waters to attack and seize Hynson's vessel as it entered the channel. The trap was set. It is puzzling why the British government should have gone to all the trouble of suborning Hynson and then being at the expense of having seven ships to hijack the diplomatic packets he was to carry for the Paris mission. That mission was so thoroughly riddled with spies that they already had access to its papers. Why did they need Hynson? Or if they needed him, why did they also need seven ships to stage a holdup? One would think that once the material was in the hands of the agent Hynson, they would have ready enough access to it; they could read it, copy it, make whatever use of it they wanted, and then send it on its way. The whole Hynson affair is confusing. Some of that confusion arises because it is the nature of spy activities to be as complicated as possible; complications being one of the spy's stocks in trade. But in the preparations made for Hynson's departure with the dispatches, we have a particularly baroque instance of a redundancy of complications.

One possible solution may be to remember that Eden thoroughly trusted very few, if any, of his agents. Carmichael reported on Bancroft, Lupton on Carmichael. Eden had set Walcot and Smith to watch over Hynson. It was one thing to be able to read syntheses of papers from the American mission. It would be far more advantageous to read the original reports. It was Hynson's task to get those reports and to turn them over to the British. And just in case he forgot that he was an agent, the ships on standby service in the Channel were there to remind him of his duty.

The tenth of March came, but Hynson's vessel did not sail into the Channel to be seized by the British. Eden was perplexed. He could not learn what had happened until 18 March when Colonel Smith returned to London. Ships had brought news to France of Washington's victory at Trenton. Franklin and Deane then decided to wait for additional information before sending their dispatches. When they did send them, the bags went with Larkin Hammond, captain of the schooner *Jenifer*. Hynson was held on leave pending a new assignment. The Secret Service's plans had to be modified and the *Dolphin* was left to rot in port.[51]

Before Colonel Smith returned to England, however, he devised an alternate plan for Hynson to use while awaiting reassignment from Franklin and Deane. Under Smith's orders, Hynson was to act the part of a thorough American patriot who nevertheless hoped to see peace come again between England and the United States. Hynson was not too good at his role. He traveled to Paris as ordered, but spent most of his time with Carmichael and Nicholson visiting the taverns and whorehouses regularly. He did meet with Lord Stormont to give him what information he knew and to tell the ambassador about his new role. Thereafter, Stormont sent an aide to Hynson twice a week to receive any further news. Stormont for some reason got the impression that Hynson was "mistrusted by Franklin and Deane and consequently knows but little." [52] Joe Hynson also regularly sent reports to Colonel Smith.[53]

Smith also instructed Hynson to tell Silas Deane and William Carmichael of his earlier meetings with John Vardill. Hynson described how this agent of the King had approached him to act as a mediator between England and America.[54] The story as such is a strange one. No agent of the King was so foolish as to believe that an unimportant ship captain could play a role in mediation between the warring powers. Carmichael, himself one of Eden's agents, heard Hynson's story and later told one of his own. To C. W. F. Dumas, during April 1777, Carmichael said that "Lately an English agent tried to bribe me heavily, if I would persuade America to accept a status quo of 1763, repeal of restrictive trade laws, and recognition of the British king." [55] The purpose of Carmichael's claim is not clear. No British agent would have been so dense as to suppose that a nonentity from Maryland would have been able to "persuade America" of anything. Carmichael's position as secretary was nearly as unimportant as Hynson's job. Neither was likely to be able to influence the course of mediation. This man who was to "persuade America" was the same one who had recently told Colonel Smith that he would steal from the Commissioners any papers Hynson might need so those documents could be forwarded to Britain.[56]

Several things may be said about these tales of Hynson's and Carmichael's. True, Carmichael could not actually "persuade America" and Hynson could not actually "act as a mediator." But what would British agents have meant in approaching these two men with such propositions? In both cases they might well have meant: "You are in a position to restore peace by helping us end the hostilities. If you will give us information we need, the war will come to an end more quickly." Indeed, this was the approach enemy propagandists used during the Second World War. In effect, they said that what we are asking may seem like treason on the face of it, but actually it would be a benefit to your country by foreshortening the bloodshed and bringing peace. It may well be that when Vardill spoke with Hynson in the coach outside Mrs. Jamp's whorehouse, this was the method he used. He flattered Hynson's vanity and hinted that he could perform a valuable service by stealing the papers of the American embassy.

No thoughtful person could have taken the surface aspects of the stories of Hynson and Carmichael seriously and there is no indication that either Franklin or Deane did so. Up to this point it is quite likely that neither of them had any reason to believe that Hynson was anything more than he seemed: "a lusty, black looking man" who was "one of the most stupid . . . fellows living," conceited, with all the marks of "an English Tar." [57] The Americans did not suspect him and the British did not trust him. Vardill wrote to Eden that "I have ever doubted whether any trust would be reposed in Hynson," and Lord Stormont also shared those sentiments.[58]

Hynson's story may have been embellished, but he had at least said something significant in telling about his earlier meetings with Vardill. He was saying that he had been contacted by the British government, and specifically by John Vardill, whose very existence he would have been unaware of if his story were not, in part, true. Did those who heard him believe that he had turned Vardill down? His story should have served to warn even the most careless person that the man who had been selected to carry American dispatches might well be a British agent. The surprising point then is that even after they were aware of Hynson's story, Franklin and Deane still considered him for future tasks. They knew little about him other than that he was a relative of Wickes and Nicholson and, with Carmichael, was their drinking

companion. They were under no moral obligation to use him.
He had knocked about England and then had had this strange
encounter with Vardill. Perhaps Hynson's confession was the
reason they overlooked so much and went to such lengths to
use him. Deane, at least, must have been overjoyed when he
learned of Hynson's talks with Vardill. As an agent himself,
it must have been comforting to know he could utilize Hynson's services if the opportunity arose.

It was at this juncture in early April 1777 that Arthur Lee
returned from his mission to Spain and sensed the coldness of
his colleagues toward him. Franklin and Deane held meetings
to which he was neither invited nor welcome. Correspondence was not shared with him. Neither Deane nor Franklin
had gone to Amsterdam as the three had earlier agreed. Both
men reacted with chilly correctness and with no hint of a desire to make him a part of a working triumvirate. Worse, neither Franklin nor Deane saw fit to brief Lee on developments
during his absence. Topping all else was the matter of the
embassy files. Lee was not allowed to have keys to the files of
the Americans, although his credentials were equal to those of
the other two. He repeatedly requested access to them, but
was put off by one excuse or another.[59]

There was another matter. When Lee left for Spain,
Franklin was already planning to move from L'Hôtel
d'Hambourg in Paris to L'Hôtel de Valentinois at Passy,
Chaumont's home. Franklin promised Lee space there for living quarters and offices. Now, back in Paris, Lee found
Deane ensconced in the quarters at Passy that Franklin had
promised to him. Temple told Lee that Deane had moved in
at his grandfather's request. Franklin made no effort to renew
his earlier offer to share rooms with Lee. With the help of
Ferdinand Grand, the Commission banker, Lee finally located a beautiful home in the suburb of Chaillot, some three
miles from Passy. At Chaillot, however, Lee felt isolated from
the business of the embassy—and with good reason, for meet-

ings were held, decisions were made, money was spent without consultation with him.

Lee was troubled by these developments. What could it all mean? The more he considered the possibilities, the more he came to see what he believed to be the true picture. At first merely suspicious, he became moved by cold anger and committed himself to the task of uncovering evidence of wrongdoing. For the time being, though, Lee held his peace.

Arthur had been back from Spain only a few days when he accepted Franklin's urgings to travel to Berlin to seek Prussian help for America. Once again Lee packed his bags. William Eden soon learned of Lee's projected mission. William Carmichael sent a letter, 24 April 1777, to "George Carlting," an alias used by Paul Wentworth.[60] Calling himself Pierre Le Maître, Carmichael brought Wentworth up to date on recent developments. "This is my 4th [letter?] and I have just rec.ᵈ the second [letter?]," he wrote. He sent along information Vergennes had given to the Americans the previous week. He told about recent appropriations by the Congress intended to increase troop strength. Carmichael asked Wentworth for a meeting at Dieppe as soon as it could be arranged, at which time "The particular explanations which you desire shall be given, but it cannot be done now." With elation, he reported that "There are now no secrets kept from me."

Carmichael then made a comment revealing much about the attitude of Franklin and Deane toward Lee. Arthur Lee, the spy wrote, "sets out about the middle of next week for Berlin. . . . There is really some Business but his Absence is also wanted. *We shall now have a clear stage.*" [61] Before Lee's departure—perhaps coincidentally, perhaps on orders from his superiors—Carmichael decided to go with him.

On the same day "Le Maître" sent his message to "Carlting," Edward Bancroft also wrote to his boss. His words were almost identical to those of his fellow agent. "Lee will not leave Paris till towards the end of the week. Till he is gone they [Franklin and Deane?] deal only in generals. They don't like him nor his connections on your side of the water." Bancroft may here have referred to William Lee, Arthur's brother, then residing in London. In a postscript, Bancroft returned to his subject. "A. Lee and Carmichael set out again for Berlin. There is really some business, but the absence of Lee is the chief object." [62]

These two letters give independent and corroborative evidence that two on-the-spot agents viewed Lee's Berlin trip as a maneuver to get him away from Paris. Neither Franklin nor Deane wanted Lee nearby. Perhaps Lee asked too many questions; perhaps Franklin and Deane felt constrained to postpone some private endeavor on which they were working so long as Lee remained in Paris. Fresh from his success in Spain and sensing that he would be able to accomplish more in Prussia than he would in Paris, given the obstructions placed in his way by Franklin and Deane, Arthur Lee made ready to leave for Berlin.

Lee, Carmichael, and Stephen Sayre, a friend of Arthur's, set out by stage for Berlin. The weather had turned balmy, and the trip was far more pleasant than Lee's earlier one to the Pyrenees. The three travelers arrived at Berlin on Wednesday, 4 June 1777. Lee set about his task of negotiating a commercial treaty for the United States with the Court of Prussia. His efforts were to no avail. Longtime allies of the English and fearful of England's anger, the Prussian ministers were not prepared to consider a relationship with the United States. Lee knocked on many doors and sat waiting long hours in official anterooms. He finally realized that both the ears and the minds of the ministers at Berlin were closed. Still he remained in the city, hoping to find some way by which he could induce consideration of his case.

The days passed. Hugh Elliot, the English representative to Prussia, learned of Lee's presence in Berlin. The Secret Service informed Elliot through channels that it wanted a look at Lee's papers. Elliot had Lee watched and quickly

learned his daily routine. He heard of the daily journal that
Lee faithfully kept and decided to have it copied.

By suborning the servants at Lee's hotel, Elliot was able to
have copies made of the keys to Lee's room and to the bureau
in which he kept his journal. The strike date was set for 26
June. On that evening Lee and Sayre set out to visit the home
of a country gentleman with whom they frequently passed
their evenings. They would, Elliot knew, be gone for some
hours, for they usually stayed quite late. Elliot personally entered Lee's room, opened the bureau, and took from it the
journal and other papers he found there. With time racing,
Elliot got the papers to a four-man team of copiers who immediately set to work. Elliot gave himself an alibi by visiting
at several places during the next few hours where he would
be sure to be remembered. At about ten o'clock, Elliot returned to Lee's hotel, just in time to see the two Americans in
the lobby preparing to go up to their rooms. They had come
back too early. The copyists could not possibly have finished
their work and even a little additional time would afford them
the opportunity to duplicate more material.

Before Sayre and Lee could leave the lobby, Elliot joined
them. For two hours he persisted in inconsequential small talk
until Lee, totally bored, excused himself and went to his
room. As soon as he left, Elliot got out of the hotel. Confer-
ring with his team, he found that they had completed copying
the most important of Lee's papers. Now the problem was to
get the papers back to Lee before they were missed.

Moments after Elliot had gone, Lee ran back downstairs in
a panic. Both his personal diary and the state secrets were
gone. A quick search of the hotel revealed nothing. It did not
take long for Lee and Sayre to recall the strange conversation
they had just had with Elliot. They realized what had happened. By this time Elliot had disguised himself as best he
could and mustered enough courage to return to the hotel and
drop the papers on the steps of the building by the front door.
An employee there soon noticed them and they were re-

turned to Lee by the hotel manager with profuse and abject apologies. The words did nothing to placate Lee.

The next morning Lee entered an official protest to the Prussian government. The embarrassed Prussians investigated. The inn's servants were shortly arrested and admitted that they had been bribed to provide someone on Elliot's staff with all the help he needed. Before the local police could act, Elliot sent his man out of the country to safety. What had begun as a quiet plot now became public knowledge. Called before the Prussian Foreign Minister, Elliot lamely confessed his role in the affair. He also admitted "excessive zeal" on the part of his servant. He affirmed that his home government had had no part in the theft and agreed to be recalled if it was felt necessary. The Prussians so notified England. Hugh Elliot was soon sent home, to be replaced by Morton Eden, William Eden's brother. The English government rebuked Elliot in mild diplomatic language and rewarded him with one thousand guineas.[63]

The documents had been copied on the night of 26 June. By 10 July William Eden sat at his desk reading them. It was a coup of major proportions. Lee's journal told of his negotiations earlier with the Spanish, of French promises of military supplies to America, of more than two million livres in subsidies already made. Eden read of the meeting of the Americans with Vergennes and of many other matters. Some of what he saw was new, and those facts of which he already had been informed received grand confirmation from the copied papers. All of it was valuable to Eden, for he now had Arthur Lee's observations as a double-check on his own spies.

Humiliated and chastened, Lee returned to Paris. His carriage clattered into the streets of that city during the late summer of 1777. Not at all anxious to receive the sneers of his colleagues, Lee nevertheless dutifully conferred with them about the recent misadventure. They listened to him, scolded him, and showed no sign of interest in briefing him on the progress of their own activities. It was the same story as on his return from Spain all over again, except that the isolation he had then felt was now heightened.

As the days passed Lee became more concerned. He saw Franklin and Deane conducting the business of the American legation without any consultation with him. Their two signatures alone were affixed to many official documents, and Lee noticed that some were signed only by Deane. To make matters worse, Lee learned that Jonathan Williams, Jr., Franklin's grandnephew, was now acting as American commercial agent at Nantes. The letter of appointment, signed only by Deane, had been issued while Arthur was in Berlin. Lee could hardly contain his anger. The appointment was unnecessarily hurried and there was no need for it to have been done in his absence. Congress had already chosen Thomas Morris for this office. Lee still wished to avoid open conflict with his colleagues and so did not insist upon his view, but he was sure that the commissioners did not have the authority to act in such a way in defiance of Congress' explicit instructions.[64]

Lee was further incensed when he discovered that mail from America was opened by Franklin and shared with Deane, but not with him. He made suggestions for ordering the affairs at Passy, for more careful record-keeping, and for excluding questionable characters from access to the files and papers of the embassy. Franklin and Deane received his ideas coolly and ignored them consistently. For the record, Lee occasionally resorted to setting forth his ideas in writing, but his letters were frequently unanswered. Franklin sometimes sent a response by way of a verbal message carried to Lee by one or another of the old doctor's servants. Lee thought this lack of formality a questionable procedure. He made appointments with Franklin. Too often they were delayed or not kept at all. It was no wonder that his suspicions of misconduct grew. Frozen out of embassy business and personally ignored, Lee wondered what he had done to warrant such treatment.

Money matters soon became another sensitive issue separating the men. When Lee returned from his abortive trip to

Berlin, he learned that Franklin and Deane, in his absences, had spent more than five million livres of public money and owed still more. As Lee well knew, in September 1776, Charles Thomson, the President of Congress, had ordered the commissioners to keep "an account of their Expenses," to have the use of an immediate sum of £10,000 and the right to hire a secretary for a yearly salary of £1,000.[65] Bookkeeping was required, yet Lee found no vouchers, no ledgers with printed columns of figures neatly explaining where all the money had gone. He found only a vast debt, and silence. In spite of heated correspondence with Franklin, he learned nothing. Arthur Lee was admittedly cantankerous, but up to this point he had showed little rancor. He had not openly quarreled with his colleagues. He had not wanted an open break among the personnel of the American mission. He had handled more than his fair share of duties since arriving in France. Only now, when he sensed the coldness of his fellow commissioners after his return from Berlin, did his anger begin to manifest itself. From this point on it never cooled, for nothing he saw or heard dissuaded him from his suspicions about the strange activities of Franklin and Deane. Certainly he believed there was enough about which to be suspicious. Among other things, Hynson was still hanging about.

Deane and Franklin continued to keep Joseph Hynson under contract. Hynson's ability to find unsuitable all vessels he was shown and Deane's craven reactions when so told were a master study of using contrived circumstances. They constantly "anticipated" one imminent departure for America after another from 10 March to 18 October, 1777. Deane wrote home of the exceptional qualities of this seaman he had procured. To the President of the Congress he described Hynson as "being a good Seaman, & of a cool, sedate and Steady Temper of Mind." [66] Franklin and Deane informed the Committee of Secret Correspondence that they had hired a "very ingenious officer" who was in all ways reliable and very suitable for carrying dispatches home.[67] Such comments

seem naive when it is remembered that Hynson's British employers thought him dense, conceited, braggardly, and a rascal.

On 20 May 1777 Deane wrote to John Hancock that
Hynson "now goes out with a ship." [68] A copy of that letter
also found its way into the British files. Deane's news was
elaborated by George Lupton. He told Eden that Hynson
was to meet a French sea captain and both would sail from
Marseilles in command of a ship.[69] John Vardill intercepted
some of Franklin's correspondence and learned that the Marseilles plan had been canceled by the French government.[70]
The French had decided not to allow a shipment of materials
from their arsenals and so the voyage had been abandoned.

On 1 June 1777 Deane sent Hynson new sailing instructions. He would leave for America from Nantes. When
Hynson saw the cutter he was to captain, the *Anonyme*, he
rejected it as too dilapidated.[71] Such concern for seaworthi-
ness was commendable, especially in one who had only a few
months before pronounced a rotting hulk like the *Dolphin* to
be fit. But then the *Dolphin* only had to sail into the Channel
before it could be allowed to sink. The *Anonyme* might actually have to cross the Atlantic. Upon Hynson's rejection of
the *Anonyme*, Deane wrote him a letter of apology and promised to find him a more suitable craft.

During July and August Hynson wasted some weeks in
half-hearted efforts to purchase, repair, and arm the *Pacifique*,
a ship owned by a friend of Beaumarchais.[72] The sale fell
through and Hynson continued to find ship after ship un-
seaworthy or deficient in one respect or another. In this way
he hoped to fulfill his promise to his masters in England by
waiting until a ship carrying the most possible dispatches
should be assigned him. Until then he could dally in France at
the expense of the Americans.

Since 5 April 1777 Deane had advanced Hynson £3,940
for salary, traveling expenses, and miscellaneous costs.[73] Another £15,169 Hynson supposedly spent in outfitting the *Dol-*

phin, which had been abandoned after the abortive mission of 10 March. The only accomplishment Deane can be credited with was the support of yet another British spy for six months.

Hynson was still cooling his heels when Lee had returned from Berlin. Lee's complaints about the vast sums of money spent during his absence without regaid for accounting procedures alarmed Deane. Worried that the Virginian might wish to pry further, Silas contemplated a change in strategy. When the sale of the *Pacifique* fell through, Deane reluctantly discharged Hynson. He had, he said, no more money for "equipping or being permitted to equip any more vessels from France since prohibitions had come from higher powers." [74] Although he felt he could no longer find a ship for Hynson's own use, he did continue efforts to locate a berth for him on someone else's vessel. On 27 September Hynson was offered a job on the *Pacifique*, which was finally sailing for the New World.[75] He turned down the offer.

Just as Hynson's task seemed hopeless, he was saved by a timely letter to Deane. In October, Jonathan Williams, Jr., at Nantes, wrote Deane that he had located a vessel which might be satisfactory to Hynson. Deane replied that he would send the captain at once. "If he is not contented with the vessel, he is at Liberty to find a better employ." [76] But Deane would have to make no more excuses for Hynson: The plot was nearly ready to unfold.

Some months earlier, Captain John Folger, a Nantucket relative of Franklin on his mother's side, had made his way to Passy after various misadventures at sea and in England. Franklin offered to give him a privateer to command. Folger, who had never captained a warship, declined. Then Franklin sent him to Havre to look over a ship the Paris mission planned to buy. At Havre, Folger found Hynson inspecting the ship he had come to see. The two became friends. They took billets at the same boardinghouse, run by a Madame Moreau. In October they each received a letter from Paris, written on the seventh by Deane. Accompanying the letters were five packet pouches of diplomatic dispatches containing the entire confidential correspondence between the French Court and the American commissioners from 12 March to 7 October 1777. Included also were the private letters of Franklin, Deane, Lee, and other American officials in Europe. The packets were addressed to the chairman of the Committee of Foreign Correspondence, Philadelphia.

The courier who brought this material found Hynson and Folger together, checked their identification, and turned his material over to them. The letter to Folger told him that the Paris mission had selected him to carry the dispatches to America on a French ship then ready to sail. He was told that Hynson would act in his stead if he could not go. Deane wrote Hynson that the ship was ready to sail from Nantes and said that inasmuch "as the publick are much interested in the safe delivery of these Dispatches, I hope you will go with them, if Captain Folger cannot." Both men received the usual warning about weighting the pouches and being constantly prepared to cast them overboard if apprehension by the British seemed imminent.[77]

This was what Hynson had been waiting for since early February, when he had sat in Vardill's carriage in the road outside Madame Jamp's whorehouse. Folger, carrying the dispatch bags, took them to his room at Moreau's boardinghouse and locked them in his sea chest. It was only long after, when he was questioned by the Congress, that he remembered he had been absent from the room a short time before he locked up the pouches. He had gone back to the dock on an errand of Hynson's design. While Folger was gone, Hynson untied the string binding the packets, extracted the dispatches, replaced them with blank paper of an equal size and thickness, and rebound the packet. Some private letters he removed, others he left. When Folger returned, Captain Hynson helpfully assisted him in locking the bags in his trunk.

It was a splendid moment for the Secret Service. Eden was

about to get his hands on all the confidential correspondence
of the past eight months between the commissioners and the
French ministry. The theft was not discovered until the
packets were opened after Folger's arrival in America. Hynson had thoroughly heeded a recent letter he had received
from Carmichael. Mixing news of pleasure with business,
William wrote that "Bancroft and I keep a decent house we
see none but ladies of the 1st Quality—I have not seen a
strumpet this 3 weeks." Then he added "keep yourself clear
of ale parties at Nantes & [don't miss] the main chance." [78]
Hynson had not missed the opportunity urged on him by
Carmichael. Supplied with sheafs of blank paper cut to the
size of the official reports, Hynson had used them to advantage. His supplies had to have previously been furnished to
him by Deane for Hynson would not have known what size
the letters would be. He would not have had the time, in the
short interval Folger was gone, to have procured a proper
supply of paper and then cut, bound, and substituted it for the
dispatches. He barely had time to search the five pouches to
find the one in which those dispatches lay. His preparations
had to have been made ahead of time.

On 19 October 1777 Captain John Folger set sail for
America and that same day Joseph Hynson left for Dieppe.
Hynson quickly traveled to London and gave the dispatches
to Colonel Smith. The colonel turned them over to Eden
who handed them on to George III.[79] In an accompanying
note Eden wrote that Hynson had "by his Conduct fully discharged his promises made some months ago—He deserves
his reward." The payoff was £200 in cash and an additional
£200 yearly. Eden also told his king that he would attempt to
use Hynson further if possible, for "He was an honest rascal
and no fool though apparently stupid." [80]

Silas Deane attempted to cover his tracks. He now committed to writing words that would later clearly show his
own duplicity in the Hynson affair. Only four days after

Hynson had turned the dispatches over to Colonel Smith and well before Folger arrived in America, Deane, knowing that Hynson had gone to England, wrote Jonathan Williams, Jr.: "This wrong-headed conceited Fool has at last turned out one of the most ungrateful of Traitors, & instead of going to Nantes, as he had wrote me, has fled into England, there to help himself by telling all & much more than he had any knowledge of. It is fortunate *for us* that he knows nothing, but this will not prevent his pretensions to knowing everything." [81]

This strange letter tells more than Deane would have been willing to reveal. Until the outbreak of war between England and France there was a steady stream of visitors—some of them tourists, some spies—crossing back and forth over the channel. Franklin had specifically instructed Hynson only a few months before to travel to England to buy a ship. Now Deane was suggesting that simply because Hynson was in England was cause for alarm. Actually if Deane was innocent, he would not even have known the whereabouts of Hynson. Nor should he have acted as if anything was amiss, for presumably the dispatches had gone off to America safely locked away. Clearly he should not have suggested that anything was wrong until the theft of those papers had been reported back from America months later. Why should he describe Hynson as an "ungrateful Traitor"? Without collusion, how would he know? If all their dealings had been aboveboard, Hynson would have been within his rights to travel to England after Folger had accepted the assignment to carry the dispatches.

Soon Hynson returned from England to Paris. He wrote Deane that he had gone to Britain to obtain some financial backing and offered to furnish the Paris mission with whatever information he could. Deane cut off his erstwhile friend in order to protect himself from suspicion. In answer to Hynson's letter Deane replied, "as you have had the assurance to

. . . propose the betraying your new Patrons . . . I must tell you that no Letters from you will hereafter be rec^d by Silas Deane." [82]

Operatives have never been known to be particularly moral and have traditionally been used by anyone able to profit from their information—no matter how gained. For Deane to cut off a source of information in those dark days was either stupid or calculated. Deane was not stupid. But he was running scared. It did not make sense to tell a man willing to spy on the enemy that his morals were inadequate. But Deane wanted it on the record that he was having nothing to do with Joseph Hynson. Soon Folger's packets would be opened in America, and the finger of suspicion would quickly point to Hynson. Foolishly, Deane must have imagined that such a letter would show that he had no involvement with the culprit.

Deane himself may have made a clandestine trip to England at this time. In the files of the Secret Service which tell the story of Hynson's treachery, there is one document entitled "First Intelligence respecting Benson's journey to Dover." It appears after a great number of other manuscripts telling of the relationship of Hynson to the Secret Service. It is placed, significantly, immediately before several of the wrappers taken from the bundles of correspondence stolen by Hynson. Benson was Deane's code name. What had taken him to Dover, England? When had he gone? For how long? What did he do while in that city? With whom did he meet? There is no further information in the files to cast any light on these questions—only the bare assertion regarding "Benson's journey to Dover." [83]

Hynson spent some time in Paris, but lived in seclusion, "cut" by most of the Americans there. The day after Hynson's return from England, Carmichael came to eat breakfast with him and delivered a message from Deane and Benjamin Franklin. They wanted to know when Colonel Edward Smith would next be in Paris. Hynson told Carmichael that the man would return soon. After Carmichael left, Hynson wrote Smith, telling him that Franklin and Deane had both advised him to remain quietly in his quarters until Smith arrived. "They at the same time said that the French Court had knowledge of my going to England and that they [Franklin and Deane] were accused of sending me there, which was the reason they could not agree to see me *at present*." [84]

In the face of the kind of perfidy Hynson had shown, why would two honest diplomats even consider *ever* seeing him again? Had not Deane already written that he would receive no more letters from Hynson? Now he sent word that "at present" he could not see him. Nor could Franklin.

Hynson remained quietly in his rooms fearing possible arrest. Carmichael occasionally called, but no others came. He did not relish the attitude of his ex-friends. "It is a carrecter I heartily despise," he wrote to Smith. "I would rather you would send me to America as a common soldier, where I might be of some use." [85] Desperate for recognition from his superiors, Hynson even forwarded to them summaries of his conversations with Carmichael.[86] Smith gave him his last task. He was to spy out sailing dates and ship cargoes. He managed to relay information on one armed ship which was carrying munitions to America. It was duly captured in the Channel by the British. By this time even Carmichael no longer visited him. On 1 November 1777 Carmichael wrote Wentworth that "J. Hynson, a Native of Maryland has quitted France in Disgust, and I am much afraid will tell what he knows: I therefore caution you against seeing him." [87] Of no further use to the Secret Service, Hynson had gone to England, where he was granted a small post in the British navy.[88] Joseph Hynson's role in the American Revolution had ended.

His actions, however, would long affect the activities of other Americans in Europe. The episode caused suspicions and provided fuel for arguments and misunderstandings among the young country's delegates.

Arthur Lee had, unknowingly, provided an opportunity

for Hugh Elliot in Berlin to steal and copy his journal and papers. Yet he misspent no money, worked energetically at his
tasks, and unquestionably furthered French and Spanish aid
to America in desperate times. His colleagues excoriated him.
Franklin and Deane sat in Paris content to wait for the
French government to act. They spent money at a fantastic
rate without voucher or receipt and with few visible results.
They staffed the Paris mission with men of low and suspicious character. They intentionally ignored Lee whenever
possible. They spent thousands of pounds supporting Joe
Hynson over a period of months, giving him opportunity to
steal vast quantities of America's secrets. They planned and
schemed for their own private benefits. Deane rested at ease
in his comfortable quarters rather than make a move toward
The Hague where he might have been able to arrange a commercial treaty helpful to his country. Yet there is evidence
that he felt well enough to make a clandestine trip to Dover,
England.

    What was Deane's motive in all this? How did he profit?
The answer may never be fully known. But the suspicious
nature of Silas Deane's activities did not escape the attention
of the more astute of his contemporaries. Despite his efforts to
disassociate himself from Hynson and to avoid any connection with the stolen dispatches, Thomas Paine was able to
trace the connection in part. In an open letter to Deane published in *The Pennsylvania Packet*, 16 February 1778, Paine
wrote: "When the supposed dispatches were brought to
York-town by Capt. Folger, who came with them from
France, they consisted of a packet for Congress of nearly the
size of a half sheet, another for Robert Morris, esq., of about
the same size, another for Mr. Barnaby Deane, brother to
Silas Deane, of about the same size, a smaller one from Mr.
Arthur Lee to his brother, Col. R. H. Lee, besides letters and
some small parcels to different persons, private, and another
packet, which I shall mention afterwards. The packet for
Congress and that for Col. R. H. Lee had both been robbed

of every article of their contents, and filled up with blank white paper; that for Mr. Morris and Mr. Barnaby Deane came safe with all their contents. Whoever was the thief, must know exactly what to take and what to leave; otherwise the packet for Mr. Morris and Mr. Barnaby Deane must have been equally as tempting as that to Col. Lee; or rather more so, because they were more bulky and promising. In short, the theft discovers such an intimate knowledge of the contents, *that it could only be done, or directed to be done* by some person originally concerned in the writing of them." [89]

A few months later, in an article dated 26 March 1779, Paine again spoke out on the Hynson affair. He charged that Deane "negotiated a proffered present amounting to two hundred thousand pounds into a purchase, and embezzled, or were privy to embezzling, the public dispatches to promote the imposition." [90]

As soon as it became generally known in France that the dispatches had been stolen, William Lee wondered about the preparations Hynson must have made. To his brother Arthur he wrote: "On reflecting about the dispatches that have been stolen, I have not a doubt of its being done by *Deane* and that *Carmichael* knows it at least, but most likely was as much concerned in the act as the other. Tho' *Dr. Franklin* may know the whole, no eclaircissement is to be expected from him; on the contrary every finesse will be used to conceal the Truth. . . . it will be proper to trace every hand through which the packets went until they came to Folger. . . ." Considering what the possibilities were, William added that "if not too late, they should on the other side carefully compare the blank paper that was put in the covers instead of the letters, with the paper on which the letters of *Deane* and *Franklin* were written . . . for if on examination the blank paper is the same with either of the others, the mistery will then be very plain." [91] The suggestion was excellent; unfortunately it was never followed up.

Historians generally have condemned Arthur Lee, upheld

Ben Franklin, and written of Deane's perfidy in this and other cases only when publication of the documents made the extent of his treachery obvious. The idea that the suspicions of Arthur Lee had any basis in fact, the idea that Franklin might have had knowledge of Deane's treachery, has been dismissed for over a century as outrageous and perhaps unpatriotic.

CHAPTER SEVEN

———•◦•———

"Moses" and Le Pot de Vin

Somewhere, in the summer of 1777, the days were lethargic. Somewhere there was a certain amount of ease and calm. Some men must have worked in harmony and friendship. Wherever those qualities and conditions existed, it was not at the American mission in Paris. Arthur Lee returned from Berlin to ask his pointed questions. Deane busied himself trying to find Hynson a ship. Bancroft, Lupton, and Carmichael sent their reports through channels to the offices of William Eden. Some of the messages Eden read seemed small talk rather than news of grave developments. In June, Lupton wrote that "Dr. Franklin keeps himself to himself, and very seldom appears at Mr. Deane's unless on some matter of consequence or just before they are sending their dispatches to America." He told of seeing Bancroft every day, and still did not know that Bancroft was a fellow spy. Lupton reported that Bancroft "says little, his chief object in my opinion is good eating & drinking, at which he is not a Bad hand." [1] The tension among the Americans in Paris tightened as incident after incident piled up. Among the three commissioners there was no longer any hope of compromise or fellowship. And America suffered.

Ben Franklin had continued his correspondence with friends in England. Since his arrival in France he had been sending such letters, often dealing with hopes for eventual success in the Vandalia project. Thomas Walpole, the English banker, wrote him 1 February 1777 about the finances of Vandalia. "When the charges are finally settled, I shall send you an account thereof, with a credit upon some House in Paris for the balance. I hope this will be speedily, as I am, and have been for some time past, very impatient to get rid of a transaction where so many different persons are concerned. . . ." Walpole did not mean he was dropping his efforts, simply that the membership of the Walpole Associates was so large that it needed to again be reshaped, as had happened so often in the past. Once more there was dead wood to be pruned away. As he indicated, he hoped to scale down the rolls "that I might be left at liberty to act for myself in it hereafter, according to my own inclination, and to the circumstances of the times." He added that "Lord Camden sends you his best compliments." [2]

A few days later, Walpole wrote again. He complained about the ineffectiveness of Sam Wharton. Under present circumstances, Walpole said, Wharton could be of no use in further applications for Ohio lands. For this reason Walpole had closed Wharton's account—that is, he had paid off Wharton for his share of stock.[3] Walpole continued his efforts to buy out those no longer of any use. On 5 March he again wrote Franklin that he had closed the accounts with other associates and enclosed Franklin's share of those accounts.[4]

Sometimes Franklin received letters from his friends in England by way of Edward Bancroft. On 4 March 1777 Bancroft sent Ben a note enclosing two letters from Walpole. In the note he commented that some people were jealous of the role he played as the courier by whom Franklin forwarded certain letters.[5] Such an extensive correspondence continued between France and England that later in 1777 the American Commissioner to Tuscany wrote that "So many ships have been carried into England, either as prizes, or by

the Villainy of the crews—having public despatches on
board—that I believe the British Ministry—have been better
informed of our affairs—from authority—than the Commissioners themselves." [6] He was more correct than he knew.

All his life Franklin loved to swim. As the cold winter days
of early 1777 moderated into the warmth of spring, Ben
began daily swims in the Seine river near his home. His
grandson Temple occasionally joined him. Ben always had
been a powerful swimmer and to keep his old bones in shape
he regularly swam along the Seine until he reached a public
bathhouse built on a river barge anchored across from the
Tuileries. Climbing aboard, Franklin sat in the clouds of
steam as the heat opened the pores of his sweating body. It
occurred to him that this was a perfect place for secret meetings. He had not identified himself to any of the intendants
and it would be safe to sit in the steaming rooms and talk with
whomever he wished. Two naked men obscured by steam
would be difficult to identify. He came to use this bathhouse,
called *Le Pot de Vin*, as a secret rendezvous point. We know
he used it in September 1777 when an English emissary, Benjamin Vaughan, came to Paris to discuss with Franklin prospects for peace. Later that year Paul Wentworth, who
wanted to see Franklin, suggested to Deane that they meet at
6:00 P.M., Friday, 12 December, at the *Pot de Vin* bathhouse
on the barge in the Seine.[7]

In September, when Vaughan arrived in town, he received
instructions to go to "a large white wooden Building upon a
Boat in the River opposite to the Tuilleries." It was the best
place he had found, Franklin later told him, where "a Meeting with me would not occasion Speculation." Vaughan went
to the baths, asked for an "old Englishman with grey Hair,"
stout, known to be a strong swimmer. The attendant to
whom he spoke immediately took him to Franklin and he and
Vaughan held their meeting shrouded by the haze of heated
air.[8] What we have evidence for in two cases may be supposed to have happened in others as well for which no docu-

ments remain. In both cases, those who came to Paris arrived from England for clandestine meetings with Franklin. Ben told one emissary to meet him at *Le Pot de Vin* for he had found it to be an excellent location. His words indicate that he had used it before. From Wentworth's notes it is clear that Silas Deane also knew of the meeting place, and the tone of Wentworth's comment allows for the possibility that Deane used the bathhouse for the same purpose as Franklin. The meetings at *Le Pot de Vin* were part of a pattern of sessions common for Franklin and Deane in that year of 1777.

Wentworth actively continued his work. The information he gathered through his agents was damning to the American cause. Some of his reports, headed "Port News," related most of the ship sailings of vessels taking supplies and dispatches to America.[9] From May 1777 to April 1778—eleven months— few ships got through to America because of the espionage ring centered in Franklin's Passy headquarters. Not only did Wentworth receive copies of commission papers, but often he got the original documents forwarded to him from the Paris mission. On one occasion he noted "Bancroft left them for my perusal. I also retained originals of those of which he brought me duplicates." Of all the personnel working out of, or associated with, the Passy embassy, only Arthur Lee can be shown to have worked wholeheartedly for the new United States.

In 1777 Arthur finally found an ally in the person of his brother, William Lee, who came to France that year as a duly appointed American commercial and naval agent to work with Thomas Morris at the city of Nantes. Nantes was a strategically located seaport on the southeast coast of the Brittany peninsula of France. From the start of hostilities between England and her colonies, Americans used Nantes as a base for privateering and for shipping supplies to America.[10] Early in the war, Robert Morris—"the financier of the Revolution"—convinced the Congress to appoint his half-brother Thomas as agent at Nantes.[11] Robert profited in two ways.

Tom was a drunk and this new job rid the family of the problems he caused. It also opened the way for huge profits for the firm of Willing and Morris if Tom could manage to guide convoys and shipments to the firm's piers in the West Indies and in America.

Tom was not the man for the job. More interested in "demon rum" than in fighting the "English devil," he allowed business at Nantes to deteriorate. In January 1777 Robert Morris wrote Silas Deane that the Secret Committee of Congress had chosen William Lee to be joint commercial agent at Nantes with Tom.[12] Morris wrote again in February, telling the commissioners that Congress had ratified the Secret Committee's choice. Deane got Morris' first letter sometime in February. He waited, however, until 30 March 1777 before writing to William Lee, who still lived in England. Even then he asked Lee only if he wished to accept the appointment. Franklin and Deane were making great plans and did not wish to see another Lee in France. The one they had was trouble enough.

At the time of these developments Arthur Lee was on his mission in Berlin. On the same day Deane wrote William in London, he proposed to Franklin's grandnephew, Jonathan Williams, Jr., then twenty-two years old, that he go to Nantes and take over the American business there. Williams accepted with alacrity. Both Franklin and Deane knew that William Lee was the congressional appointee for the post. Nevertheless, they went ahead with their own personal plans, thankful that Arthur was not around to harass them. By their appointment of young Jonathan, Franklin and Deane took the handling of prize ships, convoys, cargoes, and all the rest into their own hands. They had no authority for what they had done. If they had acted prior to receiving Robert Morris' letters, it could be argued that they took the course they did for the "good of the cause," but this was not the case. They acted in defiance of clearly stated congressional instructions. The selling of prize ships, captured by privateers, was too im-

portant and too profitable an enterprise to be allowed to remain in the hands of an uncaring drunk or to be turned over
to William Lee, who most definitely would not cooperate
with them for their private economic gain.[13]

While Jonathan Williams was settling in at Nantes,
Franklin and Deane used every possible delaying tactic to
keep William Lee out of that port city. At Nantes, Williams
sold prizes, purchased supplies for American ships, bought
and shipped arms and ammunition. All captured prizes were
consigned to him and sold at auctions where they were purchased at low prices by Williams himself, or by Deane,
Chaumont, and Franklin, and then resold at immense profits.
Williams kept a large warehouse at Nantes to use in loading
and unloading cargoes privately, far from prying eyes.
"There is no doubt," one historian has written, "that there
were opportunities in it for making a fortune." [14]

Thomas Morris, befogged by liquor fumes and neither
knowing nor caring what was happening, left for Bordeaux.
When Robert Morris learned of the commissioners' cupidity
in selling out his half-brother and replacing him with Franklin's nephew, he said: "I do not think myself in the least be-
holden to Doctor Franklin or you [Deane] for your Conduct
towards this young Man [Tom]. . . . Perhaps I have flattered
myself with the expectation of more Friendship from the
Doctor and you than I had a right to, and shall therefore Correct the Error in future." [15] Robert's anger against Franklin
and Deane quickly abated when he learned from European
associates of the sloppy way Thomas was operating the
Nantes business. He contacted John Ross, one of his agents in
Hamburg, to go to the French port to take over for Tom.
When Ross arrived, he found that Tom had kept no accounts
and that congressional matters and Morris business affairs
were arbitrarily mixed together in an entangled mess. He also
found Jonathan Williams operating there. Informed by Ross
that Tom had been endangering the lucrative profiteering
and that the commissioners had acted properly in replacing

Tom with Jonathan Williams in order to safeguard private
interests and enterprises, Morris fully accepted the ouster of
his half-brother. A drunk is nobody's friend.

It did not take long for Ross and Jonathan Williams to create a working relationship with one another. Ross protected
Robert Morris' interests while Jonathan acted on behalf of
Franklin and Deane. All of them were speculating on behalf
of their own fortunes. Arthur Lee once ran across a letter
from Jonathan Williams to Deane which told something of
the methods of the profiteers. The letter said:

> I have been on board the prize brig. Mr. Ross tells me he
> has written to you on the subject and the matter rests
> whether according to his letter you will undertake or
> not; if we take her *on private account* she must be passed
> but 13,000 livres.[16]

It was Jonathan Williams' responsibility to sell such vessels
on behalf of the Congress to the highest bidder, with the proceeds to be used to pay for the war effort. This letter shows,
however, that in this case he proposed to act as both seller and
purchaser, to share the profits with John Ross, Deane, and
Franklin, and to see to it that the bidding did not go past
13,000 livres so that the profit on resale would be as high as
possible. Franklin may have been deeply involved in all this in
spite of one author's comment that "Franklin was one of the
very few leaders of the revolution who carried on no private
business during the war." [17]

When William Lee received by ordinary post Silas
Deane's letter of 30 March 1777, several days of April already had passed. Sending the message through the ordinary
mail system was in itself a device used by Franklin and Deane
to keep Lee out of France, for such letters were often intercepted. Should the British Post Office read Deane's words to
Lee, William might well be arrested and confined rather than
permitted to begin active duties on behalf of the new States.

William read of his congressional appointment as joint naval agent, but Deane's phrases clearly indicated that there was no hurry for him to begin. He might as well stay in England as long as he wished or felt necessary inasmuch as things were being well taken care of. As a result, Lee closed his affairs in London at leisure. Pleased to have been called on by the Congress to serve his country, he left with his family for France on 7 June 1777. He got to Paris four days later, while his brother Arthur was absent on his mission to Berlin. When William Lee met with Deane and Franklin, Silas urged him to remain in Paris a little while before going to Nantes. It seemed that his commission from the Congress had not yet arrived and it would be "unsuitable" for him to begin his duties before official authorization came. Such technicalities had not stopped Franklin in January from urging Arthur Lee to go to Spain as his substitute. Deane emphasized that there was no real urgency inasmuch as both Williams and Ross were already there.[18] Such comments obviously were an attempt to protect Jonathan Williams' position as long as possible.

When Arthur Lee returned from Berlin in late summer 1777, he was appalled to find that Jonathan Williams, Jr., had been appointed to the Nantes agency without consulting with him. It seemed to him an incredibly arbitrary and wanton act and he was not hesitant to point this out to Deane. Arthur learned that Jonathan Williams received huge sums of money from the commissioners without any requirement to account for them. Jonathan constantly demanded more funds from the commission banker, Ferdinand Le Grand, and spent them on Deane's authority alone. Lee charged that Jonathan Williams, Deane, and Franklin were using the commercial agency to speculate on their own behalf. He tried to put a stop to such actions, insisting that no more orders should be signed by Deane alone. One author has said that "He was perfectly right in this." [19] Arthur Lee also urged Franklin to stop this practice, but Franklin refused to intercede, thereby lending fuel to Arthur's suspicions that he also was profiteering in the activities at Nantes.

The tenacious Virginian refused to let the matter drop, in spite of Franklin's stalling and Deane's refusal to explain what was going on. It is little wonder that they were always glad when Arthur was out of town. Worried about Lee's dogged determination, Franklin thought it best to write his grand-nephew.

> Dear Nephew: You need be under no concern as to your orders being only from Mr. Deane. As you have always acted uprightly and ably for the public service, you would be justified if you had no orders at all; but as *he generally consulted with me and had my approbation in the orders he gave,* and I know they were for the best and aimed at the public good, I hereby certify you that I approve and join in these you have received from him, and desire you to proceed in the execution of the same.[20]

He sent the letter in a frantic effort to protect the unofficial but privileged position of Williams at Nantes.

William Lee whiled away the summer of 1777 waiting for his commission to come from America. Instead of waiting in Paris, he traveled during those weeks, once to the port of Le Havre and once to Holland. While visiting the Netherlands, he learned of the activities of Paul Wentworth and immediately wrote Franklin warning him against the British agent.[21] Ben must have smiled as he read Lee's letter.

When William returned from the journey to Le Havre, he found himself so shut out at Passy that he began cultivating a friendship with Jacobus Van Zandt—alias George Lupton—not knowing the man was a spy. Lupton wrote Eden of Lee's troubles. "Alderman Lee is returned from Havre, and so much out of favour at Mr Deanes that he frequently comes to me to know what's the news." [22] The situation was nearly as bad as that portrayed by Nathaniel Hawthorne in his short

story "Young Goodman Brown," except that in Paris wherever one turned one encountered a spy rather than a witch.

William Lee's appointment from Congress finally arrived.
He left for Nantes, 2 August 1777, getting to the port city
two days later.[23] It was an uncomfortable moment for the
profiteers at Nantes when William Lee appeared, carrying
his commission from the Congress appointing him agent
there. Jonathan Williams fought to retain the right to dispose
of commercial business there. Lee found Ross guarding the
Morris business, Williams claiming authority for his actions
from the Paris mission, and both disputing his own congressional appointment. Ben Franklin, bewailing the probable
loss of personal profits that would result if William Lee exerted his proper authority there, wrote his nephew that "I
question whether there will be Flesh enough on the Bone for
two to pick." [24]

In spite of the troubles he immediately encountered at
Nantes, William Lee was glad to be out of Paris. To his
brother Francis Lightfoot Lee, then serving in Congress,
went one of the earliest warnings received in America that all
was not going well among the Americans in France. He
wrote that he had encountered too much intrigue in Paris and
that while there his letters had been opened and read "by a
certain set who unhappily have been too much trusted by
your public." He continued that "You can't at this time be
unacquainted with the faithless principles, the low, dirty intrigue, the selfish views, & the wicked arts of a certain race of
Men, &, believe me, a full crop of these qualities you sent in
the first instance from Philadelphia to Paris." [25]

Weeks passed. William Lee was frustrated at every turn in
his efforts to gain cooperation from Jonathan Williams and
John Ross. Constantly thwarted, he finally decided the best
approach would be to confront Franklin and Deane at their
seat of power in Passy. He appointed a local man, John
Schweighauser, to act as his agent during his absence and set
out for Paris, 2 October 1777.[26] When he arrived in the capi-

tal city, a letter from America finally caught up with him informing him that the previous May Congress had selected him to act as commissioner to Prussia and Austria. He was to travel to the courts of Berlin and Vienna in an attempt to procure commercial treaties and aid for the United States.

A similar letter came to another American living in France. Ralph Izard, a tall, handsome, courtly, and fiercely republican South Carolinian had moved from England to Paris in the fall of 1776 when the trouble between the mother country and America made such a journey seem wise. His intention had been to return to South Carolina, but he changed his mind and passed several months in France. Then he learned that Congress had appointed him, at the same time it chose William Lee, as commissioner to Tuscany. It would not be long before the two brothers Lee would find a third ally in Ralph Izard.

On 13 October 1777 William Lee met with Ben Franklin and Silas Deane. He asked them to take away the prize business from Jonathan Williams and they tentatively agreed. Later, when asked why they had not carried out their promise, Franklin and Deane claimed they did not have the authority to act alone inasmuch as Arthur Lee had not given his assent to the removal. It was the only time Franklin and Deane ever saw fit to refrain from acting because of the absence of Lee's consent! The excuse overlooked the fact that Lee had been protesting the appointment since it first had been brought to his attention.[27]

William Lee was incensed at the lack of help he received at the Paris meeting with Franklin and Deane on 13 October. He chafed at the ongoing difficulties he encountered with Jonathan Williams and John Ross. Ross, he quickly determined, was "an insolent meddler" and William Carmichael, the spy from Maryland and embassy secretary, was "completely untrustworthy." He wrote Francis Lightfoot Lee to urge Congress to investigate Deane's nefarious squandering of and profiteering from the public funds.[28] To another

brother, Richard Henry Lee, William wrote of persons who
"to my certain knowledge were not worth one shilling, without a prospect of ever becoming richer, that under the pretext
of serving the Public are now become men of capital fortune." He named Jonathan Williams as a war profiteer and
said "I am sure [that he] has made £40,000 sterling without
one shilling to begin with of his own, and I fancy Mr. Ross
the friend of Mr. R. M.[orris] has done much more." [29]

To Ben Franklin, William Lee complained that "I had experienced in myself that the partiality you and Mr. Deane
manifested for Mr. Williams, and the powers with which you
thought proper to invest him, had greatly impeded me in conducting the public business. . . . [I]t is known to me, and is
indeed notorious to all the world, that you . . . have put near
a million of the public money into his hands." [30]

Arthur and William Lee had debated the propriety of
writing home about their difficulties for weeks. Indeed, two
months before William's meeting with Deane and Franklin,
the brothers had decided that it was a matter of conscience
for them to speak out. Initially they both wrote to their two
brothers serving in the American Congress, and, as we already have seen, William Lee's letter to Francis Lightfoot,
sent 9 August 1777, was the first warning to be mailed to
America. Unfortunately, two of Arthur's letters were written
prematurely. Had they been composed only a few days later,
they would not have been part of the dispatches stolen by
Hynson. On 4 October 1777, Arthur wrote both to his
brother Richard Henry Lee and to Sam Adams, but it was
William Eden of the British Secret Service who received the
messages.

To Sam Adams, Arthur Lee had written that:

I have this year been at the several courts of Spain,
Vienna, and Berlin and I find this of France is the great
wheel that moves them all. Here therefore the most activity is requisite; and if it should ever be a question in

Congress about my destination, I shall be most obliged to you for remembering that I should prefer being at the Court of France.[31]

His letter written the same day to his brother was in much the same vein.

My idea therefore of adapting characters and places is this: Dr. Franklin to Vienna, as the first, most respectable and quiet; Mr. Deane to Holland; and the Alderman [William Lee] to Berlin, as the commercial department; Mr. Izard where he is; . . . France remains the centre of political activity and here therefore I should choose to be employed.[32]

The suggestions Lee made in these two letters were obviously self-serving. Lee's feud with Franklin and Deane has ruined his reputation among historians and biographers of later years, who seized on those words and magnified them out of all proportion. Yet anyone reading the whole of those messages is struck at the generally friendly tone he still maintained toward Franklin and Deane after all that had happened. Further, the reason Arthur gave for desiring to be sole commissioner was a valid one:

I should have it in my power to call those to account, through whose hands I know the public money has passed, and which will either never be accounted for, or misaccounted for, by connivance between those who are to share in the public plunder. If this scheme can be executed, it will disconcert all the plans at one stroke, without an appearance of intention, and save both the public and me.[33]

Lee's concern for being saved was real and his position would become increasingly dangerous and difficult in the months ahead. Franklin and Deane already had used every artifice at their command to rid themselves of him and his efforts to stay the plunder of public money. Some of Lee's charges, taken as a whole, were evidently wrong and misdirected. (Conversely, it is clear that he never suspected some of the things that went on around him.) An angry man, he came to be too suspicious of all actions. But his concern was well placed and his recommendation was a sound one. The scandal of that intrigue-ridden Paris mission would have been demoralizing to the nation had it become public knowledge during those difficult days. Rather than bringing charges in the open, how much better it would be for the Congress simply to change diplomatic assignments. Franklin often complained of the press of business. Then send him to Vienna. Silas Deane had long ago, in January, agreed to go to Holland. Then send him. William Lee was now credentialed to Berlin and planning to leave for that city before long. Ralph Izard had the appointment for Tuscany and was eager to begin his mission. Arthur had traveled the face of Europe, knew France and the French, and already had secured an agreement with Spain. Leave him at Paris.

Fairly mild in his letters, Arthur spoke more plainly in his diary. Regarding Jonathan Williams, he confided to those pages that "it was a most serious consideration, that a young man, without a shilling of property, was thus in a few months to be entrusted with upwards of a million of livres of the public money, of which all the account [Franklin and Deane asked to be] rendered was, that he had expended it." [34]

How soon Richard Henry Lee and Sam Adams learned of these things is unknown. We do know that William Eden read the letters addressed to them containing Arthur Lee's complaints. Franklin and Deane quickly began a correspondence with acquaintances in the United States in which they smeared the character of Arthur Lee and held up his sanity to question. In this light, a letter of 30 October from Jonathan Williams, Jr., to Ben Franklin sounds very strange when read nearly two centuries after the fact and may have had something to do with the heat Lee was putting on. He told his granduncle that he had received the letter Ben sent him on 25 October. He had read it, digested the information, and then destroyed it. Franklin usually kept copies of his correspondence, but there remains no duplicate of any letter to Williams on 25 October 1777. One wonders what warnings about William Lee's plans, what information about secret schemes, what private instructions, what compromising information Franklin's letter had in it that caused Jonathan Williams to act as decisively and swiftly as he did.[35]

On 20 December 1777, in the middle of a series of meetings with Paul Wentworth, Silas Deane suddenly found time to write home about both Lee brothers. The next day Franklin also wrote a similar message. Deane's letter sounded altogether too much like a defense before the fact. He wrote:

> You will I doubt not before the Rec^t of this have had many representations made you. I am not wholly unacquainted with the Nature or Complexion & cou'd were it necessary give you such Details of certain Gentlemen here as would at once raise your Indignation, Contempt & Laughter, but I have never wrote one Word concerning either of them untill this moment. . . . I wait only to know what these accusations are and of what Nature, that I may answer in a distinct and becoming Manner. They have declared they will complain and though *I have never taken a Single Step but by the advice of Doc^t Franklin, and have ever had his approbation,* yet I greatly fear this will not appear at once to Contradict the first Impression made by these artful and designing men in their representations. . . .
>
> I am ignorant of what kind of complaint the two Brothers here will prefer against me, I know they are implacable and indefatigable, . . . I cannot live with these Men, or do business with them, nor can I find the man in the World who can, These Characters Cannot be unknown to you, in some Degree . . . and . . . Doctor Franklin

. . . knows them. This Confidence I have the Honor of
enjoying at Court is the unhappy ground of our Difficulties, for the Minister has the most distrustful opinion of
A.L. Esq, nor will he see him but when obliged to, to do
it. . . . Not a Day passes but he ridicules & Curses the
whole French Nation in a Body before his Servants,
every Servant is a spy of the Ministry & faithfully reports all he hears to a proper Officer . . . so that the Police know by this means every thing which Passes.

. . . In this situation his Spleen is perhaps levelled as
much against Doctor Franklin as myself. But . . . I am
first levelled at.[36]

The next day, Franklin also wrote home, but in a more so-
phisticated way, using milder words, to Robert Morris.

We are now five of us in this City, all honest and Capable Men (if I may include myself in that Description)
and all meaning well for the Public, but our Tempers do
not suit, and we are got into Disputes and Contentions
that are not to our Credit, and which I have sometimes
feared would go to Extremes. You know the natural
Disposition of some of us, how jealous, how captious,
how suspicious even of real Friends, and how positive,
after suspecting a while, that the Suspicions are certain
Truths, Confirmations strong as Proofs from Holy
Writ. You will therefore, I am persuaded, if Complaints
of one another should come to your hands, make due Allowance for such Tempers, and suffer no Man to be
condemn'd unheard, I do not write thus on my own Account, as I am not apprehensive of your receiving any
Complaints of me; for tho it is difficult to live in peace
with such Characters, how much soever one esteems
them for the Virtue and Abilities they otherwise possess,
I have however done it tolerably hitherto; but as I am
not sure it can last, I wish most sincerely that we were
separated; for our being together seems of no Use, and,
as we hinted formerly in a joint Letter, is attended with
many Inconveniences. Such Inconveniences being for-

merly experienced by other States, I suppose the Reason, that no Power in Europe, for a Century past, has sent more than one Person to one Court. Possibly this desirable Event may soon take place, for if France & Spain acknowledge us as independent States the other Courts will follow, and receive our Envoys.[37]

This letter was written 21 December 1777. On either the 16th or the 17th of December, Vergennes' secretary Gérard had told Deane that a treaty with America had been decided on by the French. Franklin wrote this letter to Morris and still speaks of a French alliance as a vague possibility rather than as a nearly accomplished fact. He spent his words, instead, undercutting the mild complaints earlier voiced on 4 October by Arthur Lee. No writer then or later criticized Franklin for suggesting to a congressman that the size of the Paris delegation be cut or the personnel sent elsewhere. Lee's similar words to Sam Adams and Richard Henry Lee, however, were sufficient to send biographers of Franklin into paroxysms of shock and dismay that anyone dared to criticize the *doctorum subtilis et angelicum*. Both Deane and Franklin had written to prominent persons with no hint that the matters mentioned were of a private nature. Lee had not done so. It was not until 9 January 1778 that he enquired of Richard Henry to "Let me know whether it is not proper that I should write to the secret committee that in my judgment the public business here is turned to private emolument, that my advice and endeavors have not the least influence." [38] What he had written earlier was thus intended to be read confidentially by his brother and was not intended for delivery onto the floor of Congress. The same was true for the letter sent to Sam Adams. Adams had been Lee's friend and familiar correspondent for years. Only in 1778 did Arthur Lee begin sending official complaints about the actions of his two colleagues. Lee's patience thus allowed Franklin and Deane to get the jump on him by several months.

Ralph Izard bridled at the treatment accorded William and

Arthur Lee. It was soon clear that there was little possibility of carrying out the assignment for which the Congress had selected him. The Grand Duke of Tuscany refused to receive Izard for the same reason that Spain refused Arthur Lee permission to enter that country in 1776—fear of the British Secret Service network. The Grand Duke at Florence had no wish to involve his nation in an open confrontation with Great Britain. Consequently, Izard remained in Paris until such time as he could get permission to embark on his assignment. An intelligent, energetic man (later an able United States Senator from South Carolina in the Federal period), Izard fully expected to be consulted occasionally by Franklin and Deane, commissioners to France. Yet like Arthur and William Lee, Izard was snubbed. He claimed Franklin delayed supplying necessary papers which would have helped him make a commercial treaty with Tuscany. Ben neglected to answer Izard's letters to him and tried to make it difficult for Izard to send information home to the Congress.[39] Izard soon developed suspicions of Franklin, for he could not understand any good reason for such treatment. Franklin later admitted that he might have done better to have shown Izard some proper attention, yet his actions at the time were purposefully neglectful. His letters to Izard were the sharpest and most insulting he ever wrote and he capped this treatment by publishing a pamphlet deliberately and publicly parodying Izard. The tract read as follows:

"To the Worshipful Isaac Bickerstaff, Esquire, Censor-General

The Tatler, No. 1778

PETITION OF THE LETTER Z

The petition of the Letter Z, commonly called *Ezzard, Zed,* or *Izard,* most humbly showeth;

That your petitioner is of as high extraction, and has as good an estate, as any other letter of the Alphabet;

Lord North

This man headed the British Cabinet from 1770 to nearly the end of the Revolutionary War. He knew Franklin by his code names of "72" and "Moses."

William Eden

The head of the efficient British Secret Service, Eden directed the activities of such men as Wentworth, Bancroft, and Deane.

Silas Deane

Recalled from France by the American Congress in
1778, he remained the loyal friend and close
companion of Ben Franklin.

Richard Henry Lee

The brother of Arthur and William Lee, he was the man in whom they most often confided about the difficult situations they faced in France.

Arthur Lee

Franklin's co-equal colleague from Virginia, Lee fought stubbornly throughout his tenure in France for policies and programs beneficial to America. He was constantly opposed by Ben Franklin and Silas Deane.

John Adams

This doughty New Englander soon came to question
the situation at Passy and Franklin's role in it shortly
after his arrival in France as the replacement for
Silas Deane.

John Jay

Peace negotiator for the
United States of America
at the end of the American
Revolution.

Samuel Wharton

Long-time partner in land speculation with Ben Franklin; his crony at Passy, and later a member of the Continental Congress.

William Lee

Brother of Arthur Lee and congressionally-appointed commercial agent for America at Nantes who harbored dark suspicions about Ben Franklin.

Dr. Edward Bancroft

Spy, secretary at the
American mission, and
friend of Ben Franklin and
Silas Deane.

General
Jonathan Williams

The appointee of Silas
Deane and Ben Franklin
to the American
Commercial Agency at
Nantes.

Ben Franklin

That there is therefore no reason why he should be treated as he is, with disrespect and indignity;

That he is not only actually placed at the tail of the Alphabet, when he had as much right as any other to be at the head; but is by the injustice of his enemies totally excluded from the word WISE; and his place injuriously filled by a little hissing, crooked, serpentine, venomous letter, called S, when it must be evident to your worship, and to all the world, that W, I, S, E, do not spell *Wize,* but *Wise.*

Your petitioner therefore prays, that the Alphabet may by your censorial authority be reversed; and that in consideration of his long-suffering and patience he may be placed at the head of it; that *s* may be turned out of the word *Wise;* and the petitioner employed instead of him.

And your petitioner, as in duty bound, shall ever pray, &c. &c.

Mr. Bickerstaff, having examined the allegations of the above petition, judges and determines, that Z be admonished to be content with his station, forbear reflections upon his brother letters, and remember his own small usefulness, and the little occasion there is for him in the Republic of Letters, since S whom he so despises can so well serve instead of him." [40]

The tract by Franklin was written in the style of the British literary work, "The Tatler." The issue number appended was actually the year 1778 in which he composed and wrote the parody. The letter "S" referred to Silas Deane, whom Izard had often criticized. People read Franklin's work and chuckled at Izard and dismissed him. Thus Izard joined the war with Arthur and William Lee against the Franklin cabal.

The constant trouble among the Americans in Paris was a public disgrace. Much time, better spent on other things, was used in dispute and acrimonious accusations rather than in the service of the United States of America. All of them—Franklin, Deane, Arthur and William Lee, Ralph Izard—fought and clamored. Franklin came "nearer than ever before in his life to sinking his fame in an infamy of corruption." [41]

Before many days of 1778 had passed and probably still in 1777, Franklin began to protect his own position by accusing Arthur Lee of insanity. The first intimation of Ben's new practice came through the words of Silas Deane. Writing to Jonathan Williams, Deane revealed that he had joined forces with Franklin in this assault. "It is very charitable to impute to insanity what proceeds from the malignity of his heart: but the Doctor insists upon it that it is really his case, & I am every day more & more inclined to give in to it." [42]

A few months later Franklin wrote directly to Lee calling him insane, speaking of his "Sick Mind, which is forever tormenting itself, with its Jealousies, Suspicions & Fancies that others mean you ill, wrong you, or fail in Respect for you.— If you do not cure your self of this Temper it will end in Insanity, of which it is the Symptomatick Forerunner, as I have seen in several Instances." [43] Arthur Lee was a cantankerous man, but it is one thing to admit this and quite another to describe him as seriously paranoid, as later writers have done. Most of their "evidence" is based on assertions by Franklin and his friends, who had a great deal to gain if the charges of Arthur Lee could be discredited and were not disinterested spectators in the outcome of the war of words then raging.

Franklin long kept up the attack. On 7 April 1780 he wrote Joseph Reed of Philadelphia that "I caution you to beware of him; for in sowing Suspicions and Jealousies, and in creating Misunderstandings and Quarrels among friends, in Malice, Subtilty, and indefatigable industry, he has I think no equal." [44] If Lee could be faulted for malice, Franklin was at least his equal.

When John Adams arrived in Paris in 1778 to replace Silas Deane, Franklin almost met him at the door with complaints about Lee. As Adams remembered it, "The first moment Dr. Franklin and I happened to be alone, he began to complain. . . . He said there had been disputes between Mr. Deane and

Mr. Lee; that Mr. Lee was a man of an anxious, uneasy temper, which made it disagreeable to do business with him; that
he seemed to be one of those men, of whom he had known
many in his day, who went on through life quarrelling with
one person or another till they commonly ended with the loss
of their reason." [45] If anyone was of an "anxious, uneasy temper" at that time, it was Franklin himself, who now had to
function without his old ally Deane. Finding himself faced
with two thoroughly and implacably honest men as colleagues, it is no wonder that Ben tried to discredit the one
with the other on the moment of their first meeting. In retro-
spect, this effort sheds more doubt on Ben's motives than it
does on Lee's sanity.

The efforts continued. From America, following his recall,
Deane still tried to impugn Lee's reliability. "What I have
observed in Mr. Lee's letter confirms me in the opinion," said
Deane, "which Dr. Franklin and some others have for some
time had of him, that from a long indulgence of his jealous
and suspicious disposition and habits of mind, he at last arrived on the very borders of insanity, and at times he even
passes that line; and it gives me pleasure, though a melancholy
one, that I can attribute to the misfortune of his head what
otherwise I must place to a depravity of the heart." [46]

In 1780 Franklin wrote about a recent incident that "Dr.
Lee's accusation of Captain Landais for insanity was probably
well founded; as in my judgment would have been the same
accusation if it had been brought by Landais against Lee; for
though neither of them are permanently mad, they are both
so at times, and the insanity of the latter is the most mischievous." [47] The charges by Franklin and Deane became common shoptalk around the Passy headquarters. Sam Nicholson
once remarked to William Carmichael that "I have heard Dr.
Franklin say he thought Arthur Lee was crazy, and I am sure
it was current enough at Nantes." [48]

At the time all this began, Lee could not know how long it
would continue nor to what depths his enemies would de-

scend to smear him. He was early aware, however, of the reason for it. Early in 1778, only months after the campaign against him had begun, he wrote to his brother Richard Henry that the arguments Deane "has industriously contrived with me will render my being his accuser apparently an act of private enmity, not of public justice. And probably this was his object in quarrelling with me, being under great apprehensions from me, as well from my character as from the opportunities my situation would give me of doing it with effect." Lee did not feel the blame should rest with Deane alone. "Dr. F. has always countenanced his proceedings, I believe entirely from a consideration of the business and advantages which he artfully throws into the hands of Mr. Deane. In this situation it is not in my power to prevent every thing from being conducted according to the views and pleasure of Mr. Deane." Perhaps when Deane was "removed from the command of money the truth will come out fast enough, and the persons who, under his auspices, have been defrauding the public may be brought to account. Upon the whole these are dangerous men, and capable of any wickedness to avenge themselves on those who are suspected of counteracting their purposes." [49]

Lee thought he had reason to believe in the wickedness of Franklin and Deane. On another occasion he explained why. To Sam Adams he wrote:

The first time I came over to France . . . I was secretly informed that they had made attempts at Versailles to shut me up, which would have ended in the loss of liberty and life. I was assured that it was actually under deliberation. I at the time regarded the information as the invention of him who gave it. But I am now satisfied that, as they apprehended that I would not only complain of their conduct, but bear witness against the attempt upon the public purse, nothing is more probable than that it was true. . . . Such men . . . assisted from

hence by the old man [Franklin] and his associates, are
not to be trifled with; nor is it possible to say at what
atrocious acts they will not aim. . . . Their avarice and
bad ambition are boundless. . . . [They are] possesst of
much sophistry, and their cunning has taught them to
take their stand upon ground from which it is impossible
to drive them without such a disclosure of state secrets as
woud hazard the great cause and our national character.
Were I not restrained by this consideration, I think I
could unfold to the public such facts as woud ruin them
forever.[50]

Thus Arthur Lee believed he had reason to fear for his own
safety against the artifices of Franklin and Deane. Even para-
noids sometimes have real enemies, and whether or not Lee
was sick, as Franklin and Deane tried to make others believe,
at least it is clear that they were implacably his enemies.

"They are therefore," Arthur continued in his letter to
Richard Henry Lee, "to be acted against with great circumspection, and the proof for their detection and punishment secured before any open attempt is made. The calling for an account of the money we have expended, the taking of the
expenditure out of our hands for the future, or the removal of
him who has misapplied it, would lead to discoveries and
proofs before time has enabled him to prevent them." [51]
These things unfortunately were not done and time has
eroded almost entirely the marks once left upon it by these
men.

In earlier pages we have remarked upon the various code
names which Franklin used himself or which were used by
others to refer to him. One of those names was "Moses."
There are only two references so far located which use this
term regarding Franklin.[52] The first instance of its appearance is in connection with a letter Franklin had written 12
January 1774. That day was a Wednesday, immediately fol-

lowing the Privy Council hearing at which Ben had been castigated by Alexander Wedderburn as a public nuisance and instigator of trouble between England and America. Solicitor General Wedderburn so far had withheld his signature from the document authorizing creation of the Vandalia colony. In light of that hearing at the Cockpit, there now seemed no chance he would sign so long as Franklin remained one of the principal stockholders of the enterprise.

So on Wednesday, Franklin and Thomas Walpole worked out an agreement whereby Ben would publicly resign from the Grand Ohio Company while privately keeping his stock. Franklin wrote the following letter:

Craven Street Jan. 12, 1774

Sir,

Being told that some Persons in Administration have suggested, That my Conduct in Affairs between this Kingdom and North America do not by any means entitle me to such a Mark of Favor from Government, as that of being a Proprietor in the Grant of Lands on the Ohio, to be made to yourself and Associates, I think it necessary to inform you, That I never considered the Agreement with the Treasury for these Lands as a Matter of *Favor,* unless it was such from us to Government, by showing them that the Lands they used to give away might produce something to the publick Treasury. The Agreement for them was fair and publick, at a Price fully adequate to their Value; and as the Lords of Trade have superadded several considerable Charges more than are immediately relative to the Expense of supporting the Government of the Colony (which, besides the Purchase-money & Quit Rent, is all we contracted to pay) and have rated that Support enormously high, in my Opinion, for an infant Colony, I can never consider the Purchase of these Lands as *a Favour* from Government, nor a great Bargain to the Purchasers:—I do therefore desire that you will strike my Name out of the List of your Associates, and hereafter not look upon me as one

of them.—I wish you however all Success in your hazardous Undertaking, and am, with great Esteem,
> Sir,
> Your most obedient
> and most humble Servant
> B Franklin[53]

The letter was a ruse, for Franklin retained his shares of
stock.

Some years later, for whatever reason, Franklin remembered that letter of resignation sent to Thomas Walpole in
early 1774. In 1778 he decided to do something about it. He
asked Edward Bancroft to get the letter back for him. Bancroft contacted the English banker and on 7 July 1778 received a letter and enclosure from Walpole. Walpole's letter
is the document which ties Franklin definitely to the code
name of "Moses." Walpole said: "Pray make my best Compliments to Mr. Moses. I am always flattered when he thinks
of me and my Family. The letter you mention he wishes to
have returned totally escaped my Memory. Perhaps I may
not be able to lay my hand upon it immediately, but I will
most certainly send it back soon." Walpole must have interrupted his writing to search his files for Franklin's old letter
of resignation, for a few lines later he wrote: "I have found
Mr. Moses's Letter and will send it this Evening under [sepa-
rate] Cover . . . not chusing to inclose it in this on Acct. of
the Signature." The phraseology leaves no doubt. "Moses"
was a code name Franklin used among his speculation partners—a self-styling that by 1778 he may have been using for
years, perhaps since the time of striving for American lands
before the outbreak of war between England and the United
States.

When Ben received his old 1774 letter, Bancroft also gave
him the recent reply from Walpole. Franklin kept them together and added the following note to them:

> The Letter mention'd above, is the same that I now at-
> tach with Wafer to this Paper. It was written on Re-

quest of Mr. Walpole, to obviate an Objection made by
the Atty. General Thurloe to the Signing our Patens,
vis. my being unworthy the favours of the Crown.—But
I am still to be consider'd as an Associate, and was called
upon for my Payments as before. My Right to two
Shares, or two Parts of 72, in that Purchase, still continues, having paid all the Expense belonging to those
Shares. And I hope, that when the Troubles of America
are over, my Posterity may reap the Benefits of them.—
I write this Memorandum at Passy in France, where I
now am in the Service of the United States. July 14,
1778.

He then folded up the letters and, before filing them away,
wrote on the outside once again, "Paper that may be of Consequence to my Posterity." [54]

Several things are indicated by this document. The Grand
Ohio Company was still in operation and its shareholders
continued to hope that the colony of Vandalia would be established some day. The words make it clear that Franklin
had regularly to that point paid his portion of expenses in the
operation of the company. There seemingly would have been
but two ways in which the members of the Grand Ohio
Company might ever "reap the Benefits" of Vandalia, for it
was a *British* land firm: if the United States became independent but with boundaries restricted by the peace treaty to
the Allegheny-Appalachian mountains, England would still
control the West and would have authority to settle new colonies there; or if the United States gave up its struggle for
freedom and returned to the colonial womb, the British government would have the right to plant additional western settlements. In either case, a person primarily interested in land
speculation might think it wise to maintain his membership
and hand over his dues to the Grand Ohio Company. Franklin's connection with the Vandalia scheme, then, would make
him reluctant to insist upon American independence. Indeed,
Paul Wentworth at one point reported to William Eden that

"72 [Franklin's] cordial affection for England was most particularly Commanded to be mentioned, & his wishes to stop the progress of war in America." Wentworth said that Franklin "*wish[ed]* that the *acknowledgement* of the Independency should not be made. . . ." [55]

The reference in American archives to Franklin as "Moses" may be coupled with another instance which is equally informative and is found in English archives in the files of the Secret Service. It is a letter written by Lord North to William Eden, 29 September 1777.[56] The letter is dated only, it is unsigned, and the man to whom it was sent is not specifically identified. The handwriting indicates, however, that it was penned by Lord North.[57] The context makes it probable that the recipient was William Eden. The letter is as follows:

Dear Sir:

I am very ready to propose to his Majesty a proper reward for Mr. W[entworth] & shall be very glad to settle with E[dwards] what ought to be done for him & his correspondent. It appears by Mr. L——s [Lee's] journal that they have given us true intelligence upon several very important points, but his M—[ajesty] is not disposed to give full credit to the last information we have received, which, indeed, is so diametrically opposite to formal declarations, &, to some late measures, that it is hardly possible to believe it: On the other hand, we know that our neighbors have told us many absolute falsehoods without scruple, that they have actually assisted our enemies with arms, cloathing & money, & that *Moses* has told his intimate friends that something good is in store for them: What is still more material, is, that it appears by intercepted letters that they are *selling* for the [month?] of November. Ld. St[ormont]'s letters pacifick. He writes with a degree of confidence, which he has not express'd for some time past. He says, that M^r de [Sartine?] particularly obeys the very precise orders he

had received to remove the American privateers from
the Coast of France. That all their privateers are now
gone & that the agents of the Jamaica merchants have
been very politely received by Mr de Sartine & have the
greatest hopes of receiving their ships & cargos: He
mentions several other favorable circumstances but
amongst them, he sends one piece of intelligence not
quite of the same complexion, vis. That [Hodge?] is set
at liberty. It is impossible to reconcile Lord S—[tor-
mont] with the other gentlemen: The latter, indeed,
does not think it easy in [all?] points to reconcile his correspondent[s?] with himself. Perhaps E.[dwards] who is,
at heart, a thorough American &, at this present writing,
a *Bear* in the funds, may wish to desire us to some step
that may bring on a war, or, at least, sink the funds before November: Perhaps, he is suspected by his friends,
& deceived by them, or, Perhaps, he is well informed &
tells the truth. Among these contrarieties, we can not do
better than increase our strength gradually without em-
barking in any measure that can engage us in a dispute
with our neighbors untill it becomes absolutely inevitable, which I can not say, I think it at present.

North remarks on many things in this memorandum. He val-
ued Wentworth's and Bancroft's services and was willing to
see that they were properly rewarded. The information they
had sent in had been cross-checked for accuracy against the
entries in Arthur Lee's stolen journal. In spite of that, George
III did not feel that recent intelligence from France, warning
of impending war, was firm enough to act on. Part of his reluctance stemmed from the optimistic tone of Lord Stormont's recent dispatches. Lord North noted that Bancroft
and Stormont found it hard to get along with one another.
He pointed out his own distrust of Bancroft's stock speculations and manipulations of the London Exchange, and revealed that he believed Bancroft's sympathies were more with
the Americans than with the English. At any rate, Bancroft's

recent reports would have to be carefully analyzed and well corroborated by other agents before any policy changes toward France were based on them. In the meantime, North thought it best simply to increase England's military strength slowly and without provoking France.

That North was writing to someone intimate with the string of Secret Service agents in France is clear enough. Bancroft is mentioned by the first letter of his code name as "E." Wentworth was identified only as "W." The note mentions "Mr. L——s journal," which would mean nothing to anyone who did not know of Hugh Elliot's recent escapade in Berlin with Arthur Lee's papers. And he said, "that *Moses* has told his intimate friends that something good is in store for them. . . ." North has been referring to British personnel in France: Stormont, Wentworth, Bancroft. Then Moses. Ben Franklin's own documents relating to Vandalia identify him as "Moses." Now North has used the same term in a context which can only refer to Franklin. The wording is pointed. Franklin was not described as telling "his intimate friends" that great things were "in store" for America, but for "them." Who were his intimate friends? Bancroft. Deane. Chaumont. Three speculative partners, of whom two were British spies. What were those "great things"? Only a few months later, Paul Wentworth promised to Franklin and Deane "emoluments to the leaders, governors general, privy seals, great seals, treasurers, secretaries, councillors in the general governments, local barons, and knights" to those who helped England wind down the war.[58]

North was not always careful with his words, sometimes saying one thing while meaning quite another. Yet he chose in this letter to Eden to say that "We know . . . that *Moses* has told his intimate friends. . . ." He does not say how he came by this knowledge. Was it locked into the courier system of the Secret Service by Wentworth? Bancroft? Deane? Or did Moses himself forward it? We do not know. All we can be certain of is that North told Eden that "We know. . . ."

Lastly, it is worth noting that North made no effort of any kind in his memo to Eden to identify "Moses." Presumably, the alias was so well known and so often used that it would have been as pointless to give additional identification as it would have been to spell out "W" or "E" or "Ld St" or "his M—."

Between the time of Ben's arrival in France and the end of 1778, at least twenty couriers or agents from England made contact with him.[59] The year 1777 was a busy one in this regard. As early as March—less than three months after his arrival—a clandestine meeting between Franklin and an Englishman was noted by Beaumarchais, who reported it to Vergennes. Beaumarchais had probably learned of it through his friend Silas Deane. "A private secretary of Lord Germain's has arrived here . . . secretly sent to Deane and Franklin," Beaumarchais wrote. "He is the bearer of proposals of peace. . . . The offers of England to America are such that a deputy may send them to Philadelphia with honour." The next day, he wrote that "someone was at my house who told me England's proposals [to Franklin] are fine, acceptable." [60]

Meetings with Franklin continued. Two weeks later Beaumarchais again wrote Vergennes, this time in stronger terms, warning him about the talks Franklin was having. "I warn you that secret advances are being made by England to Mr. Franklin, which you are doubtless unaware of and which I am sure Mr. Deane has not mentioned to you." [61]

It may be that a letter written in November 1777 offers a suggestion as to why Ben Franklin so willingly received emissaries of peace from England at a time when he was charged by Congress with securing from France a treaty of alliance and commerce. On 1 November William Carmichael wrote a message to Wentworth which eventually came into Eden's hands. Carmichael said: "Our leading man"—that is, Ben

Franklin—trembled at the thought that France would accept the terms offered by America and enter upon a treaty. "He wishes no European connection. He despises France and hates England." [62] Wentworth also realized Franklin's reluctance to see France openly aid the Americans. In his sketches of the men at Passy, Wentworth described Franklin as shedding tears at the thought of separation from the mother country.[63]

At one of William Carmichael's last visits with Joseph Hynson, he told the captain of recent conversations between Deane and Franklin. Hynson forwarded the gist of Carmichael's summary on to Lieutenant Colonel Edward Smith, his Secret Service contact in England. Carmichael, Hynson wrote, "was expressing a great desire that you come to Paris." It would answer a "very great" end, for "the gentln" were "wishing to have some conversation with you." The gentlemen in the context of that letter could only be Franklin and Deane. Hynson continued that "if there was to be a meeting we might talk high at first." He asked Carmichael "did he think the Gentlemen would expect any other terms, than that of independance[?]" Carmichael replied that "there was a division about giving up their independance." The division he referred to was between Franklin and Deane on one side and Arthur Lee on the other. Hynson wrote that Carmichael had told him that "you would be surprised to hear Dr. Franklin says that whenever Great Britain would shew a disposn for peace he would be the first to give up this independance. Mr. Deane he said had made the same declaration." Carmichael had told Hynson, however, that Lee "would be against giving up independance." [64]

Sometime in early October Deane seems to have met briefly with Paul Wentworth. According to one author, there is an undated report in Wentworth's handwriting written about the middle of that month. In that message, Wentworth says that "Deane has at time been ready to say—procure me plausible means to retreat: The Vilany of the proceedings of Congress; the deceit of the French Court are insufferable—Nothing but the power of G. B. re-established can save us from the worst of evils." [65]

Eden well knew the views of Franklin and Deane. By late November or early December 1777, the chief of the Secret Service was ready to act. On 6 December he issued instructions to Wentworth to go to France and meet with Franklin and Deane in order to learn what those two men believed could be the grounds for accommodation with the Congress.[66] European agents were reporting that the French might be getting ready to sign a treaty with America and Eden wanted to forestall such a development at all costs.

Wentworth's earlier reports from the Paris mission had convinced Eden that most of those who had sparked the war were motivated by cupidity, greed, and self-interest. They might well be amenable to changing sides if the price were right and if no penalities were exacted from them for their previous "traitorous" actions. "The highest degree of political profligacy already prevails," Wentworth wrote, "and perhaps a well-timed offer of indemnity and impunity to these Cromwells and Barebones may serve, like a strong alkali, to reduce the effervescence in the mass of the people, or turn their fury on their misleaders." [67]

Eden instructed Wentworth to do whatever he could to convert those in Paris from their plastic allegiance to the United States. On the day he received his instructions, Wentworth left for Paris in the guise of an English business-man. During the remainder of December he would have several meetings in efforts to carry out his assignment. All concerned would jockey for position and advantage—Wentworth perhaps most of all. By the time he returned an event had occurred that would change the face of the war. France had agreed to sign a treaty of alliance and commerce with the United States of America.

CHAPTER EIGHT

————•~•~•————

"72" Received Me Very Kindly

When Paul Wentworth arrived in Paris in December, his first thought was to contact Edward Bancroft to be briefed by his agent on recent developments. He had just been to Paris in the middle of November to confer with Bancroft and Stormont. Bancroft criticized the ambassador for making his work more difficult. Stormont recently had sent home cargo lists of vessels being loaded for America which Bancroft had given him. When he copied them, Bancroft had followed the wording of the commissioners' records. When Stormont sent the news to London, he had used Bancroft's words verbatim. Unfortunately, so had the British government in its official protests to Vergennes. Bancroft was furious that the government had been stupid enough to use the very language of the commissioners themselves. Franklin himself professed alarm, pointing out that such exact knowledge must have come from a source "very close" to him.

Bancroft was still frightened. He could almost hear Vergennes saying "J'accuse!" to him. Angry at the ambassador for having gotten him into this mess, Bancroft insisted that Stormont supply him with a passport to use if it became necessary to escape from the French police. For his part, Vergennes complained about the lax security at the American mission. He suspected that it might be Carmichael who was

passing information and demanded that the young Marylander be fired. He was, of course, right. The problem was
that getting rid of Carmichael would not end leaks. When
Lee joined his voice to that of Vergennes, Franklin and
Deane finally and reluctantly agreed to let their young friend
go. They ordered him home.

Paul Wentworth must have chuckled as he wrote Eden a
note on Carmichael's firing. "An Express is sent off to
L'Orient to Carmichael to take under His care the duplicate
dispatches, & proceed to Nantes on board the Lion. One Stephenson had been promised this office by A Lee—who had
impeached Carmichael . . . which induced Fr: & D to do this
[justice?] to Carmichael and to quarrell with Ar Lee." [1]

Wiliam Lee hoped that now things would calm down. To
his brother, Richard Henry, he wrote on 4 February 1778:
"The uneasinesses and bickerings that have been on this side
begin to subside, and I believe will soon totally vanish as the
principal fomenter, Mr. C[armichael] is now on his way to
America. It is inconceivable the mischief this man has been
the cause of by telling untruths from one to another, whis-
pering and insinuating what never happened, or was said, and
a thousand other little artifices. . . ." [2]

At any rate, when Wentworth got to the French capital
city, he was more than irritated to learn that Bancroft had left
the city on a speculating trip to London. He would have preferred to deal with Franklin and Deane through Bancroft.
Now there was nothing left but to contact the man he was
most sure of, Silas Deane. He sent an unsigned note to Deane
early on Friday, 12 December 1777. "A Gentleman who has
some acquaintance with Mr. Deane wishes to improve it," he
wrote, and suggested they meet that day at noon in the Lux-
embourg Gallery or at 6:00 P.M. at the Pot de Vin baths on
the Seine.[3]

Several hours later Wentworth learned that Deane would
be unable to see him that day. He would, however, be able to
meet Wentworth in his own quarters the next morning, Sat-

urday, or at Passy Saturday evening with Franklin.[4] Wentworth did not make the contact. On the following Monday,
15 December 1777, Wentworth tried again. "I could not be
in Paris without asking the honour of paying you my Re-
spects, especially as I shall be returning to London in a very
little while, where you may have wishes to make me usefull,
in which I shall be Happy if they promote Peace." He signed
only his initials, sufficient identification to allow Deane to
recognize the author of the note.[5] They met for the first time
that day. Deane told Wentworth how he loathed the French
—people, court, and country—and he was pleased when
Wentworth suggested that between the two of them they
might lay the foundation for a union of America and England.[6]

After the meeting adjourned, Deane hurried to Franklin
and told him of Wentworth's arrival and of their first contact.
They then sent word to Vergennes of the arrival of an English "businessman" with whom they would be visiting. They
gave no more details than necessary about who he was or
why he had come.

Vergennes was intrigued. He wanted to know more about
this visitor and asked Beaumarchais for information. The
playwright replied that "He is related to the Marquis of
Rockingham; he is a particular friend of Lord Suffolk, is employed by the Ministers in difficult matters. M. Wintweth
speaks French like you, and better than I do; he is one of the
cleverest men in England." [7] Vergennes was worried. France
had postponed open action on behalf of America for months
while waiting for Spain to agree to a united front. Yet it was
necessary for England to be humiliated if France was ever to
regain her prestige. Now a man like Wentworth was in
town, surely—if Beaumarchais were correct—in a more important capacity than it seemed. It would be a calamity if
America and England patched up their differences. Perhaps
France should act even without Spain.

Deane meanwhile arranged to meet with Wentworth for

dinner on Wednesday, 17 December. When Vergennes
heard of the assignation he instructed Gérard to see Deane
prior to the American's conference with Wentworth and to
inform him of Vergennes' decision to form an alliance.
When Gérard requested this meeting Deane told him that he
could see him on Wednesday at Chaumont's home in Passy,
a more private place than Franklin's quarters there. Gérard
quickly replied, calling for a meeting on Tuesday. Deane
agreed. At 5:00 P.M., Tuesday, Deane and Gérard conferred.[8] Either that day or the next, Gérard informed Deane
that the French government planned to make the treaty of
commerce and alliance with America. It would no longer
wait for common action against the English by Spain. There
was one condition: America must agree that she would not
make a separate peace with the British.[9]

On Wednesday, 17 December, Deane and Wentworth
met again. Wentworth told Deane of certain plans which, if
the fighting could be stopped, Britain could use to tie American commerce to the Empire and bring in a revenue to the
Exchequer in inoffensive ways. Deane liked the idea. When
they parted that day they agreed to meet the following morning, Thursday, 18 December, at the Café St. Honoré for
breakfast.

Franklin, Deane, and Lee were breakfasting together when
Wentworth arrived, but Deane excused himself to his two
colleagues and left to join the British agent, whom he did not
attempt to introduce to Franklin or Lee. Soon Wentworth
and Deane walked off together in deep conversation.[10] In
their conversation that day, Wentworth decided to do his best
to scuttle any projected Franco-American alliance. He told
Deane of the rewards that might belong to him and to anyone
who helped settle the present conflict, "which Great Britain
only can give permanently." [11] Such helpful persons might
become governors, principal secretaries of the Cabinet, or
holders of the privy seal, might receive baronetcies or knight-
hoods. Such emoluments tickled Deane's fancy. Only a few

days later, the rewards for Deane became manifest. Lord North wrote to George III about trade goods which Wentworth would purchase in London for shipment to America for "Mr. D." The King spoke of Deane's "proposals, to which are added some pieces of intelligence Mr. W. received from him," and mentioned that "undoubtedly if the intelligence sent by Benson [Deane] is founded, France has taken her part and a war with Great Britain must soon follow." [12]

After visiting with Deane, Wentworth wrote William Eden about the private financial operations of Ben Franklin and Silas Deane. He said that *"They are deeply concerned in the Cargoes going out,* which is a great capital furnished by a company of Merchants—Chaumont, Holker, Sabatier, Frigeuix Horneca & Co., Monthieu, Bernier, Grand, Beaumarchais, &c. &c. &c." [13] On Christmas Day Wentworth wrote again, filling in details he had neglected in his earlier report. He told his chief he felt it had been wise to promise the American commissioners anything, no matter whether or not the promises were actually kept. The important goal to achieve was prevention of the now distinctly probable Franco-American alliance.[14]

Deane had promised to arrange a meeting between Franklin and Wentworth. Days passed. Wentworth waited on in his hotel room. He noticed French agents kept him under constant surveillance and he was frightened. One day, while he was absent from his quarters, his strongbox was jimmied but the intruder had been unable to force it open. When Wentworth saw the signs of the illegal entry and the attempt to open his lockbox, he opened it and burned his papers as a precautionary measure. He had always rationalized his activities as those of a loyal son of his country; he did not feel like a common spy, and now these events thoroughly frightened him. As he wrote to Eden: "I frankly confess it is not a situation for a man who aims at honour to be kept in—unavowed and neglected—regarded as a spy—suspected by friends." [15] He appealed to Stormont. In order to safeguard this agent,

the ambassador presented Wentworth to Louis XVI as a
friend and businessman on a trip to Paris. Vergennes, probably with tongue in cheek, gave Wentworth a dinner.

While Wentworth worried away the days, Ralph Izard
called on Arthur Lee. Izard had somehow learned of Wentworth's visit. He asked Lee "if he had heard anything of a
proposal to the commissioners, within a few days, from England." Lee answered that he had heard nothing, either from
Franklin and Deane or from anyone else, and Izard replied,
"then you are ill-treated, and you ought to call Mr. D. to a severe account for his conduct; for that Paul Wentworth had a
meeting with Mr. D., to whom he made propositions, which
Mr. D. gave to the French ministry." Lee could only stam-
mer that "he had not heard one syllable of it; that he would
enquire into it." [16]

Lee now knew who it was he had seen leaving with Deane
from the Café St. Honoré the week before. Smoldering suspicions were confirmed. He had known of Wentworth since
his visit to Spain, and had then warned the other two commissioners about the man. He well knew what kind of man
the English agent was, and now Deane was fraternizing with
him! What business did they have together?

Lee now recalled something that Franklin had said to him:
"both Sunday [21 December 1777] and this day [22 December 1777], that Dr. Bankcroft was expected from London, for
he had written on the 9th that he should set out in a few days;
that he, Dr. F., was therefore apprehensive that he was
seized." Lee told Izard that that had been his first hint that
Bancroft was out of Paris. It was hard for him to understand
what possible business Bancroft could have in London "if Dr.
Bankcroft was in any office of trust under the commissioners." If he was so employed, "it was a little surprising
such a step should have been taken without his [Lee's] knowledge." If Bancroft was not an employee of the Paris station,
then "he could not understand why he had access to their pa-

pers, and even had the key" which Lee himself "had repeatedly asked for in vain." [17]

Bancroft must have gone to London in November if he had written to Franklin 9 December telling him he would soon return. For Lee it was all beginning to add up. First Bancroft's quiet trip to London, then the sudden appearance of Wentworth in Paris, then Wentworth's meeting with Deane at the Café St. Honoré. Whatever Franklin, Deane, Bancroft, and Wentworth were up to, it foreshadowed no good for the United States of America.

Bancroft returned to Paris and met with Wentworth. Deane already had informed Wentworth that Bancroft had gone to London with £300,000 to invest in "great Business." [18] Even if he exaggerated, Bancroft must have had a considerable sum to use in stock manipulations on the London market. A friend of Arthur Lee later wrote him that "very considerable sums were done in the stocks by the friends of a certain quondam commissioner . . . in which it was very visible Mr. Deane was concerned, and that Dr. Franklin was not absolutely ignorant of it." [19] Wentworth refused Bancroft's offer of repayment and encouraged him to do what he could to help arrange a meeting with Franklin. It took Wentworth almost four weeks after his arrival in Paris, until 6 January 1778, before the meeting could be set up. Everything had to be done in strictest confidence and secrecy.

While Wentworth waited, he learned a great deal. Later he would report on his findings to Eden. When he had been in Paris on an earlier trip he had used a particular coachman to drive him on his errands. Now the man worked for "72." Wentworth made it a point to talk with him. Why did he talk with the coachman and what were the circumstances under which the conversation was carried on? Looking up a former chauffeur and maintaining a liaison with him was not a particularly common practice. For that matter, it was strange that both "72" and Wentworth had employed the same man. In a city the size of Paris there must have been thousands of coachmen available for hire. Was the fact that both Franklin and Wentworth had employed the same one coincidental or accidental? Wentworth gives no answer. He simply wrote that "72['s] Coachman who was mine some months ago—told me Milord Dr. 72. [Franklin] has been twice to see me at my lodgings." After having taken so long to arrange a conference with Franklin, Wentworth must have been disgusted to hear that he had missed his target on two separate occasions. He also told Eden that Deane visited "almost every night" with Vergennes at Versailles, "& returns sometimes at 2 o'clock in the morning . . . the reason was to avoid" Arthur Lee, "who is kept out of *the Secret,* tho informed eno' to keep him quiet. . . . There are many Circumstances more of this kind, but . . . I shall not swell this Letter." [20]

On Sunday, 4 January 1778, Wentworth met with Deane and Bancroft, who "promised to procure an interview with 72." During the meeting Lee walked in, which considerably dampened the conversation, for no one said much "in presence of A. Lee." The talk resumed when he left. Wentworth was told that "72['s] cordial affection for England was most particularly Commanded to be mentioned, & his wishes to stop the progress of war in America, & prevent it in Europe, to do which G Britain must go before Fr. & Spain, who would gladly see the Independency of the Colonies, without the Necessity of a war in Europe to produce & support it." Deane continued relaying Franklin's views. Franklin, Deane said, felt that "His duty to one & affection for the other, equally bid Him to *wish* that the *acknowledgement* of the Independency should not be made. . . . He *wished* rather, that it may be implyed or arise out of the Essence of the objects of the [proposed] Treaty [with France]; than Expressed by any formal words."

Wentworth learned that the French Court had suspected Carmichael as the one leaking secrets from the Paris mission and that, under duress, Franklin and Deane had agreed to send him back to America. Beaumarchais had indicated that Carmichael's recall was acceptable, for in the United States the young agent would be able "to assist their affairs." Wentworth also learned from Bancroft that "nothing in there [sic] letters was said of the Treaty between France & Spain & America as that was a private joint letter in 72 own possession," a copy of which Bancroft had made to forward to England.[21]

Wentworth was finally going to get his meeting with Franklin. Deane and Bancroft had set it up for 6 January. Wentworth almost got his chance to talk with Franklin on Monday, 5 January, rather than on Tuesday the sixth. To Eden he reported that "If I had known of opportunity, I should have seen 72 yesterday—but your desire of the issue, will suffice & postpone but one day longer." [22] The proper moment finally came on Tuesday. Wentworth took with him an unsigned letter from Eden to use as bait. He had been authorized to say only that its author was someone high in government. Basically, the note stated that while England could agree to almost anything, it could not approve independence.[23]

When Wentworth arrived at L'Hôtel des Valentinois for his rendezvous with Franklin, he met Chaumont "at the Garden door, who reproached me for not coming to see him lately—I told him His porter book would show his last years debt to me, but I was willing old debts should be erased with a sponge & Contract new ones with the Year." This unqualified statement to Eden clearly reveals that this was not Wentworth's first visit to that home, for the "porter book" would show several entries for visits there in 1777. Wentworth and Chaumont knew one another well enough to joke, for one to complain that the other did not come often enough. On those occasions, had Wentworth come only to see Chaumont? Or had he seen Franklin and Deane as well? A few lines later, Wentworth told how he asked Franklin that day to "recall Ideas which had passed between us." When had they exchanged those ideas? Before the war when both were agents in England for various colonies? Or in the months just passed when Wentworth made those stopovers at Chaumont's home recorded in the porter book? Had not the coachman reported that "72" had been twice to see Wentworth at his lodgings? Later Wentworth had to remind Franklin that "He [Franklin] wished to meet me [Wentworth]," showing that the desire for talks was not entirely unilateral.

In his report to Eden, Wentworth wrote with a scandalized tone that Deane and Bancroft regularly dined at Chaumont's and along with "72 are quartered there at the Publick Expense as well as [maintaining] their House in Town." Jonathan Williams, Jr., seems to have been in Paris for a conference with Franklin, for when Wentworth called on "72" he "found him very busy with His Nephew." Franklin told Williams to leave the room and for two hours Wentworth and he talked, before they were joined by Silas Deane. Prior to the meeting Franklin, exactingly careful as usual, had passed word to Wentworth to refrain "in any part of the conversation" from any mention of the rewards he had spoken about with Deane.[24] Throughout the long talk, Wentworth tried to abide by Franklin's wish; that point had, at any rate, already been sufficiently covered in conversations with Deane. Franklin knew what the rewards for cooperation would be.

Wentworth was pleased that "72 received me very kindly." The British agent opened the conversation with complimentary remarks about Franklin, "to which he is very open." Then Wentworth asked his aged friend several questions: "How much short of Independence He wished?" Was the emphasis on independence simply a measure of expediency? What were the "Terms & the means he would suggest to induce reconciliation?" Wentworth indicated that Franklin's opinion on these matters "would be that of the Congress."

Franklin reacted angrily. Time after time, he said, he had set forth opinions on how to settle the differences between England and America; each time he had done so it had "only subjected Him to abuse," so that in the present situation he wanted "to be very cautious of what he said." He would not set forth "propositions in writing" and verbal opinions were liable to misconstruction. If he could have the opportunity to set forth his views personally to the English government, that might be more satisfactory, for "discussion was necessary to develop the tendency of probable Consequences of many Principles which at first might appear unfavorable—But He being present at the objection, He might remove it, & shew the Effect to be advantageous."

By this time Franklin had worked himself into a rage of "passion & resentment." Wentworth tried to soothe him, arguing that even though he had been ill used, "His resentments should be lost in the Cause of His Country; . . . that if the great Breach was made up He, in the share of Glory he might acquire, should be thankfull to have suffered evil, to produce so great a good, yet in His day."

Franklin replied "that His warmth did not proceed from a feeling of personal injuries" but from "the Barbarities inflicted on his Country." At that point, noted Wentworth, "he lost Breath in relating the burning of Towns, the neglect or ill treatment of Provinces," and other complaints. Wentworth countered that Britain was sorry for such misdeeds and wanted to repent. It was too late, thought Franklin. "True, but late repentance if sincere was more lasting in its Effects— and what must his portion be if he could turn the Torrent of rigor & revolution of an opulent & courageous people, into affection, union & prosperity," declaimed Wentworth. At such a point, "Britain & America would be the greatest Empire on Earth."

Franklin answered that he might be agreeable to helping, although the greatest difficulty facing them was that "the Spirit of America was High." Nothing but independence "would be at all listened to" at that point. Once again Franklin lapsed into a diatribe listing the personal and national injuries inflicted by Britain. Wentworth cautioned him. "I could not wait upon him for that sort of instruction, & must beg to moderate him by calling his attention to the Humanity, the Benevolence, the Reputation of a remedy." He reminded Franklin that, after all, "He wished to meet [with] me" and such outbursts could do no one any good.

It was at this moment that Wentworth showed Franklin the letter he had brought with him. Wentworth read the first two pages, to which Franklin "paid great attention." It was, he said, "a very interesting sensible letter," and "a pity it did not come a little sooner." Franklin "applauded the Candor, good sense & Benevolent spirit of it" and asked who had written it. Wentworth refused to comment except to say that the writer was "Concerned, Cordially disposed, as He was Happily situated to turn such principles to the most benevolent purposes." Franklin stated that "He was glad to find Honour & That so near the Throne—He was afraid it was banished" from England. He then went on to reminisce about a recent visit from a British emissary, about which Wentworth comments in his report: "He enlarged needless to repeat. I never knew him so excentric—no body says less generally & keeps a point more closely in View—but was diffuse . . . today."

The talk rambled on for some time with Wentworth becoming more and more discouraged. He seemed to be unable to come to a meeting of minds with Franklin. Finally he interrupted the old man to ask, "would you Sir save a great deal of Time, by going to the spot you loved so much, if proper passports were granted?"

"Yes, I should have no objections," replied Franklin, "but I could not answer for my Colleagues." Franklin cried out that he would talk "Peace—I say Peace" with any agent so authorized by the British government.

Two hours had gone by. Deane came in and the three men talked for some time. The meeting ended. Wentworth stayed for dinner that evening at the invitation of Chaumont. Franklin and Deane were present also. In his report the next day, Wentworth told Eden that during the table talk that evening those present "was offering betts" that America would become independent and that "Vandalia was to be the Paradise on Earth." Chaumont remarked "that His whole family were determined to go there." Western speculation thus still seemed to be an important topic of conversation at Passy.

As soon as he could wind up his affairs after his meeting with Franklin, Wentworth left Paris. He still felt strongly the danger from Vergennes' watchers. He may have been right.

It is difficult to tell what fruit, if any, that meeting had borne.[25] Franklin and Deane, through Carmichael to Hynson and through him to the British Secret Service hierarchy in London, had called for a meeting. Wentworth had gone to Paris. He had learned some things and had promised Deane rewards which were soon forthcoming in the form of shipments of trade goods to "Mr. D." in Connecticut. Franklin drove twice to Wentworth's lodgings to see him. They met for two hours on 6 January. Wentworth's description of Franklin sounds almost as if he believed the old man had become senile, but other authors have written that Franklin was just playing a cagey game with the British agent. Wentworth's reports to Eden imply that he had gained nothing from the weeks in Paris. Yet emissaries continued to come to Passy to meet with Franklin. During that meeting with Wentworth, Franklin lamented that the contact had not been made with him earlier. Perhaps Franklin would have been willing, prior to the French agreement to an alliance, to declare publicly for peace with England. Even after Vergennes announced the impending alliance, the idea of concluding a peace with England still appealed to him. Naturally cautious, Franklin needed time to weigh the risks. The conclusion he reached was that, prior to the French announcement, peace negotiations with England might well have ultiimately enhanced his career. Now they could only endanger his reputation.

After Wentworth left, things settled back into the usual routine of operations at Passy. Perhaps life now was a little smoother for Ben Franklin and Silas Deane, although Arthur Lee continued to put pressure on the two of them and Jonathan Williams, asking them to justify the huge expenditures that had been made. Williams finally forwarded some accounts to Paris. Lee studied them, marking some entries as "manifestly unjust," "plainly exorbitant," and "altogether unsatisfactory for want of names, dates, or receipts." [26] He called on Williams to send supporting cash vouchers to Paris for examination, but, according to Lee, Williams never did so. Lee simply refused to approve the muddled records and forwarded them to Congress.

Then, on the last day of January 1778, Thomas Morris died. His papers finally ended up in the hands of Franklin. In November 1778 he finally gave them to John Ross to deliver to Robert Morris. They never again saw the light of day.[27] As late as 1787 Congress was still puzzling over Tom Morris' accounts. The following year, the Finance Committee issued a statement that approximately 20 million livres spent in France during the late war could not be accounted for.[28] Ten years earlier, in March 1778, in a comment to Franklin, Arthur Lee accused Jonathan Williams of squirreling away 100,000 livres that he could not properly account for. Then, in June, Lee wrote to the Congress that "It now appears that for the expenditure of a million of livres he has given no account as yet." [29]

Ben Franklin finally agreed to select accountants to audit the Nantes books, but according to Arthur Lee, the job they did was not a thorough one. Pressured by Lee, Franklin also

called for John Ross' accounts to be audited. The "accountants" he chose for the task were Samuel Wharton and Edward Bancroft! The shepherd was asking the wolves to tend
his sheep. Bancroft and Wharton certified that Ross' accounts
were accurate and that the United States should pay the balance "owed" to him.[30] William Lee, suspicious of the accounts of Silas Deane, wrote Richard Henry Lee from
Frankfurt: "Remember, I pray you, not to let any of his accounts for the expenditure of publick money finally pass
without the most authentic vouchers; upon proper inquiry
into this business, I can boldly assert that most infamous
transactions will be brought to light." Upon reflection, William Lee then added the words: "From this apprehension
arises Mr. Deane's and Dr. Franklin's mortal hatred to my
brother and myself." [31]

Arthur Lee contended that Franklin connived at both
Deane's and Jonathan Williams' nefarious activities and
shielded them from investigation. He charged that Franklin's
intervention allowed Jonathan Williams to draw still more
funds he claimed were due him. Lee noted with sarcastic fury
that Jonathan Williams, who had been a penniless clerk to a
sugar baker in England, had become so self-important as
naval agent at Nantes that he styled himself as a merchant
and charged the commissioners five Louis d'ors daily for his
time when he came to Paris to "consult" with them.

William Lee waited on in Frankfurt, still looking for a
change in European politics that would allow him to present
his country's case to the courts of Austria and Prussia. Finally, rather than continue wasting his time, he decided to
seek aid for the United States from the Dutch. The powerful
burgomeisters of Amsterdam, sympathetic to America, instructed the Grand Pensioner, Engelbert van Berckel, to inquire into the matter. He appointed a merchant, Jean de
Neufville, to correspond with Lee. Later the two men met at
Aix-la-Chapelle. William had with him a copy of the recent

treaty France had signed with the United States and the agreement the two of them worked out was based on this document, with a few minor changes to fit it to the Dutch situation. (When John Adams later sought a treaty of amity and commerce from Holland, the Lee-Neufville agreement was used as its basis.)

William Lee was pleased with his accomplishment. He returned to Paris 12 September 1778 to show his work to Franklin.[32] Ben seemed hostile to him and ungracious about what he had accomplished. In a curt note Franklin complained that any such agreement should have been made by an accredited commissioner, rather than by Lee acting in a private capacity. On another occasion, "The Doctor replyed that it was a matter to be considered whether it was worth our while to ask any of the Courts of Europe to acknowledge our Independence." William Lee noted that "This, I confess, astonished me greatly." [33] And so it should have. If Franklin were not in Europe for the purpose of getting those nations to recognize the independence of the United States, he was not there for any official reason at all! So William dispiritedly sent a copy of his work to Congress. To his brother Richard Henry he wrote, "You will see by my letter to Congress of this date how far I have gone in negotiating a treaty of Commerce with . . . Holland, etc; but it is really a lamentable circumstance that I forsee the business will be obstructed, and I am afraid fatally because I have not power to sign it, and if communicated here, where the only power of signing is at present vested, it is most probable, that intelligence of it will speedily get to England; as has for a long time been the case with all the most important and critical transactions relative to America." [34] At the end of September 1778, William Lee returned to Frankfurt to continue waiting for an opportunity to begin his diplomatic duties at either Berlin or Vienna.

In 1779, when Henry Laurens was sent by Congress to Holland to procure a $10 million loan, his ship was seized enroute and he was captured. Laurens tried to sink his official papers in a bag before the English could get hold of them. The enemy ship lowered a boat and managed to retrieve one of several weighted bags thrown overboard. Inside was a copy of the Lee-Neufville agreement. When news of this incident reached London, the Ministry demanded that the Dutch disavow the agreement, which they promptly did. Whitehall also asked for the punishment of the Grand Pensioner, Engelbert van Berckel, who had acted as middleman between the burgomeisters and Lee. This the Dutch would not do. Whereupon Britain declared war. In this roundabout way, William Lee had brought another enemy of Britain into the war.

But this development was still far in the future when, early in 1778, Franklin and Deane hit upon a way to undercut any objections the Lee brothers might make to the Congress about their operations. The tool was handed to them when William Eden assigned another agent, Major John Thornton, to the Paris mission. In the closing weeks of 1777, Franklin used Thornton to investigate the conditions of American prisoners of war. Ben sent him on trips back to England, supposedly to distribute funds to needy POWs.

The presence of Thornton gave Franklin an idea which, if carried off properly, would thoroughly discredit Lee with Vergennes once for all.[35] Arthur Lee had not had a secretary since his trip to Berlin. Noting this, Franklin suggested to him that John Thornton might be a suitable person for such a position. Lee should have been more wary, but he took the bait and employed Thornton. Soon after, in hopes of gathering information useful to the American cause, Lee sent Thornton to England to spy out the land. Of course, Lee did not suspect that Thornton was one of Eden's agents.

When Thornton arrived in London on the task given him by Lee, he contacted Samuel and Joseph Wharton and told them of the plan Franklin and Deane had concocted to ruin Lee's reputation. The two brothers decided to aid in the scheme. Lee had to be discredited for he had come too close to the truth. He already had charged that Bancroft was a spy and was supplying secret information to the English. At that time Bancroft had "boldly and indignantly" repudiated Lee's assertion, "a feat that scarcely could have succeeded if it had not been countenanced by Franklin." [36] But Lee was not a man to be stopped so easily: hence the importance of Franklin's scheme for ruining his reputation.

After their talk with John Thornton, Sam and Joseph Wharton sent along to the Paris Mission the news that Thornton had been leaking secret information to official persons while in England. When Franklin and Deane received this communication, they immediately reported to Vergennes. Lee had employed a British spy and had sent him to London where he was spilling state secrets. They also made certain that Vergennes received a letter Thornton had forged. In this document, purportedly from Lee to Lord Shelburne, "Lee" regretted the fact that there had to be a Franco-American alliance.[37] Vergennes was already concerned at the massive security leaks at the Paris Mission and had requested Franklin to send Carmichael home.[38] Now he sent word to his ambassador at Philadelphia to express to the Congress that the French Foreign Ministry could no longer trust Arthur Lee.[39] In this way Franklin accomplished his object of discrediting his colleague. Who could believe or take seriously the charges of such a knave? Thus Lee's charges were left unexplored for the most part by the Congress and by later writers. Needless to say, Ben carefully kept quiet about the fact that Thornton had been hired by Lee on his recommendation.

Franklin used this incident as justification for not including Lee in the work of the mission any more than was absolutely necessary. When Arthur Lee learned that Thornton was not all he should be, he quickly fired him, but the damage had been done.[40] Now Franklin had the perfect excuse for excluding him from commission activities. Frustrated, Lee continued to send now-tainted intelligence to the Congress. But no one was listening.

CHAPTER NINE

———•◦•———

Conversations With Pulteney

The month of January 1778 was filled with negotiations between Franklin, Deane, and Lee and the diplomats of the French Foreign Ministry as to the wording and intent of the proposed French treaties. Franklin and Deane tried to take control of the American portion of the complicated maneuvers. Ralph Izard had hoped to be consulted on the issues of the treaties and was angered when he was not. Perhaps as a consequence, he wrote to Henry Laurens that power too long held and too little checked had given Franklin and Deane the feeling that they were infallible.[1]

Izard also wrote Franklin himself. He charged that "a friend of yours was in the month of January made acquainted with the very day the treaty was to be signed; that this information was transmitted to London; and in consequence of it that insurances to a great amount were made, for whose benefit I will not take upon me to say. If these things can be proved, the world will judge by what motive you have been actuated."[2] There is now no way of testing Izard's charge except to note that Edward Bancroft on 22 January sent Wentworth an outline of the terms of the prospective treaties. On 4 March he sent a careful summary of the actual terms.[3] Thus they were known in England long before they were officially announced there by the French ambassador.

The long-standing quarrel between Franklin and Deane and Arthur Lee once more burst into open antagonism during discussions of the proposed treaties. When the French Ministry submitted the first draft of the Treaty of Alliance to the American Commissioners, it guaranteed the "liberty" of the United States but contained no mention of its sovereignty or independence. This wording accorded with Franklin's hope that no specific mention of "independence" might be made—that it "may be implyed or arise out of the Essence of the objects of the Treaty; [rather] than Expressed by any formal words." [4] Lee could not agree. He considered those words to be indispensable and protested against their omission. He cited the example of the French treaty with the Swiss cantons as a precedent for their inclusion. [5]

Franklin and Deane sided with the French by pointing out that even Congress had not suggested that the treaty include words supportive of America's sovereignty and independence. Stubbornly, Lee held on, and Franklin and Deane finally gave in only after Lee had warned them that their stance might well have dangerous consequences with the Congress. [6] "It was with the greatest difficulty I persuaded them to insist on the recognition of our sovereignty, and the acknowledgement of our independence. These were proposed by your friend [Lee], evaded by his colleagues." [7] In its final wording, Article Two of the Treaty declared that "the essential and direct end of the present defensive alliance is to maintain effectually the liberty, sovereignty and independence absolute and unlimited of the said United States as well in matters of government as of commerce."

There was also a difference of opinion among the commissioners regarding the Commercial Treaty. Lee argued against making it perpetual, urging that it should be for a limited time only on the grounds that this might save embarrassments in the future—as indeed it would have done for President Washington a few years later. But on this point Lee lost.

Lee also questioned the matter of molasses. In the first draft of the Commercial Treaty it was stated that France would not lay export duties on molasses shipped to America from the islands of the French West Indies. Vergennes objected, for there was no equivalent restriction on American exports. So Franklin interposed that if France would not tax molasses, the United States would agree to levy no duty on any item taken by France from America. Vergennes quickly agreed.

Lee objected strongly. While Franklin's formula would bind America on all exported goods, France would be bound on but one, molasses. Such a clause would violate the principle of reciprocity on which all treaties should be based. Whether or not Congress ever laid an export tax, Lee argued, this was giving permission to France "to tie both our hands for the privilege of tying one of her little fingers." [8] Franklin and Deane fumed at Lee's recalcitrance, but at least one writer has noted that Arthur Lee was absolutely right to object. His behavior "was not an officious interference, as Franklin's biographers have maintained." [9] He was simply trying to protect the rights of America in the face of an uncaring attitude shown by Franklin and Deane. The French Ministry sought to retain the wording of the first draft. Lee adamantly objected, but finally waived his disagreement, for it seemed more important to conclude the negotiations speedily than to have the agreements in as advantageous form as one might have wished.

Upon further reflection Lee had second thoughts and restated his objections to the molasses article. He refused to budge no matter how angry and exasperated Franklin and Deane became. Lee refused to sign the Treaty unless there should be an explicit understanding with the French Court that Congress might have the liberty to accept or to reject the Franklin "compromise" on molasses, without endangering the actual ratification of the rest of the treaties. The French Foreign Ministry agreed. When the treaties reached Congress, the articles in question were debated and unanimously rejected as not in the best interest of the nation. Thus in the end Congress unanimously upheld Lee's position and repudiated Franklin's.[10]

In England, Lord North, the King's prime minister, was sick at the thought that France might enter the war on the side of the colonies. He suggested to George III that it might be wise to send a commission to America to treat with the rebels. Repeal the tea duty. Repeal the Massachusetts Acts of 1774. Realizing that such suggestions might offend his monarch, North offered to resign his office, but George refused to accept the resignation. Indeed, he was intrigued by the possibilities in North's ideas, and by 9 February he directed North to pursue discussions in and out of Parliament on the American question with all dispatch.

In one sense it was already too late and the British knew it. On 6 February 1778, a Friday evening, five men had gathered at the Hôtel de Lautrec, the headquarters of the French Foreign Ministry. They were Gérard, Franklin, Deane, Lee, and Bancroft. The final copies of the treaties had been prepared. Gérard and the three American commissioners signed them. The ceremony was brief and at its conclusion Franklin handed the secret documents to Edward Bancroft for "safekeeping." Ralph Izard later charged that the next day Franklin wrote a London correspondent giving him the information in the Treaties.[11] Whether or not Izard's charge is valid, it is certain that forty-two hours after the ceremony, thanks to the swift work of Bancroft, those documents were copied and in the offices of the British government, there to be analyzed and evaluated.

Perhaps there was still time for the British to act. The American Congress would have to study and debate the treaties after receiving them, and they might not be sent from France immediately. Passage across the Atlantic was a matter of weeks. Thus there was opportunity still remaining for the British. Perhaps ratification would be refused if the members

of Congress knew that England had at last had a change of
heart.

So North pushed ahead. He ordered Stormont home from
France with such haste that the ambassador was required "to
quit this Court without taking leave." [12] North quickly introduced conciliatory bills into Parliament; by 16 March they
were passed and on their way to America. In fact, the bills allowed America all it asked short of actual independence. A
near race across the Atlantic developed. The English ship,
H.M.S. *Andromeda*, carried drafts of North's conciliatory
bills; the French *Sensible* bore the Franco-American treaties.

North needed a committee to negotiate with the Americans for England. For this purpose he established the Carlisle
Commission. The powerhouse of the commission was William Eden, soon to be withdrawn from active leadership of
the Secret Service. He drew up one of the original plans for
the commission, was involved in most of the detailed planning, and was the contact for others engaged in contingency
planning. Eden was not officially named to the commission
until 7 March, although four days earlier he had been given
£1,000 "to fit himself" for his new duties.[13] Alexander Wedderburn heard the good news about his kinsman and wrote
congratulations: "A more important trust was never put in
any hands, or on a more delicate occasion." [14]

The Earl of Carlisle, the nominal head of the mission, was
a front for Eden. The Earl was still under thirty, a dilettante,
and a minor poet. He was a treasurer of the King's household
and a privy councillor. The third member of the group was
George Johnstone, former governor of West Florida. These
three would be joined in America by the Howe brothers,
making a total of five on the commission. The Carlisle Commission was to treat first with the American Congress and
General Washington. If such meetings bore no fruit, it was
authorized to approach directly any of the former colonies in
an effort to end the war on a piecemeal basis. The Commis-

sion, begun with high hopes, was ultimately doomed to failure. Although its members spent months in America, they
had little success and finally, discouraged, returned to England to announce their failures.

During his last days as head of the British Secret Service,
William Eden continued to send agents to France. Through
such continuing contacts, Eden still hoped to find the correct
touchstone that would allow Franklin publicly to throw his
weight behind a move for reunification of the colonies and
the mother country.

After Wentworth visited with "72" in early January, another emissary from England came to France to visit Franklin. This was James Hutton, an eminent Moravian leader and
a long-time friend of Franklin. Through Eden, Lord North
empowered Hutton to hold out to Franklin and the American
Congress anything short of declared independence. Wentworth knew of Hutton's visit to Franklin and told Eden that
Franklin suspected Hutton to be of "very high authority." In
a letter to Hutton, written shortly after Wentworth's departure, Franklin stated that "I cannot, as you seem again to desire, make Propositions. . . . But we can treat, if any are
made to us; which however we do not expect." Franklin had
not forgotten about Wentworth's propositions; he simply saw
fit not to mention them. A few days earlier, Franklin had suggested his own view to Hutton, which must have gladdened
the old Moravian's heart. Franklin wrote him that "Perhaps
you might by your [peace] Treaty retain all Canada, Nova
Scotia and the Floridas." The words did not seem to be those
of a man dedicated to wresting for America the best terms
possible at the end of the war. In their talks during Hutton's
visit, Franklin told Hutton that indeed he had the authority to
negotiate peace terms and to recommend a reasonable settlement to the Congress.[15] Shortly afterward, when Franklin
got hold of copies of North's conciliatory bills, he wrote a
friend in England, David Hartley: "Whenever you shall be
disposed to make peace upon equal and reasonable terms, you

will find little difficulty. . . ." [16] A few days later he added: "I am of opinion that if wise and honest men . . . were to come over here immediately with powers to treat, you might not only obtain peace with America but prevent a war with France." [17] Presumably Hutton was no longer "wise and honest."

Such comments from Franklin, given weeks after the signing of the Franco-American treaties, could only encourage Eden to continue his efforts to bring a settlement to the war before France could actively engage her armies. In what may well have been a response to Franklin's promises, William Eden twice sent William Pulteney, a wealthy Whig and member of Parliament for Shrewsbury, to France to meet with the old doctor and his Connecticut cohort, Silas Deane.

Pulteney had wanted to do what he could to bring the war to a halt since the news of Saratoga had reached England late in 1777. His private views harmonized perfectly with Eden's task of sounding out the Paris mission. On 6 December 1777 Pulteney told authorities of his willingness to go to France. "Dr. Franklyn knows that I have always respected him when it was the fashion to entertain other opinions," Pulteney declared.[18] For a time he was put off, for Paul Wentworth was already in Paris and there might be no need to use another agent. Pulteney learned of Wentworth's activities in France on 3 January 1778, when his European business agent wrote him:

I have your very obliging letter of the 22nd past by the last Mail, and am not at all sorry that Messrs. W:[entworth] and E:[den] have yet sent no message to Mr. S.[ilas Deane]. It shews me that the overtures have met with Consideration, and as a great body [Parliament? Privy Council?] must be Consulted whose motions are slow, if an Answer had come soon, I woud have been Certain it was negative, before perusal. I shall now however give but a week or two more, and Then desire

S:[ilas Deane] to insist on a peremptory answer. Otherways the proposals will be consider'd as rejected, and Consequently as never having existed.[19]

Wentworth's mission bore little fruit and Hutton did not achieve what he wanted. Yet Franklin still called for properly credentialed emissaries who could officially negotiate to visit him. Thus, only a few days after Franklin wrote Hartley, Eden sent William Pulteney to Paris. The specific terms he was empowered to offer were the best given by the British prior to Yorktown. Upon arriving in Paris, Pulteney's first move was to get in touch with his European business agent, William Alexander. Alexander had known Franklin since the American's trip to Edinburgh in 1774. By 1776, the Scot was living in Dijon, France. It was he, we may recall, who warned Franklin, soon after the doctor's arrival in France, not to leave his papers so carelessly scattered because of the numerous spies surrounding him. Now, with Pulteney's urging, Alexander had himself become one of the spies he had so earnestly warned Ben against. He moved from Dijon to a home near Passy, where he established a "listening post" from which he could keep Pulteney, and through him the Secret Service, apprised of the latest developments at the American mission.

Pulteney arrived in Paris early in March and stayed in a hotel in the Latin Quarter under the name of "Mr. Williams." Franklin and Pulteney secretly met about the middle of the month. The American, thinking of the recent signing of the Franco-American treaties, told his visitor that "every Proposition, which implied our voluntarily agreeing to return to a Dependence on Britain, was now become impossible," although "A Peace on equal Terms undoubtedly might be made." Franklin also told Pulteney that the American mission in Paris had authority to conclude such a peace.[20] Understanding this as a promise, Pulteney prepared to return to England, telling Franklin he would return as soon as possible with specific offers from his government.

William Alexander wrote Pulteney that "You will find, I am Sure, as sincere a disposition as ever to Conciliate and reconcile differences of Sentiment so far as is consistent with the Essential Security of America." He added that he could say this because "I write with Confidence and under the Eye of a very wise Man." [21] Seven days later, 26 March, the Scot wrote again to Pulteney. On the subject of peace, he reported, Ben "spoke indeed Cautiously and as a Man unwilling to make concessions that might expose him to Censure from his friends where the Interest of the whole family [i.e., America] is concerned. . . . He even said in words 'I have still some remaining affection for Him [England] and woud be happy on reasonable terms to make Him [England] easy.' " Alexander added that Franklin was willing that all this should be made known to Lord North.[22] Alexander's words were corroborated by Edward Bancroft. After the first meeting of Franklin and Pulteney, Bancroft had forwarded through the network a message to Wentworth indicating that Pulteney's "hints for a negotiation are adopted." [23]

Learning of these things after his return to London, Pulteney remained hopeful of success. North was less so and told the king of his feelings in a memorandum of 25 March. Answering his prime minister on the following day, George did not bother to hide his own feelings toward Franklin. He felt it "proper to keep open the channel of intercourse with that insidious man" and ordered another meeting of "the agents employed in this dangerous business." [24] Pulteney set out once more for France, with eighteen proposals approved by Lord North and the king.[25] On 29 March 1778 he contacted Franklin. "Mr. Williams returned this morning to Paris and will be glad to see Dr. Franklin, whenever it is convenient for the Doctor, at the Hôtel Frasilière, rue Tournon. It is near the hotel where he lodged when the Doctor saw him a fortnight ago. He does not propose to go abroad, and therefore the Doctor will find him at any hour." [26] On 30 March, Franklin and Pulteney met for the second time. On this occa-

202 CODE NUMBER 72

sion they were joined by William Alexander. The English agent gave the eighteen propositions to Franklin, who scanned them and handed them back. By Franklin's own account, he claimed to have told Pulteney that "the ministers cannot yet divest themselves of the idea that the power of Parliament over us is constitutionally absolute and unlimited; and that the limitations they may be willing now to put to it by treaty are so many favours, or so many benefits, for which we are to make compensation." [27]

Franklin reportedly went on to tell Pulteney that he did not think America would agree to a treaty on terms such as these and that the commissioners certainly did not have the authority to do so.[28]

Then, in the midst of his conversation with Pulteney, Franklin allegedly told his visitor that he "did not approve of them, nor did he think they would be approved in America. But there are two other Commissioners here; I will, if you please, show your Propositions to them and you will hear their Opinion." To which, according to Franklin's account, Pulteney answered, "No, as you do not approve of them, it can answer no purpose to show them to anybody else; the reasons that weigh with you will weigh with them; therefore I now pray that no mention may be made of my having been here or my business." Franklin added, "To which I agreed."[29]

Franklin did not set down the gist of the conversation with Pulteney until 19 March 1780—two years after it had occurred. The conversation may or may not have been limited, as Franklin described it, to discussions of North's eighteen points. Franklin's summation of the talk shows clearly that the English offer to America had been insufficient. Yet a few days later, on 8 April, George III wrote to Lord North that "I do not think much is to be built on the note from Mr. Pulteney, probably the Old Doctor may wish to keep a door open, but as it does not delay the [Carlisle] Commissioners it can be of no disservice." [30] What was the "door" that Franklin wished to keep open?

Another question may be asked. Did Franklin agree, as he himself stated, not to tell the other commissioners about Pulteney's visit? If so, it was a promise he did not long keep. Either the same day he met with Pulteney, or the next day, 31 March, Franklin passed along to Silas Deane either North's eighteen points or private propositions on other matters made to him by Pulteney, or both. The latter is most likely. On 31 March Silas Deane set out for a journey to the port city of Toulon. Pulteney was still in Paris. Deane carried with him a copy of Pulteney's proposals. On 7 April, Franklin wrote to him at Toulon. "The negotiator is gone back, apparently much chagrined at his little success. I have promised him faithfully that since his propositions could not be accepted they should be buried in oblivion. I therefore earnestly desire that you would put that paper immediately into the fire on receipt of this, without taking or suffering to be taken any copy of it, or communicating its contents." [31] Deane complied.

Did the memorandum contain only North's eighteen proposals given Franklin by a duly credentialed British agent in search of peace?

Did that note reveal something too personal for Franklin to take such a risk? Perhaps Pulteney had offered Franklin and Deane bribes, as some have thought. [32] If this came to light, Lee and his friends would immediately seize upon it and shout it heavenward. Or was Franklin simply a man of deep personal honor who had given his word to a clandestine British agent not to reveal to anyone the eighteen proposals of Lord North? Perhaps this was why he had to write to Silas Deane to destroy the copy he had given him, breaching his honor as he did so.

Another piece of information may shed light on this episode. In America, at a meeting of the Carlisle Commissioners on 6 May, George Johnstone presented his "Heads of Accommodation" which he claimed were based on information derived from the meetings between Franklin and Pulteney. Johnstone stated that he had "secret information" from

Franklin suggesting that if the Carlisle Commissioners offered seats in Parliament to American leaders, such a bribe "would be more alluring than any other." [33] It should be noted that William Pulteney had been born William Johnstone, but had changed his name when he married Frances Pulteney, a rich heiress. George Johnstone, the Carlisle Commissioner, was Pulteney's brother, and it was entirely likely that Pulteney would send such information on to his brother in America at the earliest opportunity. He told George Johnstone something else as well, for Johnstone, in a letter to the American congressman Francis Dana, revealed that "Dr. Franklin on the 29th of March last in discussing the Several Articles we wish to make the Basis of our Treaty, was perfectly Satisfied they were beneficial to North America and such as *they should accept*." Congress printed the letter. Franklin was livid when he learned of it. Such information could only have come straight from William Pulteney. Ben handed a copy of the letter to William Alexander, "with marks of Indignation which I never saw in him but on a like occasion." Franklin said: "What trust or Confidence coud ever be put in Men who thus violated the most solemn engagements—and to whom breach of faith and falshood were equally easy?" Franklin insisted that he had "Never discovered to any Mortal alive any one circumstance that Had passed," and was utterly contemptuous of Pulteney for doing so. His protestations were off the mark, as was his air of injured innocence, for the records clearly show that he had wasted no time in breaking his promise to Pulteney not to reveal the substance of their meeting.[34] He was threatened because of the public embarrassment of having Congress learn how much he had told Pulteney in spite of his efforts to forestall that occurrence by asking Deane to burn the memorandum of that conversation.

Pulteney had gone home after his meeting with Franklin in March 1778, but he left Alexander behind to keep him in touch with any new developments. The man who had warned against spies now himself became a full-time employee of Eden's Secret Service. He lived at Auteuil, within walking distance of Franklin's home at L'Hôtel des Valentinois. Alexander and Pulteney devised a cipher in which to code their letters, on a level with those created by boy scouts, in which they simply stated the opposite of what they actually meant.[35]

Over the next several months, Alexander sent to Britain considerable information dealing with economic conditions in America, the character of the new envoy, John Adams, and recent activities of the Carlisle Commission in America. His mission lasted until about the middle of November 1778. After that he closed up his spy shop and sometime later moved back to Dijon. In September 1779 Jonathan Williams, Jr., married Alexander's daughter Mariamne.[36]

The new year of 1778 had not been a good one for Franklin and Deane. From the opening days, Deane felt too deeply the pressures resulting from his clandestine activities and Arthur Lee's inquiries into them. As early as 15 January, Deane wrote to his brother Simeon that "I am most heartily tired of public Business, & only wish to retire without Loss or Disgrace." [37] It would not be possible. He had become mired too deeply in matters he could not cope with. Already a message from Congress was enroute to him. The preceding 21 November 1777, a suspicious Congress—angered over the number and quality of European soldiers Deane had sent as officers for the American army, and outraged over the possibility that Deane and Beaumarchais were trying to defraud the United States Treasury—resolved that Deane should return to America.

According to Deane, he received the notification of his recall on 4 March 1778.[38] It must have been a shocking blow to him. One moment an important diplomat, the next a recalled politician. For a time the news was kept quiet by Franklin and Deane. Thus Deane was presented to Louis XVI on 20 March as still one of the three American commissioners at the

ceremony in which the French Monarch publicly acknowledged the recently signed treaties.

Franklin also allowed Deane to continue to draw as much
money as he wished from the commission funds. Indeed,
Deane could not have done so without Franklin's connivance.
During his last two weeks in Paris, from 15 to 30 March—
long after he had received notification that he had been relieved—Deane drew 38,715 livres (£1,700), for which he
gave no accounting.[39]

Worried about the reception he would meet with from the
Congress, Deane asked Franklin to write him a letter of recommendation to show at home. Ben was only too happy to
comply with the request. In the recommendation Franklin
spoke of Deane's "great and important service to his country." [40]

For as long as possible, Franklin and Deane kept quiet the
news of the latter's recall. Lee eventually learned of it, however, and again began his concerted clamor to have the accounts settled prior to Deane's departure. He never did learn
the date on which Deane planned to sail, nor was he included
in the discussions which led to the choosing of Gérard as the
first French minister to America, nor did he know that the
two men planned to leave for America on the same vessel.
Receiving no response to his repeated requests for a meeting
to audit the accounts, Arthur Lee finally wrote a desperate
letter of entreaty to both Franklin and Deane. He cried out
"to repeat the request I long ago and repeatedly made that we
should settle the public accounts relating to the expenditure
of the money entrusted to us for the public." [41] Lee wrote the
letter, he said, because of recent rumors of Deane's impending departure. He was too late. The secret had been successfully kept, and on the very day he wrote, Deane slipped out
of Paris carrying a copy of Pulteney's propositions, on his
way to Toulon to join Gérard and the French fleet which
would take them to America.

On April Fool's Day, 1778, Franklin replied to Arthur

Lee's request. "Sir," he wrote, "There is a Stile in some of your Letters, I observe it particularly in the last, whereby superior Merit is assumed to yourself in point of Care and Attention to Business, and Blame is insinuated on your Colleagues without making yourself accountable by a direct Charge, of Negligence or Unfaithfulness, which has the Appearance of being as artful as it is unkind. In the present Case I think the Insinuation groundless."

With his tongue firmly pressed into his cheek, Ben went on to add that "I do not know that either Mr. Deane or myself ever show'd an Unwillingness to settle the Public Accounts. The Banker's Book always contain'd the whole. You could at any time as easily have obtain'd the Account from them as either of us." This was simply untrue. The demonstrated unwillingness of Franklin and Deane to talk about accounts extended as far back as Lee's return from his mission to Spain early in 1777. "And you had abundantly more Leisure," Franklin commented, in a gratuitous slap at the hardest working of the three commissioners. "Mr. Deane, however, had left with me, before the Receipt of your Letter, both the Public Papers, and Explications of the several Articles in the Account that came within his Knowledge. With these Materials I suppose we can settle the Account whenever you please. You have only to name the Day and Place, and I will attend the Business with you." [42]

Franklin's letter was more artful than any act of which he accused Lee. As a matter of record, Lee had sought an account audit for nearly a year, only to be rebuffed repeatedly. Even John Adams, who certainly tried hard enough, could make no sense of the accounts, and several generations of historians have thrown up their hands in despair at ever untangling the skein of those financial transactions.

Lee's reply was written the next day.

It was with the utmost surprise, that I learned yesterday that M. Gérard was to set out in the evening for America, in a public character, and that Mr. Deane was to accompany him, without either you or he having condescended to answer my letter of the preceeding day.

That a measure of such moment, as M. Gérard's mission, should have been taken without any communication with the Commissioners is hardly credible. That, if it was communicated, you should do such violence to the authority that constituted us, together with so great an injury and injustice to me, is equally astonishing. If success to the mission and unanimity on the subject in Congress, were your wish, with what propriety could you make it a party business, and not unite all the Commissioners in the advising and approving a measure, in which you desired their friends and constituents might be unanimous?

I do not live ten minutes' distance from you. The communication, therefore, could not be attended with delay or difficulty. Within these few days, I have seen you frequently, as usual. Particularly, on Monday I was with you at your house for some time. I asked you about the sailing of the ships at Nantes, expressing my desire to know when we should have an opportunity of writing [the Congress]. You said you did not know when they sailed. I asked if there were no letters, none but one from M. Dumas having been shown to me for some time. You answered, No. I had, at a former meeting, asked you whether it was not proper for us to send an express to give intelligence of such consequential events as our being acknowledged here, and the treaty avowed. You told me, it would be sufficient to write by the ship from Nantes, (for it was afterwards you mentioned there were two,) as the news being public would find its way fast enough.

Upon M. Amiel, who came from your house to mine, mentioning, on Tuesday, that Mr. Deane was to go away in a few days, I wrote to you and him to repeat what I have so often requested, that the public accounts might be settled, for which Mr. Deane had taken possession of all the vouchers, and that the public papers might

be delivered to us before his departure. You made no answer. I sent my secretary again yesterday to desire an
answer. You sent me a verbal one, that you would settle
the accounts with me any day after to-morrow. Your
reason for not doing it before was, that it was not your
business. Now it seemed your business only, and Mr.
Deane had no concern with it. The delivery of the public papers, which are the property of all, not of any one
of the Commissioners, though you and Mr. Deane have
constantly taken them to yourselves, was too immaterial
to answer.

During all this time, and with these circumstances,
you have been totally silent to me about the present opportunity of writing to Congress, about the important
public measure in agitation, and about Mr. Deane's departure. Nay, more, what you have said, and the manner
in which you acted, tended to mislead me from imag-
ining that you knew of any such thing. Had you studied
to deceive the most distrusted and dangerous enemy of
the public, you could not have done it more effectually.

I trust, Sir, that you will think with me, that I have a
right to know your reasons for treating me thus. If you
have anything to accuse me of, avow it, and I will answer you. If you have not, why do you act so inconsist-
ently with your duty to the public, and injuriously to
me? Is the present state of Europe of so little moment to
our constituents, as not to require our joint consideration, and information to them? Is the character of the
court here, and of the person sent to negotiate with our
constituents, of no consequence for them to be apprized
of? Is this the example, you in your superior wisdom
think proper to set, of order, decorum, confidence, and
justice?

I trust too, Sir, that you will not treat this letter, as
you have done many others, with the indignity of not
answering it. Though I have been silent, I have not felt
the less the many affronts of this kind, which you have
thought proper to offer me.[43]

This letter of Lee's sounded a clear note of petulance, childishness, and bad-tempered annoyance. Lee should have known that a message of this kind could not possibly serve either him or his cause, yet his frustrated reaction may have been understandable. Since his arrival in France, Lee had been systematically treated with scorn, made to suffer exclusion from official business, had his sanity questioned, and now found himself again the object of deceit. He had accused Franklin of keeping him in ignorance of the date of Deane's departure. This was obviously true. The avowed reason for doing so was the "public good," Franklin later claimed.[44] The real reason was that neither Franklin nor Deane wanted Lee to remain in the confidence of the French Foreign Ministry. They already had informed Vergennes that Lee had employed the spy, Thornton, as his secretary. Shortly after his arrival in America, Gérard told the Congress that his government did not trust Lee.[45]

To Lee's series of requests, which upon reflection seem well within the bounds of propriety, Franklin reacted with angry haste. On 3 April, he replied to Lee, bringing up once again intimations of his colleague's insanity.

> It is true I have omitted answering some of your Letters. I do not like to answer angry Letters. I hate Disputes. I am old, cannot have long to live, have much to do and no time for Altercation. If I have often receiv'd and borne your Magisterial Snubbings and Rebukes without Reply, ascribe it to the right Causes, my Concern for the Honour & Success of our Mission, which would be hurt by our Quarrelling, my Love of Peace, my Respect for your good Qualities, and my Pity of your Sick Mind, which is forever tormenting itself, with its Jealousies, Suspicions & Fancies that others mean you ill, wrong you, or fail in Respect for you.—If you do not cure your self of this Temper it will end in Insanity, of which it is the Symptomatick Forerunner, as I have seen in several Instances. God preserve you from so terrible an Evil: and for his sake pray suffer me to live in quiet.[46]

Franklin sent Lee a second letter on 4 April, in which he repeated his answer as to why he had not earlier replied to requests from Lee. "It is true, that I have omitted answering some of your Letters. . . . I saw your jealous, suspicious, malignant and quarrelsome Temper, which was daily manifesting itself against Mr. Deane," and for that reason "pass'd your Affronts in Silence" and "burnt your angry Letters." Deane had just been recalled to America to respond to charges. He had been in the employ of the British from the moment of his landing in France. Yet Lee's curiosity about his activities were regarded by Franklin as "jealous, suspicious, malignant."

Franklin told Lee that if Deane had left without informing him, that was really Deane's business, not his. As for his own role in the affair, it simply was not the proper time to explain matters to Lee, for the "public good" was involved. Then, speaking of Lee's letter to him, he wrote: "When this comes to be read by the committee [of Congress] for whom it seems to be calculated rather than for me, who knows the circumstances, what can they understand by it . . . ?" [47] Whether or not putting Lee's letter before the Congress was Lee's intention, it certainly seems to have been Franklin's.

That same day, while on the subject of expenses, Franklin challenged Lee by declaring that, inasmuch as the Virginian was so exercised about money, perhaps the two should compare personal spending. The old doctor claimed that his own disbursements were very moderate, "having only the necessaries of life, and [having] purchased nothing besides except the encyclopedia, nor sent a sixpence worth of anything to my friends or family in America."

He told Lee that he lived simply, frugally, almost in a spartan style. Yet his wine cellar at Passy contained some 260 bottles of red Bordeaux, over one hundred of red Burgundy, approximately four hundred of various white wines, including champagne, two hundred vin ordinaire for use by his servants, and forty-five bottles of rum. His maître d'hotel supervised an entire staff of servants hired to cater to the "ambassador" and his official family of spies. Franklin often dined out. When he did not, however, his meals were likely to consist of beef, veal, or mutton, after which he would be served either poultry or game. Also placed before him were two vegetables, two sweets, one pastry. In winter he had only two kinds of fruit although in summer he regularly had four varieties. He was served ices once each week in winter, twice during the summer. He topped his meals with a choice of cheeses, biscuits, and bonbons.[48] Franklin obviously had his own way of defining "the necessaries of life."

Immediately after this series of angry exchanges with Lee, Franklin seems to have undergone a change. As long as Silas Deane had been available, the two seem to have worked closely on a multitude of private and clandestine matters. They had defended the spies in their household to the Lees and others and continued to employ them. They had allowed special access to state information by those not entitled to it. Until Deane's last day in Paris, they had continued to use Congressional funds without discretion. They had tried to destroy the reputations of Arthur and William Lee and Ralph Izard. Unbeknownst to their compatriots, they had met with a series of British agents at clandestine locations. They had listened to offers of honors and emoluments that would be theirs if they came out publicly for reunion with Britain. They had made the port city of Nantes a private enclave for their personal interests. They had speculated in British stocks by using privileged information. They continued to manipulate events so as to further land speculation in the American West.

Yet Deane was now gone and John Adams would replace him. Lee was clamoring throughout the land that something nefarious was going on. His voice was joined by those of his brother and of Izard. Franklin may well have been frightened that his reputation, carefully protected over the years in spite of many possible pitfalls, might at last suffer irreparable damage. This he could not allow. And so, slowly he began a series of retrenchments. It was not easy. His enemies bayed at his heels in full voice. Whenever he had the opportunity, he would stand firm. As chances occurred, he would push his own interests. But the halcyon days were over. From now on, when faced with solid opposition by his colleagues, Franklin would find ways of working with them so as not to arouse their curiosity too much about certain chapters of his life now better hidden.

CHAPTER TEN

_____·•·_____

Silas Deane—the "Wild Boar"

As he considered his new situation, Franklin thought it might be best to gain John Adams as his ally at the first opportunity. To this end he would have to talk things over with the man from Massachusetts before he could be "poisoned" against him by Arthur Lee's suspicions.

John Adams arrived 8 April 1778. His diary entry, written two days later, shows something of Franklin's tactics. "The first moment Dr. Franklin and I happened to be alone, he began to complain of the coolness . . . between the American ministers." Franklin told Adams "that Mr. Lee was a man of an anxious, uneasy temper, which made it disagreeable to do business with him; that he seemed to be one of those men, of whom he had known many in his day, who went on through life quarrelling with one person or another till they commonly ended with the loss of their reason." Franklin also pointed out Izard as a troublemaker, "a man of violent and ungoverned passions," and suggested that neither Izard nor Lee "was liked by the French."

Adams was unhappy to hear Franklin's report. "I heard all this with inward grief and external patience and composure. I only answered that I was . . . extremely sorry to hear of any misunderstanding among the Americans . . . that it would not become me to take any part in them." [1] Since Franklin had talked so readily, Adams expected to hear next from Lee

with his version of events. He was surprised when this was
not forthcoming. Some days later Adams confided to his
diary that "Mr. Lee had, as yet, said nothing to me concerning these controversies. I was informed, afterwards, by
others, that he had said he would be silent on this subject, and
leave me to learn by experience the state and course of the
public business, and judge for myself whether it had been or
was likely to be done right or wrong." [2] Once again, Lee had
not acted in the way his biographical characterizations would
indicate. Indeed, Franklin's talk with Adams is more suggestive of the way later writers have described Arthur Lee than
were Lee's own actions. But Ben was in a spot, casting about
for allies now that he was bereft of the support of Silas Deane.

Izard kept up his end of the barrage against Franklin. He
wrote complaining that he was too often obliged to ask for
the reasons causing the old man to act toward him in the way
he did. He said the cautious and quiet departure of Deane and
Gérard should not have been concealed from those who had a
right to know of it. He "begged" Franklin not to amuse him
with further promises or excuses, but either to give him the
explanation for his conduct or to be man enough to refuse
outright.[3] From Frankfurt, William Lee wrote Arthur that "I
am convinced that *Deane* and the tribe have corrupted *Franklin*," whom he also described as "the Old Fox." [4]

Arthur Lee encapsulated his own feelings about his elder
colleague in these words: Franklin's "abilities are great and
his reputation high; removed as he is to so considerable a distance from the observation of his constituents, if he is not
guided by principles of virtue and honor, those abilities and
that reputation may produce the most mischievous effects. In
my conscience I declare to you, that I believe him under no
such internal restraints, and God knows that I speak the real
unprejudiced sentiments of my heart." [5] Convinced that both
Franklin and Deane had been stealing from the public funds,
Lee wrote that because Franklin was "concerned in the plunder . . . in time we shall collect the proofs." [6]

In late Spring 1778 Arthur Lee discovered that Franklin

was still deeply involved in land speculation activities. To an American acquaintance, Lee wrote: "Since I last wrote to you I have discovered that a company, which has at its head, and which obtained some time since from the crown of Great Britain, an immense grant on the Ohio, within the Dominion of Virginia, are intriguing to interest members of Congress in it so as to get a confirmation of their grant from Congress, which would be invading the right of our state. The grant was called Vandalia. Many Englishmen are members of the company and the Americans are Dr. Franklin, Mr. Joseph Wharton, in London and a Dr. Bankcroft. These are the persons by whose intrigues it is expected the business may be affected." [7]

Shortly after his arrival in Paris, Adams wrote:

> It is with much grief and concern that I have learned, from my first landing in France, the disputes between the Americans in this kingdom; the animosities between Mr. Deane and Mr. Lee; between Dr. Franklin and Mr. Lee; between Mr. Izard and Dr. Franklin; between Dr. Bancroft and Mr. Lee; between Mr. Carmichael and all. It is a rope of sand. I am at present wholly untainted with these prejudices, and will endeavor to keep myself so. Parties and divisions among the Americans here must have disagreeable, if not pernicious, effects. . . . Mr. Deane had been at least as attentive to his own interest, in dabbling in the English funds and in trade, and in fitting out privateers, as to the public; . . . and . . . Dr. Bancroft too had made a fortune. . . . What shall I say? What shall I think?" [8]

One of the first problems to catch Adams' eye was the situation in Nantes. There Jonathan Williams, Jr., still held sway with John Ross, in spite of the earlier efforts of William Lee to gain control of the situation. Adams described the matter in his diary as follows:

> Mr. Jonathan Williams, a relation of Dr. Franklin, . . .
> I had the best disposition to favor, as far as the public

service and my own sense of propriety would permit. Dr. Franklin and Mr. Deane had employed him in transactions which appeared to me to be commercial, and, in this, had differed with Mr. Arthur Lee, and interfered with the province of Mr. William Lee. I, therefore, united with Mr. Lee in this and many subsequent proceedings, requiring the settlement of Mr. Williams's accounts. Dr. Franklin, finding that two of us were agreed in opinion, subscribed the letter with us.

Mr. Ross was neither appointed by Congress, by the public ministers in France, nor by Mr. William Lee, but, I suppose, was connected in trade with Mr. Robert Morris, and might have orders from him to purchase arms, or clothing, or other articles for public use, as Mr. Morris was then chairman of the commercial committee of Congress, and, some time after, appointed financier. Mr. Ross expected us to advance him money to pay for his purchases, and yet did not think himself responsible to us, or obliged to send us his accounts, vouchers, or even his powers or orders. Whatever Mr. Deane or Dr. Franklin had done before my arrival, I thought this procedure more irregular, more inconsistent with the arrangement of Congress, and every way more unjustifiable, then even the case of Mr. Williams. Mr. Arthur Lee's opinion and mine were perfectly in unison upon this point, which, Dr. Franklin perceiving, united with us in subscribing the letter. But these were grievous disappointments to Mr. Williams and Mr. Ross, and all their friends, and, consequently, occasioned grumblings against Mr. Lee and Mr. Adams.[9]

This much Adams had seen and determined to act upon only five days after his arrival! Determinedly neutral at the onset, he had quickly perceived the rightness of an action that Arthur Lee had been calling for over a period of months. At long last, John Ross was gotten rid of. Jonathan Williams would be next.

On 25 May 1778, Adams wrote from Passy to Jonathan Williams. "The necessities of our country demand the utmost frugality, which can never be obtained without the utmost simplicity in the management of her affairs. And . . . we think it prudent and necessary, for the public service, to revoke, and we do hereby revoke, all the powers and authorities heretofore granted to you by the commissioners plenipotentiary of the United States of America, at Paris, or any of them, to the end that hereafter the management of the affairs, maritime and commercial, of America, may be under one sole direction, that of Mr. Schweighauser, within his district [of Nantes]." [10]

William Lee had won. Schweighauser was the man he had chosen to act in his stead when he left Nantes to take up his place in Frankfurt on his mission to Austria and Prussia. Jonathan Williams was now out. Franklin had resisted this move, for Nantes was simply too sweet a sugar plum to allow to fall from the hands of his family without regrets. Adams, however, had been adamant. Not only did he want Williams to resign, but he was careful to insist that allowing Williams to resign in no way was to be understood as indicating approval of his mixed-up accounts. For those he would have to answer to Congress alone. A reluctant Franklin then joined Adams in authorizing Williams to draw the money he claimed was due him, prior to his resignation, so long as it was clearly understood that this did not in any way validate his claim to that money.

Adams shortly confessed that the quarreling he found around him, "the uncandor, the prejudices, the rage among several persons here make me sick as death." He wrote Sam Adams that embassy affairs were confused, huge amounts of money were being spent, large debts were owed, and no documents or accounts were kept. The commissioners prodigiously spent on their own support from three to six thousand pounds yearly. He hoped Congress would separate the offices of envoy and commercial agent, recall all the mission except for one man, set his salary, and supervise accounts so that he had no chance to profiteer.[11] While this letter was sailing across the Atlantic, Adams turned to the accounts of the Paris mission.

"There never was, before I came," wrote Adams, "a minute-book, a letter-book, or an account-book; or, if there had been, Mr. Deane and Dr. Franklin had concealed them from Mr. Lee and they were now nowhere to be found. It was utterly impossible to acquire any clear idea of our affairs. I was now determined to procure some blank books; and to apply myself with diligence to business, in which Mr. Lee cordially joined me." [12]

"The business of the commission had been delayed and neglected in a manner that gave me much uneasiness. . . ." Adams said a few days later. "I had now procured my blank books, and I took the letters which we had received into my own hands; and, after, making all the inquiries into the subject which I could, I wrote in my blank book the following answers . . . to show the number of persons who had their eyes fixed upon our little treasury, and under what a variety of pretences and pretended authorities they set up their claims upon us for money." Franklin was unwilling to do anything about this situation and argued against Adams' measures as best he could. But there soon came a time when he no longer felt safe in continuing his arguments. As Adams put it, "Dr. Franklin, after he found that Mr. Lee and I agreed in opinion, and were determined to sign and send them, did not choose to let them go without his name." [13] Two such letters written by Adams went to Williams and Ross. "By these letters the die was cast and one great scene of controversy closed for the present. I had written all of them myself, and produced them to my colleagues as soon as I could get them together. I was doubtful whether Mr. Franklin would sign them, but when he saw that Mr. Lee and I would sign them without him if he refused . . . he very composedly put his signature to them all. . . ." [14]

On the matter of accounts, Adams learned that the situation was at least as bad as he feared. "I made a strict inquiry

of Dr. Franklin, Mr. Lee, and others, for the books of accounts, the letter books, the letters received, the copies of letters sent; but nobody knew of any. Mr. Lee said there had
been no regular accounts, nor any letter book. All agreed that
Mr. Deane had done the business; that he consulted Dr.
Franklin only when he pleased, and Mr. Lee rarely, if ever;
and that all accounts, if any had been kept, and all letters, if
any had been written, were carried off, or concealed by
him." [15] Adams' conclusion may have been accurate as far as
Lee was concerned, but unknown to Adams and Franklin, in
America Silas Deane was busy explaining that "he had not
taken a single step but by the advice of Doctor Franklin"! [16]

Adams was further troubled that Franklin had been living
in Chaumont's home for so long without paying rent. Such
open taking of gifts from an interested foreigner shocked
him. Clearly, a conflict of interest was involved. As Adams
put it: "I know very well that the company we had [as guests
at Passy], and the society with which Dr. Franklin generally
associated, were disliked and disapproved by a great body of
the first and soundest people in the kingdom. . . . These
great people I now speak of, were, I know, very much disgusted at our living at Passy, and in the house of M. Chaumont. But this step had been taken before my arrival; and
what could we do?" [17] One thing he could do was to raise a
fuss. Indeed, Adams complained of the situation so loudly and
at such length that during Franklin's last years in France a
yearly sum was paid to Chaumont for the space occupied by
the American mission.

The early siding of Adams with the Lees and Izard has
bothered many historians, who have been unsure how to treat
it. One writer has described the situation in the following
terms:

> Franklin's biographers have been sorely puzzled to
> know what to do with [Adams'] criticisms; but any one
> who will take the trouble to read impartially all that
> Adams has said, and not merely extracts from it, will

easily be convinced of his fairness. He makes no mistake about Lee; speaks of him as a man very difficult to get on with, and describes Izard in the same way. There is not the slightest evidence that these two men poisoned his mind against Franklin. He does not side with them entirely; but, on the contrary, in the changes he undertook to make was sometimes on their side and sometimes against them. He held the scales very evenly.[18]

While Adams was still trying to get things straightened out, Franklin may have received another contact from the British Secret Service, about which Adams learned some of the details. Near the end of June 1778, someone threw into Franklin's quarters in Passy a letter written at Brussels on 16 June. The message was signed Charles de Weissenstein.[19] Franklin showed the letter to Adams. Its author claimed to be of English birth, but asserted that he sided with America in its struggle with the mother country. The writer also referred slightingly to France. The gist of the rather lengthy message was the hope that Franklin would "offer some conditions directly to the king himself," that might be used to end the war. Weissenstein would "undertake through a most eligible mediator to transmit into the king's own hands any proposals on your part which are not couched in offensive terms."

Franklin was asked to deliver his proposals, if any, in a devious way. He was to take his "preliminaries in writing" to Notre Dame between 12:00 and 1:00 P.M., Monday, 6 July, or Thursday, 9 July, where he would meet a man to whom he could deliver them. "You will ascertain my friend by his having a paper in his hand, as if drawing or taking notes. On any one's coming near him, he will either huddle it up precipitately or, folding it up, tear it with an appearance of peevishness, and walk away. At that very altar where he stood, place your packet within reach, or if there is nobody else near, throw it on the ground and walk away instantly. Don't if you can avoid it, let even him see it is you that bring it, much less anybody else. As soon as he sees the coast clear, he will re-

turn and look for the packet." To complete the identification
of the contact, the agent in the cathedral was to wear a red
rose either in his hatband or in his button hole.

In an accompanying enclosure, Weissenstein spoke of perquisites that would accrue to Franklin for aiding in this
scheme. The note was reminiscent of the offers made months
earlier by Wentworth when he came to Passy. Franklin, and
anyone helping him, would have "offices or pensions for life
at their option, according to the sums opposite their respec-
tive names," which were left blank, to be filled in by those directly concerned. Franklin, additionally, would be made an
American peer. The offer of a peerage recalls the information
William Pulteney sent to his brother George Johnstone of
the Carlisle Commission, after his visits with Franklin. According to Pulteney, Franklin had suggested that an offer of
seats in Parliament to American leaders might go a long way
toward separating such men from their loyalties and bringing
them more quickly to the bargaining table.

Told about this letter, Adams wrote of it to Elbridge
Gerry, a member of Congress from Massachusetts, and in-
closed in his diary an extract of his thoughts. "This letter re-
quires a commentary. The reasons for believing that it came
with the privity of the King, were derived wholly from Dr.
Franklin, who affirmed to me, that there were in the letter infallible marks, by which he knew that it came from the King,
and that it could not have come from any other, without the
King's knowledge." [20] Adams' statement was curious. Franklin had been present in 1760 at the coronation of George III.
He may have been present at a state dinner in 1768 at which
the king appeared, a celebration in honor of the visit to London of the king's brother-in-law, King Christian VII of Den-
mark.[21] Surely these two meetings were not sufficient for
Franklin, years later, to identify "infallible marks" in a letter
pinpointing its origin to the king. Yet Franklin insisted. "I
was not impertinently inquisitive," wrote Adams, "and he
affected to have reasons for avoiding any more particular de-

velopment of the mystery. Many other hints have been dropped by Franklin to me of some mysterious intercourse or correspondence between the King and him, personally." [22] The answers might have been very interesting if Adams had pressed Franklin for a more definite explanation or, barring that, if he even had elaborated in his diary upon these comments. Unfortunately, he did neither.

Franklin never clarified the matter, and other available records cast no additional light on the subject. Ben made no response to Weissenstein's offer, or if he did it was in such a way that no traces were left behind.

He did show the message from Weissenstein to the French, for he no longer seemed willing, as he had in the past, to take the risk of meeting English agents in secret ways and places. Nevertheless, it was this episode that led Adams to begin "to entertain doubts of Franklin's sincerity," as one biographer has noted. [23]

Adams must surely have soon come to doubt some of Franklin's other perceptions. Ben had an apoplectic view of Ralph Izard, yet Adams found the South Carolinian to be entirely different from the way Franklin had portrayed him. In the summer of 1778 Adams wrote to America that Izard "did me the honor of a visit yesterday, when we had much sweet communion, as the phrase is, upon American affairs." [24] What, Adams must have wondered, had been going on prior to his arrival to cause Franklin to look upon Izard with such jaundiced eyes? And why did Izard insist, regarding Franklin, that "His tricks are in general carried on with so much cunning that it is exceedingly difficult to fix them on him"? [25]

Adams' views began to harden. In October, Lee wrote to him urging that he be allowed to act as the secretary for the American mission in Paris and to keep its papers. Adams replied that it might be better for Lee to move out of his quarters at Chaillot and come to live at Passy with him and Franklin. If that were done, Adams suggested, Franklin "may be of more service to us than he is at present. We shall then have a right to call upon him to do business, and we shall know what situation he is in, and what reward he is to have." [26] If both Adams and Lee lived in the same quarters with him, they could, when necessary, insist that he pay attention to his duties.

Lee, however, would have none of it. He told Adams that "The living upon the bounty of a common individual I always objected to; besides, in the best of my judgment, that individual [Franklin] appears to me justly chargeable with the foul play used with our despatches. Till I see reason to think otherwise, I should hold myself inexcusable, both to my constituents and myself, if I were to put myself so much in his power." [27]

Even though he could not corroborate details, Adams was forced to concur in at least the basic charge of misconduct on Franklin's part. A few weeks later, writing to James Lovell, he commented that "most of the old connections of the doctor and Mr. Deane were filled with prejudice" against both Lee and Izard. He added that, in his view, "there was a monopoly of reputation here and an indecency in displaying it which did great injustice to the real merit of others that I do not wonder was resented. There was an indolence, there was a dissipation, which gave just occasion of complaint, and there was a complaisance to interested adventurers. There was an intimacy with stock-jobbers; there was an acquaintance with persons from England which gave just occasion of jealousy, however innocent the intentions were. I have learned that total silence is enough to procure a character for prudence, whatever indiscretions a man [i.e., Franklin] may commit." To remedy the situation, Adams urged that the Congress should pass a resolution "forbidding every man, in the most positive terms, who has any connection with your minister here, from having any connection with English stocks, insurances, etc., and forbidding all correspondence with them." [28]

Lee echoed these sentiments. To a friend in America, Ar-

thur wrote that "it is not a little unpleasant to be deprived of
that praise that constant toil and assiduity in the public service
have deserved, and submit to be traduced by those who, instead of consulting the public interest when in office, have
made immense private fortunes for themselves and their de-
pendants; who are occupied in two things only, their own
gain and the abuse of every one who will not sacrifice the
public to their views." Lee charged that Deane was "generally understood to have made £60,000 while he was employed
here, and Dr. Bancroft his clerk, from being penniless, keeps
his [illegible], his house, and his carriage." Franklin's nephew,
Williams, had gone "from being a clerk in a sugar-bake house
in London" to being "a capital merchant here, loading a
number of ships on his own account, while gentlemen of the
first fortunes in America cannot get remittances on credit for
their subsistence. These things are notorious, and there are no
visible sources of this prosperity, but the public money, and
state secrets to trade upon. It may be useful to you to know
these things as they concern the public. My opposition to
these proceedings have made all that are concerned in them
my bitter enemies." [29]

The situation continued to develop in this way until the re-
lationships among the American commissioners in Europe
had become so tense that Congress resolved on 22 October
1778 that the Committee of Foreign Affairs should inform
Franklin, Lee, Adams, and the others in France that "the desire of congress [is] that 'harmony and good understanding
should be cultivated between them.'" [30] It was a sorry and
low moment for American diplomacy.

This congressional resolution was not the only sign of the
squabble visible in America. Silas Deane had long since returned home. He had left France early in April 1778. Enroute, at Aix, he wrote back to Franklin asking his mentor to
say goodbye to certain friends in Paris. He had not done so
before leaving, he claimed, from lack of time.[31] Why time

should have been a factor, when he had known for weeks that
he would leave, he did not explain. He carried with him a
certificate from Franklin:

> My colleague, Mr. Deane, being recalled by Congress,
> and no reasons given that have yet appeared here, it is
> apprehended to be the effect of some misrepresentation
> from an enemy or two at Paris and at Nantes. I have no
> doubt that he will be able clearly to justify himself; but
> having lived *intimately* with him now fifteen months,
> (the greatest part of the time in the same house), and a
> constant witness of this public conduct, I cannot avoid
> giving this testimony, tho' unasked, in his behalf, that I
> esteem him a *faithful, active,* and *able* minister, who to
> my knowledge has done in various ways great and im-
> portant services to his country, whose interests I wish
> may always by every one in her employ be as much and
> as efficiently promoted.[32]

How Franklin could so have stretched the truth about
Deane's activities boggles the mind. James Lovell, in America, put the matter a different way in a letter to Sam Adams:
"Deane owns he got his recall the 4th of March, yet he imposed himself on the public so as to be presented [to the
French King] on the 20th. He disposed of public money to
others and took largely of it himself [during that time]. . . .
Thus Mr. Deane, no longer a Commissioner, takes out of
public treasure entrusted to the Commissioners only, in the
space of 13 days, 38,718 livres." [33]

Deane knew he would be called upon for a report when he
got to Philadelphia, yet he took no ledgers with him that
would have explained his financial transactions. He took only
his baggage, Franklin's certificate on his behalf, a commenda-
tory letter written for him by Vergennes and procured
through the good offices of Deane's friend, Beaumarchais, and
a jewel-studded miniature of Louis XVI. When he arrived in
America he presented Congress with a statement of money

he claimed that body owed him. This claim was substantiated by no vouchers and listed indiscriminately public and private expenses. The auditor-general of Congress later pointed this fact out and added that it would have been helpful if Deane had given some indication of the cargoes forwarded for public use and the names of those to whom they had been consigned. It was, said the officer of Congress, as important to account properly for merchandise as for cash.

Congress never did get exact figures from Deane. Franklin and Deane had so entangled the finances of the Paris mission that it is probable that even if they had tried neither one of them could have accounted for the money spent. At least it is clear that the tangles were beyond Franklin's comprehension. He later admitted that "As to the accounts of that gentleman . . . if I had them I should not be able to do much with them, or to controvert anything I might doubt in them, being unacquainted with the transactions and agreements on which they must be founded, and having small skill in accounts." [34]

Silas Deane was called twice before a committee of Congress during August to answer questions about his financial dealings. He had no account books. He could only claim that he had left France hurriedly, which was untrue, and so had not had time to prepare his accounts and bring them home with him. He further claimed he had been unaware that questions as to his economic transactions would be brought against him by the Congress. The necessary papers, Deane said, had been safely deposited in France awaiting his return. "Previous to my setting out [for home], I obtained of M. Grand, our banker, an account of all the moneys received or paid out on the public account, which I brought with me, and which has for some time been before Congress; which account must, nevertheless, be liable to be misunderstood without my personal presence, complicated, extensive, and unsettled as they naturally were. Duplicates were also given to Dr. Franklin and Mr. Lee, and I left with the former what public papers were in my hands and an explanation of the account. It was all that the little time I had would permit me to do." [35]

Deane's account of the situation deliberately misled his listeners. Not only had he not given copies of his accounts to Lee, but he even had done his best to keep the time of his departure a secret from that man. And if Franklin supposedly had copies of the papers, they had mysteriously disappeared. As to receipts, Franklin wrote the president of the Congress in 1779 that some "equipment for two frigates" was still in a warehouse and claimed that "it was the only case, out of all the goods shipped from France, in which the Paris mission had been given a receipt." [36]

The statement Deane submitted from Grand gave simply a total of money spent: 4,046,988 livres. No vouchers, no receipts explained the entries. One curious entry, however, shows that Samuel Wharton, on 17 February 1778, had received 19,520 livres from Deane. Deane could never satisfactorily explain this entry or why he had sent this money to a private individual in an enemy country during wartime. At about the time of this transaction, speculators—of whom he and Wharton were chief—were manipulating the London stock market as the news of Saratoga reached Europe. But Deane chose not to enlighten Congress with this explanation.

Here the matter of Deane and his accounts rested at dead center for weeks. Arthur Lee wrote friends in America about the mishandling of funds at the Paris mission. Millions had been spent, he claimed, and yet nearly everything still remained to be paid for. On 12 October, Deane replied to the suspicious Virginian in a letter to the Congress. "Mr. Lee has in his hands the accounts of all the monies received and paid out on the public account. He knows that the total amount received by the Commissioners, to the time of my leaving Paris, was 3,753,250 livres, and the whole expense to that day was 4,046,293 livres; the greater part of this was expended by and with Mr. Lee's orders. The whole is well known to him, and I sent him in writing an explanation of every payment made in his absence." [37] Surely these new facts must have been news to Lee, who had clamored in vain for an opportunity to participate in the affairs of the Paris mission.

Deane loudly called for a congressional hearing at which he might at last receive the money "owing" him and have his name cleared. On 1 December 1778 he was finally ordered to return for an appearance before the Congress. On 5 December he was told to appear a second time. That same day, however, he had printed in the *Pennsylvania Packet* a lengthy diatribe against Arthur Lee. Henry Laurens, the president of the Congress, was so angry when he read this article that he argued to his colleagues that Deane's conduct had been so unbecoming that he should not be allowed to reappear personally before the government. The matter was put to the test and Laurens lost by one vote. Angry, he resigned the presidency of the Congress, to be succeeded by John Jay.[38]

While waiting to be heard by the Congress, Silas Deane and Robert Morris continued the active commercial relationship they had maintained since Deane's departure for France in 1776. They talked of profits, of lands for sale in the American West. They learned that Samuel Wharton had at last arrived in Paris, there to rejoin his old partner, Benjamin Franklin, for the first time since 1775. Wharton, Chaumont, Bancroft—Franklin's closest companions—all partners in the old and continuing Vandalia enterprise. With Deane and Morris, these men became increasingly interested in the area to the north of the proposed Vandalia grant, the vast acres across the Ohio River. And all involved seem to have continued their efforts to profit on the London stock exchange.

While continuing to wait for Congress to clear his name, Deane was dismayed to learn that Arthur Lee had sent that body a full statement of his own interpretation of the affairs in France. The report, which contained a complete narrative refutation of most of Deane's claims, was a political bombshell. The necessity of rebutting it occupied most of Deane's time for weeks and the answers he gave brought about a tract and newspaper war as detractors and supporters alike leaped into the fray. Charges and countercharges, fact and wild allegation—all were presented to the reading public as the nation chose sides in this contest. The dispute split Congress, lost seats for some of its members and gained seats for new men, sadly divided the attention of this beleaguered body from its major task of prosecuting the war, and forever sullied the reputations of otherwise honorable men.

Throughout the quarrel Deane maintained that "I confess I feel a pride in having my name joined with so great a patriot and so venerable a character [as Benjamin Franklin], and am content that the present age and posterity also should be informed that Mr. A. Lee and Mr. Izard complained of me, if at the same time it be known that a Franklin was my guide, my philosopher and friend." [39] When criticized for exceeding the bounds of his authority, he rejoined that at least he had good company, for "In the execution of . . . every . . . part of the business executed by me, I was assisted and directed by the advice and concurrence of my colleague, Dr. Franklin." [40]

John Adams felt otherwise. In 1779, when Deane issued a tract called *An Address to the People of America*, Adams told Franklin "with great freedom, and perhaps, with too much warmth . . . that it was one of the most wicked and abominable productions that ever sprang from a human heart." He complained to Bancroft that Deane was "like a wild boar, that ought to be hunted down for the benefit of mankind." [41]

Adams' views, however, were no longer that important. Some months before, he had written the Congress urging it to recall all its mission at Paris except for one man, to set his salary, and to supervise his accounts so that he had no chance to profiteer. [42] Congress liked the idea, recalled both Lee and Adams, and, on 14 September 1778, made Franklin minister plenipotentiary. The committee which decided this came within a couple of votes recalling Franklin and leaving Lee in his stead, but pressure from Gérard, the French ambassador to the United States, saved Franklin from this fate. Franklin now held in his hands sole American authority and was no longer obliged to explain his actions to troublesome colleagues. Henry Laurens, however, made available to Congress letters he had received from his fellow South Carolinian, Ralph Izard, which, as Laurens said, reflected the public character of Franklin in a very unfortunate way.[43] In Europe, William Lee wrote to Izard to claim that "The plot formed at *Passy* before the *departure of Deane* seems to have taken by the appointment of Franklin. It seems to me likely that the whole will [now] succeed." [44]

In America, the partisans of Arthur Lee and Silas Deane continued to rage at one another. On 17 October 1779, writing to James Lovell, Franklin maintained his belief in the innocence of Silas Deane. He added a sentence which completely rewrote recent history: "I have never meddled with [the quarrel you mention between Mr. Deane and Mr. Lee] and have no intention to take any part in it whatever." [45] As one historian has commented, "If being a consistent partisan of Deane was not intermeddling, then his statement was correct." [46]

Throughout most of 1779, Congress refused to deal directly with the Deane case. Deane, for his part, was unwilling or unable to make an accounting of his expenditures. Still he sought for a resolution from that body "excusing" him from further attendance upon it or from further action by it. He waited in vain. Congress refused to end the case. The most the Deane supporters in Congress could accomplish occurred on 6 August 1779 when the United States government resolved to "discharge" the ex-commissioner to France. Embarrassed and angry, Deane laid plans to return to Europe at the first opportunity.

Relieved from his official position, Arthur Lee set about winding up his European affairs so that he might return to the United States. Concerned that Lee would carry home with him official documents that might incriminate not only Silas

Deane but himself as well, Franklin began to hassle Arthur for the return of any papers in his possession. This episode is the first time since his arrival in France in 1776 that Benjamin Franklin publicly showed an interest in preserving and ordering American state papers. The timing reveals that he had more in mind than a simple desire to retain proper files of official documents. On 18 February he made the first request to Lee for the return of "all the public papers in your hands belonging to this department." [47] Lee replied a few days later, wondering why Franklin should suddenly be interested in such papers when that had never before been the case. He refused to return the few he had in his files, most of which, he claimed, were copies rather than original drafts. He would need them in order to refute Deane's charges against him. [48]

Again in March Franklin made an effort to retrieve Lee's papers, and for the second time Lee refused. On 27 March, Franklin wrote Lee for the third time. To the stubborn Virginian, Franklin said that "Mr. Adams did not, as you insinuate, exact any promise of me to arrange and keep in order the papers he sent me. He knew such a promise unnecessary, for that I had always kept in order and by themselves the public papers that were in my hands, without having them so confounded among a multitude of other papers 'that they could not be found when called for.'" [49]

To Sam Adams some weeks later Lee explained in detail what the problem was regarding the papers Franklin had so assiduously been calling for.

> I have look'd near, long, and narrowly at a person who has been, and is, the Father of all this shameful business. Neither my reading, experience, nor imagination can furnish me with the Idea of a mind more corrupt, nor that labors with more cunning, and systematic constancy to carry that depravity into execution. . . . The meanest of all mean men, the most corrupt of all corrupt men is assimilating every thing to his own nature.

. . . those papers . . . Mr. Deane left with Dr. Franklin, and . . . the latter put [them] into my hands, not knowing, I presume, what evidence they contain'd against him and his associates. The great sollicitude which Dr. Franklin shews to retrieve them, is a proof of his sorely repenting what he did. The fact is, that these men were put off their usual guard, which is cunning and concealment, by the vain persuasion they had, that the eclat of a French fleet and recommendatory letters obtain'd by intrigue, in which M. G[érard] had no small hand, woud stifle all enquiry, and send Mr. Deane back honor'd and trusted as before. The vanity of their Under Agents prompted them to boast of this, and Dr. Franklin himself insinuated it in this way. But when the enquiry was likely to come forward, Mr. Deane, I suppose, wrote to him to secure those papers, upon which, tho' he had never given himself the smallest trouble about them before, he apply'd to Mr. J. Adams, unknown to me, to deliver them into his hands. Having got them, and finding from the list I had made, that the very papers he wished to suppress were not there, he suspected I had them, and apply'd for them with a sollicitude which he never shews but when there is some selfish object in view.

. . . unless this universal complaint of public depredation be stopt, unless the expenditure of the public money by the various Agents be fairly and fully accounted for, the temptation of plunder will be so increased by the prosperity and impunity of the plunderers, that they will soon become numerous and powerful enough, not only to protect themselves and continue their corrupt practises, but to destroy by intrigue, subornation and influence every person that opposes their measures. Of one thing you may be assur'd . . . that he who is the father and prompter of all this business will not hesitate at the utmost extremity of wickedness, to spread and maintain that corruption by which alone his influence and objects can be long supported.[50]

Although Lee was not yet ready to sail for home in midsummer of 1779, John Adams returned to the United States
on board a vessel on which there also traveled a Frenchman,
François Barbé-Marbois, with whom he struck up an acquaintance. On one occasion, Marbois, who was to become
the Secretary of their Legation, remarked to Adams that
Franklin, whom he knew well, "had beaucoup d'agrément,
beaucoup de charlatanerie." [51] A few days later Marbois
asked Adams what was the reason for Dr. Franklin's support
of and attachment to Edward Bancroft. "Because," said
Adams, "B. is devoted to Mr. D[eane] and because he is the
only American at Paris who loves him; all the Americans but
him are, at present, very bitter against Franklin; he would
probably be very glad to get his grandson [William Temple]
secretary [of the American mission], but as I fancy he must
think him too young to obtain the appointment, he will join
with Mr. D. in endeavoring to get B. D. I know, from
authentic information, is endeavoring to get B. appointed;
that B. was so irregular and eccentric a cháracter, and his
conduct in American affairs had been such, that I confessed I
had an entire distrust of him." [52] Where Adams got his information is unknown, but his words spoke strongly of Deane's
audacity. Under fire himself, Deane was still trying to serve
his British masters by using whatever influence remained to
him to get Bancroft an official congressional appointment as
Secretary to the American mission in France.

Arthur Lee remained in Paris until 1780. He was still there
when a friend of Franklin and Wharton, Thomas Hutchins,
was arrested by the British government for his speculating activities. They also seized much of the correspondence he had
conducted with Samuel Wharton. For a time Hutchins was
allowed to languish in prison, until suddenly he was released
and given orders to locate his military unit and join the
fighting in America. Instead, Hutchins hied himself to Passy.
There Franklin wrote him a letter of recommendation to present to the American Congress, and Hutchins sailed for the

United States. The Congress shortly afterward commissioned him as the official geographer of the nation.[53]

In the spring of 1780, Lee finally arranged to leave France for America on the privateer frigate *Alliance*. He brought with him carefully prepared reports of his accounts, which he gave to Congress 17 October 1780. He also asked for a hearing before that body, for he believed that his own recall, like that of Deane, indicated that at one level or another he was under censure for his European activities from the government of the United States.[54] On 1 December 1780, the committee charged with looking over this matter reported that no supportable charges could be made against Arthur Lee and that he had conducted himself while in Europe in a creditable fashion. Lee then submitted to the Congress charges against Franklin, emphasizing his peculiar attitude toward commercial relations. On 2 January 1781 the committee to whom Lee had submitted his charges made its report, calling for the scheduling of a congressional session to consider Franklin's recall.[55] Hearing of this, Franklin offered in April to resign his office, but Congress refused either to accept his offer or to act on the call for his removal.

Had everything gone according to plan, Franklin should have been pleased when Arthur Lee sailed for America in the spring of 1780. He had finally gotten rid of an enemy who would no longer be able to sit carping upon his doorstep, watching his every move. Unfortunately, even before Lee left on board the *Alliance*, John Adams had returned to Paris —this time as a peace negotiator for Congress. Franklin was never certain what the sharp-eyed Adams might discern. Perhaps he was secretly pleased when, shortly after Adams' return to Paris, the doughty patriot from Massachusetts quarreled with Vergennes and thus found himself unwanted and unwelcome at Versailles.[56] Never one to be daunted, Adams decided to leave France and travel to The Hague, where he hoped to negotiate a loan for the United States from the Dutch. Franklin argued against asking for a loan if not against the trip itself. Consistent with the stand he had taken ever since he sat in the halls of Congress in 1776, Franklin complained that "I have long been humiliated with the idea of our running from court to court begging for money and friendship, which are the more withheld the more eagerly they are solicited, and would perhaps have been offered, if they had not been asked." [57] Despite Franklin's objections, Adams left Paris on 27 July.

With Lee gone and Adams come and gone, other ghosts turned up to haunt Franklin. Silas Deane had decided to return to Paris. Still devoted to speculation, he wrote his partner, Robert Morris, before he sailed. It was a long letter, telling of the advantages to be gained through land speculation and suggesting which areas in the West might be sought out for the best advantage. Of them all, the Vandalia area was probably the best. "If you approve of these outlines, I will take an Interest with you in any purchases you make of lands, with the view of disposing of them in this way." [58] In May he wrote Joseph Wharton, Samuel's brother, that "It will be a very easy task to clear up the money transaction between your brother Samuel Wharton and me." [59] When he arrived in France, however, he was disappointed to learn that Samuel had sailed for America. "It is a great disappointment," he wrote to Samuel, "not to have had the pleasure of meeting you here, as it, with many other subjects might have been adjusted and closed." [60]

Arriving in Paris in late summer 1780, Silas Deane immediately visited Franklin, who opened both his arms and his dwelling to the arch-traitor.[61] To John Jay, Deane described the situation as he had found it in Paris. "I have taken up my old lodgings with Doctor Franklin. My meeting with him and my other friends here has given me the most sincere pleasure; and being happily freed from every political concern whatever, hope, that whilst I enjoy the society of my friends here, my enemies in America will forget me." [62] Whether or not Franklin was actually glad to see Deane, he could hardly turn him away—even after the disclosures made public about Deane in the tract war in America. Deane had been his partner for too long. Franklin surely must have missed Deane's earlier official standing, for the old doctor now had to write many of his own letters, signing his own name to documents that formerly would have gone out over the seal of Silas Deane. Such of these papers as are still available show how completely involved Franklin was in the various commercial ventures which formerly had been the province of Silas Deane.[63] Thus Franklin's headquarters now consisted of himself, his grandson William Temple, who acted as his secretary, the spy Bancroft (when he was not traveling on his own private business), and Silas Deane. It was hardly a roster of luminaries of which America could be proud.

Deane promptly began using Franklin's home as his mailing address and as the center from which he pursued his speculative ventures. To one interested person, Deane wrote that "I have a prospect of doing something with the shares of the Illinois and Wabash lands. . . . I shall from time to time acquaint you, through our mutual friends Messrs. Morris and Wilson, of my proceeding in this affair." [64]

At one time or another after Deane had moved into his home, Franklin may have shared with Deane his worries about John Adams. At any rate, Deane soon wrote to John Jay to poison his mind against any news he might hear from Adams. "I have not seen him, but Franklin and Bancroft assure me he is actually mad, and more so, though in a different way, than ever Lee was." [65] What had worked once against Arthur Lee might well be made to work a second time against John Adams. At least there was no harm in trying.

For his part, Franklin did what he could to support his partner in his enterprises and to protect him against unfortunate slanders against his honesty emanating from America. To C. W. F. Dumas in Holland, Franklin sent a recommendation for Deane, "who has a great regard for you, and whom

I recommend to your civilities, though the gentlemen at present with you [William Lee and John Adams] may be prejudiced against him, prejudices that time will cause to vanish by showing they were groundless." [66]

Franklin hoped to retain total control over the European aspects of American affairs, for by so doing he could command considerable profit for himself. This was especially the case if loans for the American Congress from foreign courts and bankers and the income derived from American privateering and sale of prize ships were channeled through his hands alone. This was why he had so tenaciously held onto the commercial agency at Nantes for his nephew Jonathan Williams, Jr. This was why he had tried to discourage John Adams from attempting a Dutch loan. Yet there were so many avenues for money to be siphoned into America other than through him that it must have been discouraging. Not only did the American Congress need money, so also did the individual states. Often they had to borrow from European bankers in order to continue operating. One hint of Franklin's operating methods is shown in the attempt of Pennsylvania to arrange a European loan. That state appointed James Searle as its agent, under orders to proceed to France to borrow money. He later reported that Franklin did all in his power to prevent him from gaining this objective, because Franklin and his friends hoped to be the sole channel through which money flowed. Searle wrote Joseph Reed of Philadelphia regarding this situation: ". . . unless some speedy and effectual measures are taken on our side the water to counteract the baneful influence that the conversation of the disappointed, mortified, and scheming G [Silas Deane] has upon the minds of many people here, I fear very bad consequences may attend it.

"This man [Deane] has the countenance and protection of C [Benjamin Franklin] to a very great degree, by which means he is attended to, and he is doing the greatest injury to 16 [Arthur Lee] in every company he can get admittance to.

"There are others also, who make no scruple to treat the counsel of 16 [Lee] with every possible insult and misrepresentation, I mean a certain Doctor Bancroft, who does it openly at the public table of C [Franklin]. Mr. Cha-m-t [Chaumont], the great patron of O [C, i.e., Franklin?], has also become outrageous and open-mouthed against the measures of A Z [Congress], which he represents and calls wicked and villainous, and has even threatened to expose, as he terms it, their base conduct to the world. All this is done in the most open manner at the place of residence of C. I find Mr. C. the declared enemy of private state loans, and have therefore not been able to get any assistance, or the offer of any, through that channel, and the two persons above mentioned, I mean G [Deane] and Bancroft, are using every means in their power to counteract the public as well as private loans, which loans, if effected through any other than a particular channel, would interfere with their connection in the public supply of our army, etc. Alas Sir, there are, I fear, Arnolds in France, natives of America." [67] This letter described Franklin's continued protection of Deane; the ongoing ridicule and scorn heaped on Arthur Lee; the open and public vilification by Chaumont of the American Congress, which that body's Minister Plenipotentiary, Benjamin Franklin, freely allowed to continue without criticism or challenge; and the private peculations of Deane and Bancroft even when they endeavored to obstruct America's financing of its war against the mother country.

With Adams in Holland, Franklin and his coterie were able to continue their own personal and private pursuits unchecked. In their never-ending quest for success in western speculation, Samuel Wharton published in Philadelphia a pamphlet extolling the rights of speculators to lands in the West to which they had gained title by grant from the Indians. Worked out by Franklin and Wharton before the latter left France for America, the work was entitled *Plain Facts: Being an Examination Into the Rights of the Indian Nations.*[68]

Although Franklin and Wharton had hoped that this publication might stir the American Congress into action on western grants, once again they were doomed to be sorely disappointed.

Until late spring 1781, only John Adams had been selected by the Congress as a peace negotiator. On 15 June that body resolved to add to the number of those so appointed; it chose Benjamin Franklin, John Jay, Henry Laurens, and Thomas Jefferson. Their instructions allowed them to negotiate all preliminary details of a peace with England. The only strict requirement was insistence upon Britain's recognition of the independence of the United States.

Then, in 1781, Silas Deane dropped his bombshell. In concert with Paul Wentworth of the British Secret Service, he agreed to write a number of letters to friends and acquaintances in America urging the futility of the war and the desirability of a return to imperial status for the American states. Where Wentworth and Deane met to work out the details for this "correspondence" is not known, but it was during a time when Deane was still domiciled at Franklin's home. The letters were dated as of May and June 1781, but had to have been prepared before that time, for they were previewed by Lord North and King George III prior to their use. Both North and the King believed the tone of the letters sounded too much as if they had been dictated to Deane, but decided to go ahead with the plan in spite of that.[69] They were published in North America, in the state of New York, by James Rivington, editor of the newspaper *The Gazette*. As the letters appeared, one by one, from 24 October through 12 December 1781, outraged cries of Americans rose skyward. Arnold had been guilty of but one act of duplicity. Deane had planned and executed his treachery over a period of months and was as out of reach of punishment as Arnold had been.[70]

One American who visited with Benjamin Franklin told him that he "felt constrained . . . to announce . . . my conviction that Mr. Deane must be regarded an enemy alike to

France and America. He [Franklin] observed to me that simi-lar reports had reached him before, but that he had been un-willing to admit their truth." [71] Far from repudiating Deane, Franklin continued to support his cause. He wrote to the Congress, commenting about Deane's actions but still urging that the American government settle the bills Deane claimed it owed him. Franklin never criticized or condemned Deane in any clear-cut manner. Indeed, it would have been danger-ous for him to do so.[72]

That the letters may have been written for Deane rather than by him is suggested in a note he sent Paul Wentworth early in 1782. In that message he reiterated his willingness to continue serving the Secret Service in any way open to him: "if you should have anything of greater or less importance in which I can serve you hope that you will honor me with your commands. . . . I have never been able to get a sight of the letters published by Rivington in New York, which have made such a noise in America; if you can send them to me by some private hand coming this way, it will greatly oblige me." [73]

Even Franklin was unwilling to countenance Deane's re-maining as his guest any longer, and so the luckless Deane moved away from Passy and by 1782 had settled in rented lodgings in Ghent. He kept up a steady stream of corre-spondence with Wentworth and Bancroft, and borrowed money from Franklin. As he wrote to his brother Barnabas, "I am at this moment indebted to Doctor Franklin and others at Paris for sums borrowed for my support, and, being unable to pay, am obliged to their kindness even for my personal lib-erty." [74]

Franklin continued to defend Deane. To Robert R. Liv-ingston, he maintained that "I had an exceeding good opinion of him when he acted with me, and I believe he was then sin-cere and hearty in our cause." [75] Now, with Deane heartily despised by most Americans, people were willing to listen to the charges Arthur Lee had been making for years about the

disreputable arms purchases Deane had made in France for
the American army. Such charges even were printed in the
English newspapers. Franklin felt, at last, that he had to make
an answer to those allegations. He drew up a certificate vindi-
cating Deane's actions which read: "Certain paragraphs having lately appeared in the English newspapers, imputing that
Silas Deane, Esq., formerly Agent and Commissioner Plenipotentiary of the United States of America, had, some time
after his first 'arrival in France, purchased in that kingdom,
for the use of his countrymen, 30,000 muskets, &c.; that he
gave three livres for each of them, being old condemned
arms; that he had them cleaned and vamped up, which cost
near three livres more; and that for each of these he charged
and received a louis d'or'; and that he also committed similar
frauds in the purchase of other articles for the use of his country; and Mr. Deane having represented that the said paragraphs are likely to injure him in the opinions of many persons unacquainted with his conduct whilst in the public
service. . . ." Franklin now summed up his view: "I think it
my duty, in compliance with his request, to certify and declare that the paragraphs in question, according to my best
knowledge and belief, are entirely false, and that I have never
known or suspected any cause to charge the said Silas Deane
with any want of probity, in any purchase, or bargain, whatever, made by him for the use or account of the United
States." [76]

William Lee snorted in derision when he learned what
Franklin had done. To a friend, he "observed that Dr. F. has
given a certificate in vindication of Silas Deane, relative to the
charge against him about the magazine of old firelocks. Was I
in London, I would make the following reply in the public
papers:
    'A correspondent who has read Dr. B. Franklin's certifi-
cate, published in the London papers, in vindication of Mr.
Silas Deane from a charge bro't against him, the said S. D.,
for a gross imposition on the Congress of the United States of

America, in the purchase of a magazine of old iron, and old, useless musquets, says it puts him in mind of an associate appearing at the Old Bailey in support of the character and honesty of his fellow laborer in the same vocation, who stood arraign'd for a highway robbery; for he has seen a publication in America, wherein Dr. B. Franklin is publicly charged with being as deep in the mud as Mr. Silas Deane is in the mire, about the same magazine of old rusty iron; and to this public charge Dr. B. Franklin has never yet found it expedient to make any reply.'

". . . The doctor, is, however, protected, for reasons obvious, by the Court of Versailles, and until there is full peace, he can't be bro't to the punishment he has too deeply merited. But I have more than one written proof, even under his own handwriting, that he carried his hand to a direct falsehood." [77]

In letters such as this, William Lee made no effort to hide his detestation of Franklin. Such charges by old enemies, however, did nothing to dissuade Franklin from continuing to give what support he could to Silas Deane. In April 1783, Deane still reminded his correspondents that they could always contact him by way of Franklin's Passy address.[78] Deane remained on friendly terms not only with Benjamin Franklin, but also with Edward Bancroft and Paul Wentworth.[79] This strange quartet had tied itself too closely during past years to sever easily the ties that bound its members together. All the old Vandalia partners—Deane, Bancroft, Wharton, Trent, Walpole—were bound together by correspondence which demonstrates their interest in profit from speculation in the American West.[80] The suspicion will not die that if these long-time partners of Franklin continued vying for public lands, then the old doctor was also aware of what was happening and was voluntarily involved. Further, there is a hint in some of Deane's letters that William Franklin, an early partner with his father in land speculation, a Tory during the Revolution, and the president of the United

Loyalists, had once again plunged deeply into the schemes of his old associates. In 1783 Deane wrote to Bancroft to "take no notice for the present of W. F., as I suspect his fidelity." [81] On several occasions during this period, the initials "W. F." are used to refer to some partner in speculation. It was the practice of that era to use a man's initials in correspondence, as a sort of code to disguise partially his identity if the wrong person read the letter. Of all those over the years who had been identified with the Vandalia project, only William Franklin's name would fit those initials. It would not be surprising to find William interested once again in land: it seemed to be a family trait. His father's efforts at speculation continued at least almost until 1789. Two days before that year began, Benjamin Franklin wrote to an old acquaintance asking him to forward a letter to the President of the Congress. In that letter, Ben urged that he be granted a tract of western land because of his "services" during the war. Such a grant would be "of use and some honour to my Posterity." [82] He had used almost exactly the same phrase years earlier, in 1778, when he wrote to Thomas Walpole to retrieve the letter of resignation from the Vandalia Company that awkward publicity had forced him to write just prior to the outbreak of the Revolution.

All of this, however, was still in the future. The time was still 1782, Arthur Lee had returned home to America, John Adams had arrived in France as a peace negotiator soon to leave for Holland, Silas Deane had also returned to Europe to write his dismal letters and flee to Ghent. Yorktown had been besieged and Cornwallis' great army had surrendered. The fighting was nearly over, the time of peace was at hand.

CHAPTER ELEVEN

Mr. Adams, Mr. Jay, and Mr. Franklin—Peace in Paris

When news of Cornwallis' defeat at Yorktown reached England, opposition voices in Parliament—seldom muted and of late extremely clamorous—renewed their call for the resignation of Lord North and for the formation of a new government. The opposition also demanded that at the first opportunity peace should be made with the Americans. George III still hoped to salvage something from the last years of conflict and so stood firmly in support of Lord North. North might have been saved had the war taken a better turn at this juncture, but this was not to be. The war news continued to bring accounts of British disasters: Minorca fell to the Spanish; St. Eustatius, St. Christopher, Nevis, and Montserrat were captured by the French.

On 27 February 1782 Parliament passed a resolution authorizing peace with the thirteen American colonies. Without new ideas, bereft of support, Lord North announced his intention to resign on 20 March. Few attempted to persuade him otherwise. He left office a week later. King George reluctantly accepted the next government, a coalition of the parliamentary forces of Lord Shelburne, Lord Rockingham, and Charles James Fox. Formed in March, the new government was from the beginning rent with internal dissension. Both Shelburne and Fox wished to control peace negotiations, but Shelburne managed to steal a march on his colleague. He sent a Scottish merchant, Richard Oswald, to Paris to contact Benjamin Franklin. Adams was in Holland and Jay still at his post at Madrid. Franklin's situation was sensitive. He had fit well into French society and had become the darling of the *ancien régime*. His low-key activities of earlier years and his contacts with British agents had not come to the keen ears of Vergennes. As the war wound down, Franklin determined to ingratiate himself firmly with Vergennes by supporting the French line whenever possible—even if that meant taking positions harmful to the United States of America. One author has said that it was not that "the Sage of Passy was lacking in perception as to America's interests, but he always managed to cloak his sentiments in agreeable deference to the French court." He was "adaptable, even devious." ¹ With the colonies thoroughly lost to England, a stance supporting the French Court would be the one most likely to advance Franklin's own interests.

Parliament had now voted for peace; France had privately indicated that peace would not displease her. Now Franklin could glory in his new role of peacemaker. He had his first meeting with Shelburne's emissary, Richard Oswald, at Passy, 12 April 1782. The two men began preliminary discussions. Franklin was so taken with the man that a few days later he wrote Shelburne to say: "I desire no other channel of communication between us than that of Mr. Oswald, whom I think your Lordshp has chosen with much judgment." ²

On 17 April, Franklin took Oswald to Versailles and presented him to Vergennes. The following day he gave a memorandum to Oswald, about which Vergennes knew nothing, listing "hints" for ending the war on an equitable basis. One suggestion was that Great Britain cede Canada to the United States. Out of such a grant might come funds providing money both to pay for American civil losses during the war and to compensate Loyalists for confiscated property. Such an offering might well hold promise for speculation. Franklin

soon feared that his suggestion might be used to harm him politically, for many in the United States would not take kindly
to measures which would benefit Tories. For this reason, although he later told Adams the "gist" of his memorandum, he
omitted reference to asking for Canada. As Franklin put it, "I
was not pleased with my having hinted a reparation to Tories
for their forfeited estates and I was a little ashamed of my
weakness." [3] Whatever the reason, when Franklin later sent
Vergennes the substance of the suggestions he had made to
Oswald, he also neglected to tell him about the paragraph on
Canada.[4]

Shelburne, ever the supporter of empire, hoped that Franklin might be persuaded to treat with Britain on terms short of
independence.[5] The King supported him in this. "I do not
possibly see," George III wrote his Minister, "how the present Ministry can consent to Independency but as the price of
a certain peace." [6] As late as September 1782, Franklin was
willing to go along with Shelburne's hopes. At that time he
was reported as "not for Standing out for the previous acknowledgement of Independancy etc. and says it is a pity to
keep 3 or 4 millions of People in War for the sake of Form
etc." [7]

About the end of April 1782, Franklin wrote to Jay to
"Come hither as soon as possible." [8] Jay did not arrive from
Spain until 23 June, and after getting to Paris was very ill
with influenza for some days. By July, however, he was ready
to exert his own views on the shaping of the peace and actively participated in discussions after that time. John Adams
had returned 26 October from an extremely successful mission to Holland. Whereas earlier he was often mistaken for
his cousin Sam, and introduced as "le collègue de Monsieur
Franklin," he now gained new fame in France because of his
work in the Low Countries. He was given a party at Versailles when he returned to Paris and the guests crowded
around to praise him. One told him: "Monsieur, vous êtes le
Washington de la Négotiation!" Another person claimed:

"Monsieur, ma foi, vous avez réussi merveilleusement!"
Adams was pleased to hear another guest remark that "You
have shown in Holland that the Americans understand negotiation as well as war." At the close of the evening, finally
alone in his room, Adams wrote in his diary of his gratifica-
tion at receiving such compliments and sniffed that "A few of
these compliments would kill Franklin if they should come to
his ears." [9]

To Adams, Franklin was always "the old conjurer." It
took neither Adams nor Jay very many days to come to a
meeting of the minds on the subject of Benjamin Franklin.
Adams had been strongly censorious of Franklin since 1778,
when he had arrived in Passy to replace Silas Deane, and the
intervening years had done nothing to alter his opinions. Both
Jay and Adams were concerned that Vergennes would willingly sacrifice America's interests to those of France and they
became increasingly convinced that Franklin would support
him in this. Adams commented that "If Mr. Jay and I had
yielded the punctilio of rank, and taken the advice of the
Count de Vergennes and Dr. Franklin, by treating with the
English or Spaniards, before we were put upon the equal
footing that our rank demanded, we should have sunk in the
minds of the English, French, Spaniards, Dutch, and all the
neutral powers. The Count de Vergennes certainly knows
this; if he does not, he is not even a European statesman; if he
does know it, what inference can we draw, but that he means
to keep us down if he can; to keep his hand under our chin to
prevent us from drowning, but not to lift our heads out of the
water?" [10] At least as startling as this realization about Vergennes was their awareness that Franklin would support him
in such policies. Some years later, Adams recalled that moment of understanding. "It is impossible," Adams said, "for
any man but Mr. Jay and myself to conceive our mutual feelings upon this sudden discovery, that we had both formed the
same opinions of the policy of the Comte de Vergennes and
of Dr. Franklin." [11]

Formal meetings of the peace negotiators began 29 October 1782, only three days after John Adams returned from Holland. By this time the fragile government in England had changed once again. The Rockingham administration had lasted only from March to July 1782, when Rockingham unexpectedly died. Shelburne, who had been the most powerful figure in the Rockingham ministry, and the one most favored by George III, now took over and from July 1782 until April 1783 was the chief minister.[12]

When Adams arrived for the peace talks, he was extremely disgruntled to learn that Franklin—ever aware of the needs of his own family—had persuaded a reluctant Jay to join him in appointing William Temple Franklin as the official secretary of the peace negotiators. Temple previously had served as secretary to his grandfather where he gained the only such experience of which he could boast. It did not take Temple long to begin to use his office for family advantage. He soon expressed a wish, which was quickly relayed to Lord Shelburne, that Britain ought to do something "for his father, Gov. Franklin, as being the only Governor that gave to his Court plain and wholesome advice before the war." [13] His upholding of his father's "plain and wholesome advice" bespoke strange sympathies for one holding a position of trust from a nation just concluding its war for independence. When Arthur Lee heard of Temple's appointment, he dismissed him as that "young insignificant boy," a not-unrealistic analysis.[14]

The Franklins—grandfather and grandson—continued to support one another's ambitions. A few weeks after his appointment, Temple went to see John Adams. "He showed me an extract of a letter of Dr. Franklin to Congress concerning him, containing a studied and long eulogium—sagacity beyond his years, diligence, activity, fidelity, genteel address, facility in speaking French; recommends him to be secretary of some mission; thinks he would make an excellent minister, but does not propose him for it as yet." The letter of which Temple boasted had been written two years earlier, in

March 1781, and had been sent by his grandfather to the President of the Congress.[15] Since nothing had come from his recommendation, Benjamin Franklin had taken it upon himself to find a governmental post for his relation; hence the appointment of Temple as secretary of the peace commission. Adams, however, did not believe that to be the end of it. "This letter and other circumstances," he wrote, "convince me that the plan is laid between the Count de Vergennes and the Doctor, to get Billy made minister to this Court, and, not improbably, the Doctor to London. Time will show." [16] Whether or not Adams' guesses were correct, at least it is certain that it would have been very difficult for Temple to proceed with his improprieties without the permission or knowledge of his grandfather. Such incidents alarmed Adams about the probable course of the negotiations just beginning.

Adams soon confided his worries to his diary. He did not know how Jay and Franklin would work together and hoped that he might be of some use as a mediator. "Between two as subtle spirits as any in this world, the one malicious, the other I think honest, I shall have a delicate, a nice, critical part to act. F's cunning will be to divide us. To this end, he will provoke, he will insinuate, he will intrigue, he will maneuvre. My curiosity will at least be employed in observing his invention and his artifice." [17]

John Jay was also concerned. All those present in Paris knew that France would not look with pleasure upon acquisition by the United States of the country west of the Allegheny-Appalachian ridgelines. Spain also opposed such growth in the boundaries of America. As Jay put it: "This Court, as well as Spain, will dispute our extension to the Mississippi. You see how necessary prudence and entire circumspection will be on your side, and if possible secrecy. I ought to add that Dr. Franklin does not see the conduct of this Court in the light I do, and that he believes they mean nothing in their proceedings but what is friendly, fair, and honourable. Facts and future events must determine which of us is mistaken." [18]

The peace commissioners had long since received their instructions from the American Congress. They were to insist on independence, to make no peace separate from France, and other matters such as boundaries, fishing rights, and so forth were to be worked out in consultation with the French and British. The commissioners, in turn, gave to Oswald their understanding of what the peace terms should be: complete independence, the shrinking of Canada's boundaries to those of before the Quebec Act of 1774, fishing rights on the Newfoundland banks, and a proper boundary settlement.[19]

Vergennes soon let it be known he would not support a Mississippi boundary for the United States. One American on the scene noted that "The affair of the back Country is I imagine to favor the pretentions of Spain. Though this Affair has been communicated to Dr. Franklin he affects not to see the drift of it and says Marbois may have written these things in his Zeal but he does not believe he is encouraged by the Comte de Vergennes—nothing can be clearer than that it is the wish to play us off as the puppets of the War." [20] Franklin's support of the policies of the French Court was placing him once more on dangerous ground. "There seems to be a general dissatisfaction with Dr. F. and no scruples are made in saying the time will come when his Character will be known that he is an intriguing unfeeling Man"—so Americans in Paris were saying.[21]

Vergennes also let it be known that he thought insistence upon American independence was much ado about very little. By his lights, there was no hurry about British recognition of such status; let it be deferred until the end of the war, when Gibraltar had been secured for Spain. Adams and Jay, on the other hand, insisted on immediate recognition of themselves by Britain as ministers plenipotentiary of the United States of America. The British government finally

commissioned Richard Oswald to treat with such representatives of the United States and the way was cleared for real
progress toward peace.

Adams hoped to arrange matters so that in the future the
new nation would need few dealings with either England or
France. America had been, in his words, a "football" between
them long enough. In the future, America should be "completely independent, and to have nothing to do with either,
but in commerce. . . . My hopes of success are stronger now
than they ever have been, because I find Mr. Jay precisely in
the same sentiments, after all the observations and reflections
he has made in Europe, and Dr. Franklin, at last, at least appears to coincide with us." [22]

Encouraged both by the softening of Britain's position and
by the cooperation forthcoming from Franklin, John Jay declared that it was in the interests of the United States to treat
with Great Britain separately from and without consultations
with the French Court. Franklin reacted strongly against
such a position and his "support" threatened to vanish. He
once again expressed his confidence in the French and reminded Jay of the steady benefits to America which France
had granted. He did not believe the commissioners should de-
part from their congressional instructions, he said; they had
their orders from home, and they should have no dealings
with England separate and secret from France. He met a
worthy opponent in Jay who was, on this point, inflexible. A
later writer commented that "Franklin made a great mistake
in not agreeing with him, for in the suspicious state of people's minds at that time his conduct in this respect was taken
as proof positive of his subserviency to the French court." [23]

A recent author has vividly recreated the confrontation
scene on this matter between old Doctor Franklin and John
Jay. They argued at some length about the intentions of
France and Spain. Jay contended that France was not acting
in good faith about American independence; Vergennes
hoped to dominate the American negotiations and to delay

them until France had achieved its own aims and Spain was in a position to exclude all foreign influence from the area of the Gulf of Mexico and the Mississippi River basin. During the heated conversation, when Jay claimed that France was more interested in supporting Spain's pretensions than America's claims, "The old doctor snapped back at Jay, 'Forget about technicalities. Let us be mindful of the generosity of France to us in the past.' " Franklin went on to remind Jay of Congress' instructions "to take the advice of the French court, [and] the New Yorker reminded the doctor: 'We have another instruction which sets independence as a pre-condition to entering into a treaty.'

" 'Have we any reason to doubt the good faith of the King of France?' asked Franklin.

" 'We can depend upon the French,' Jay countered, 'only to see that we are separated from England, but it is not in their interest that we should become a great and formidable people, and therefore they will not help us to become so.'

" 'If we cannot count upon France, upon whom else may we depend?' Franklin inquired.

" 'We have no rational dependence except on God and ourselves,' Jay replied.

" 'Would you deliberately break Congress' instructions?' Franklin pressed.

"Jay did not hesitate. 'Unless we violate these instructions the dignity of Congress will be in the dust,' he asserted. 'I do not mean to imply that we should deviate in the least from our treaty with France,' Jay added. 'Our honor and our interests are concerned in inviolably adhering to it, but if we lean on her love of liberty, her affection for Americans, or her interested magnanimity, we shall lean on a broken reed that will sooner or later pierce our hands. If you don't believe that, consider the fates of Geneva and Corsica!'

" 'Then you are prepared to break our instructions,' Franklin pressed, 'if you intend to take an independence course now.'

"Jay had made up his mind. 'If the instructions conflict with America's honor and dignity I would break them—like this!' Family tradition has it that Jay stood up and hurled his long clay pipe into the fireplace. Strewn among the ashes and embers, the shattered pieces might well have betokened the grand alliance itself. With Jay's impulsive gesture, 'independence,' for which America had fought long and bitterly, suddenly attained a new meaning and dimension." [24]

What Franklin's real purposes were in this episode are shrouded in obscurity. It is certain that before the war he had argued for colonial policies that ultimately emphasized separation from England. He had sat in Congress and, as a member of one of its committees, had helped to draw up the actual Declaration of Independence in 1776. But his record in the years that followed make clear that independence was certainly not a matter of principle with him. Indeed, the opposite is more nearly true. He had argued against foreign alliances and commercial loans which would have strengthened America in her fight against the mother country, and he had done so both while in Congress and as commissioner to France. In fact, he had berated Arthur Lee for his dogged pursuit of European aid for the United States. Franklin had done very little, in spite of the tradition extolling his virtues, to bring France into the war as an ally of America. Throughout 1777 he met with a series of known and unknown British agents of the Secret Service. Franklin reportedly "trembled" at the possibility of a French alliance and "shed tears" at the thought of absolute separation from England. He called for a meeting with the British agent Wentworth, and listened to his enumeration of the blandishments and inducements that would be given to anyone who helped to heal the breach with America. Thereafter he met with Pulteney and reputedly suggested that the Carlisle Commission would do well to offer American leaders seats in Parliament as bribes for them to lay down their arms and their cause. On several occasions, Franklin allegedly told those whom he could trust that he would be happy to see the war stopped and that America's independence was not a crucial goal for him. Now, in the very course of the peace negotiations, he argued and pitted himself against Jay, who insisted on initial recognition of America's independence as a *sine qua non* for further discussions.

Franklin may have believed that his actions would ultimately best serve America. He may have retained a sense of loyalty to England that bent him toward any course that might tend to preserve some relationship between America and the mother country. He also may have been so completely self-centered that he cared neither about the United States—or England—or France, but simply chose to pursue those options which would best serve his own highly personalistic aims.

King Louis XVI, for one, may not have been very impressed with Franklin's service. At one point toward the end of the war, Louis presented to the Countess Diane de Polignac a valuable Sèvres *vase de nuit*—a chamberpot—on the bottom of which he had had painted a portrait of Franklin and the motto by Turgot which was generally reputed to refer to Franklin: "Eripuit fulmen coelo sceptrumque tyrannis"— "He snatched the thunderbolt from the sky and the scepter from tyrants." [25] In this gift, Louis may well have been expressing his own attitude toward Franklin.

During the winter of 1781–1782, Ben Franklin's old friend William Alexander—resident of Edinburgh, Dijon, and Passy, employee of the British Secret Service, and sometime watcher of Franklin's headquarters at Passy—returned to England. Claiming authority from Franklin for his words, he contacted the British government and told how it need not be too concerned about making a formal recognition of America's independence. Implicit recognition would be sufficient. When Adams heard of this, he became so furious he considered submitting his resignation as a peace negotiator, but changed his mind before sending the letter to America. [26]

Despite their difficulties and the constant internecine war-

fare, the American negotiators made progress and the preliminary articles of peace were signed by the diplomats of the
United States and Great Britain on 30 November 1782.
Franklin, as was his wont, continued to use his official position and inside knowledge for family profit. When his
nephew, Jonathan Williams, Jr., learned that the preliminary
peace had been signed, he asked Franklin to be allowed to use
one of his own ships to notify Congress of the peace terms.
"This," Williams said, "will be making the public pay what I
should otherways lose & what no Man can think unreasonable. . . . It is proper to inform you my Brig has a Cargo on
board her. . . . I suppose there can be no objection to her
having on board enough to ballast her; & whether this be
Brandy or stones is of no Consequence." [27] In this way, Williams could bill Congress for the expenses of the ship's voyage
while making a handsome and undiminished profit on the
vessel's cargo. It had taken Williams only seven days after the
preliminary signing of the peace to figure out a method for
making an income from that good news.

Meanwhile Franklin was doing what he could to let Vergennes know that the preliminary articles of peace had been
worked out over his own objections.[28] Between the signing of
the preliminary articles of peace in 1782 and the final treaty
in 1783, Franklin may have continued to use his influence to
prevent congressional acceptance of the work of the Paris negotiators. A modern scholar has uncovered an old rumor, current at the time and brought to life again after Franklin's
death, that Ben "worked secretly against the treaty. Right
after the signing of the preliminaries, according to these allegations, the doctor had written James Moylan, the agent of
the United States at L'Orient, along with his kinsman Jonathan Williams, that the treaty had been negotiated 'without
his privity,' and would not be confirmed by Congress. Accordingly, he was reputed to have advised them both to continue their commercial speculations, and both were ruined by
following this tip. Jasper Moylan . . . told the story to Timo-

thy Pickering, the High Federalist critic of all things French.
John Jay was shocked by the story. He still insisted that 'Dr.
Franklin cooperated with me fairly in obtaining the best
terms that we could for our country,' and told Pickering that
such 'strong' accusations needed substantiation. Such substan-
tiating evidence is not found [this author claims] among the
extant Franklin papers. . . . What is significant is not that
Franklin was in fact guilty as charged but rather that the suspicion of conflict of interest would not down despite dis-
claimers by the doctor, and that in his case the ghost still
haunts the peacemaking." [29]

Over the years in France, Ben Franklin had given recommendations by the dozens to others. He had even made the
art of writing such letters into a fine science, which he called
a "Model of a Letter of Recommendation of a person you are
unacquainted with." Temple later reported that Ben occasionally used his "model" in efforts "to shame the persons
making such indiscreet applications; and to endeavour in
some measure to put a stop to them." Franklin's model letter
of recommendation read as follows:

Sir: The bearer of this, who is going to America, presses
me to give him a letter of recommendation, though I
know nothing of him, not even his name. This may
seem extraordinary, but I assure you it is not uncommon
here. Sometimes, indeed one unknown person brings
another equally unknown, to recommend him; and
sometimes they recommend one another! As to this gentleman, I must refer you to himself for his character and
merits, with which he is certainly better acquainted than
I can possibly be. I recommend him however to those
civilities which every stranger of whom one knows no
harm has a right to; and I request you will do him all the
good offices and show him all the favour that, on further
acquaintance, you shall find him to deserve. I have the
honour to be, etc.[30]

In a more serious vein, Franklin had written a certificate of probity, or uprightness and complete honesty in his dealings, for Silas Deane when that worthy individual left France for America after his recall.[31] Then again, in December 1782, Franklin had penned another certificate of vindication for Deane, who had been charged with purchasing useless weapons for the American army while he served the United States in France.[32] Not quite a year later, after the peace negotiators had completed their work in Paris, Franklin felt so threatened by charges that he was only a tool of the French court that he wrote to John Jay about the matter. Now *he* needed a letter of recommendation, a certificate of probity, a penned word of vindication. Franklin said to Jay that it "is confidently reported, propagated and believed by some among us, that the Court of France was at bottom against our obtaining the fishery and territory in that great extent in which both are secured to us by the treaty; that our Minister at that Court [Franklin] favoured, or did not oppose this design against us; and that it was entirely owing to the firmness, sagacity and disinterestedness of Mr. Adams, with whom Mr. Jay united, that we have obtained those important advantages.

"It is not my purpose to dispute any share of the honour of that treaty which the friends of my Colleagues may be disposed to give them; but, having now spent fifty years of my life in public offices and trusts, and having still one ambition left, that of carrying the character of fidelity at least to the grave with me, I cannot allow that I was behind any of them in zealous faithfulness. I therefore think that I ought not to suffer an accusation, which falls little short of treason to my Country, to pass without notice, when the means of effectual vindication are at hand. You, Sir, were a witness of my conduct in that affair. To you and my other Colleagues I appeal by sending to each a similar letter with this, and I have no doubt of your readiness to do a brother Commissioner justice, by certificates that will entirely destroy the effect of that accusation." [33]

Old and declining, Franklin certainly hoped to carry his reputation intact at least to the grave. His wording in the letter to Jay leaves some doubt that he believed it would be maintained much longer than that. He was also correct in his assessment that many of the accusations against him stopped just short of charges of treason, and some, privately, went the complete distance. Never before in his life had Franklin been in such straitened circumstances that he needed character witnesses to attest for him. The very fact that he now needed them testifies to the reality of the many suspicions that haunted others about him. No such charges were levied against John Adams or John Jay; no, not even against the harried and frenetic Arthur Lee. Franklin alone was singled out. One wonders why?

The next day Jay replied to Franklin's request. His answer was at best lukewarm. "I have no reason whatever to believe," wrote Jay, "that you were averse to our obtaining the full extent of boundary and fishery secured to us by the treaty. Your conduct respecting them throughout the negotiation indicated a strong and steady attachment to both these objects, and in my opinion promoted the attainment of them." [34]

The war was over. The peace had been resolved. Nearly a year had passed since the preliminary articles had been signed on 30 November 1782. Gathering at the L'Hôtel d'York, on 3 September 1783, the diplomats of the United States and Great Britain prepared to sign their names to the definitive articles of peace. There were ten such articles in all. Britain recognized the independence of the United States of America. The boundaries were set for the new nation. America was to be allowed to continue to use the fisheries of the Grand Banks and to dry and cure such catches on the beaches of Newfoundland and Nova Scotia. No "lawful impediment" was to be placed by Congress in the way of British merchants seeking to collect prewar debts from Americans. Congress would "earnestly recommend" restitution of confiscated Loyalist property. No further punishment would be given or damages claimed from Loyalists because they had supported England during the war. Hostilities were to cease, prisoners were to be set free, troops were to be withdrawn, papers seized from archives were to be restored. Conquered territory was to be returned. Navigation on the Mississippi was to be open for the peoples of both Britain and the United States. Ratification by Parliament and by Congress was to proceed with all possible dispatch.

It was a good and generous peace. The Definitive Articles of Peace were signed and sealed on behalf of England by David Hartley. The document was attested to for the United States of America by John Adams, Benjamin Franklin, and John Jay. The war had lasted from 19 April 1775 until 3 September 1783—eight years, four months, and fifteen days. England had lost a portion of empire; the United States of America had been established out of the agonies of conflict.

CHAPTER TWELVE

———◆———

"*Muzzle Not the Ox*"

The cannon were silenced. Bayonets were sheathed and once again muskets rested in racks in European and American arsenals. Men now plowed and reaped from fields over which they had earlier fought. The sounds of war had ceased and the calming sense of peace touched the land of North America. No soldiers crouched behind breastworks. No sailors frantically grabbed pails of sand and slow match to prepare to repel an enemy ship. The diplomats had rustled the last of their endless memoranda at the highly polished tables at Versailles. Even the last great battle, the siege of Yorktown, dimmed in the memories of those who had surrounded that embattled community. The Revolutionary War had brought the birthing of the United States of America and the years winnowed away.

Peace served in many ways the men who had been in the forefront of the silent struggle during the war. Paul Wentworth had hoped for a baronetcy and a seat in the Parliament. The title never was bestowed, but he did get a seat in the Commons, which lasted exactly six weeks during the year 1780 before the voters replaced him with someone else. In 1790 he retreated to his plantation fields in Surinam and died there three years later. William Eden went on from his work as head of the Secret Service and as member of the Carlisle Commission to fulfill an important and worthy place in the governmental and diplomatic service of his nation; he died as Baron Auckland in 1814. John Vardill, Anglican priest and agent of Eden who directed the activities of Joe Hynson, was rewarded by a grateful administration with a living in Lincolnshire, where he remained until his death in 1811.

William Carmichael returned to the United States, served briefly in the government as a congressman from Maryland during 1779, and left for Spain with John Jay as his secretary. In 1783 he was appointed as minister to Spain, where he served until 1794. Under suspicion for certain of his activities, the government recalled him, but he died in Madrid, 9 February 1795, before he could return.

In 1779, Jonathan Williams, Jr., married Marianne, the daughter of William Alexander, the British spy and friend of his granduncle, Ben Franklin. The fortunes of war and bad advice caused his mercantile business in France to fail in 1784. Bankrupt, with nothing longer holding him in France, he returned to America with Franklin in 1785. Years later, he was appointed the first superintendent of the new military academy at West Point, which opened 4 July 1802 with ten cadets.

Recalled from France in June 1779, Ralph Izard's conduct while in Europe was cleared by Congress, 9 August 1780, the same month he returned to America. During 1782 and 1783 he served in the Congress and later became a legislator in his home state of South Carolina. In 1789 he was chosen as a United States Senator. Izard retired in 1795 and suffered several years of poor health before he died in 1804.

Then there were the cantankerous Lees. William Lee had his commission to Prussia and Austria withdrawn by the Congress in June 1779. He remained in Europe four more years without any official status, living in Brussels. In September 1783 he returned to his home in Virginia. Having seen so much, he spent the last years of his life in near darkness, his sight almost gone. He passed away in 1795. His brother Arthur returned to America after his own recall, arriving in September 1780. He became a member of the Virginia House of Delegates in 1781 and from 1782 until 1784 was a member of the American Congress. For a time he held the post of Northwest Indian Commissioner and in July 1785 became a member of the congressional treasury board. Arthur Lee died in 1792.

After the war, on 24 February 1785, John Adams became ambassador to the British Court of St. James. He remained there until 1788. In 1789 he became the first Vice-President of the United States and in 1796 was elected the second President of the new nation. He died on 4 July 1826, the fiftieth anniversary of the Declaration of Independence.

Edward Bancroft carefully hid his Janus-faced character. He drew a pension from a grateful British government until he died in 1821. Nearly seventy more years would pass before the first hints of his astounding record of duplicity became known. Even when the records revealing his status as a double agent during the Revolution were made public, some historians found it difficult to admit that this tireless, hardworking man could have been a traitor.

Bancroft's friend Silas Deane long maintained his innocence of the charges made against him and dreamed of the day he might return to his native land to make a new start. For years he lived in Ghent and London in near poverty. Perhaps he was sustained by memories of his early days in Paris when he rode through the streets in fine carriages and lived in splendor at L'Hôtel des Valentinois. In 1789, while living in England, Silas Deane laid plans for returning to America to restore his good name and recoup his fortunes. As he was about to sail for home, there are indications that he was murdered by his good friend Bancroft, who wished to insure that Deane's lips would forever be sealed about the wartime activities of the Paris mission headquartered in Benjamin Franklin's home. In 1842, without necessarily judging the

merits of Deane's earlier claim that the government owed
him money upon his return to America, the United States
Congress voted his descendants $37,000.[1]

And what of Benjamin Franklin? As early as 26 December
1783, Ben wrote home asking to be allowed to return soon to
the New World.[2] A year and a half would pass before Congress honored his request. During that interim there is evidence that Franklin was no more careful with public funds
than he had been in earlier days while the nations were at
war. At one point after the signing of the peace, Chaumont
seems to have approached Franklin to ask for money. On 2
May 1784, Franklin replied: "If we agree and make a settlement so that the state of our accounts may appear clear to my
constituents, I shall make no difficulty of advancing the sum
you require." [3] His only concern seems to have been that his
account books should look good to later auditors. It was of no
importance that such an advance to Chaumont might be
viewed as misuse of the government money with which he
was entrusted.

After many more months in France, on 2 May 1785,
Franklin received authorization to go home. Laden with
trunks, carrying gifts from the royal government of France,
surrounded by sad-eyed friends and well-wishers, Franklin
left Passy forever on 12 July 1785. His ship, the *London
Packet,* made landfall at Market Street wharf in Philadelphia
on Wednesday, 14 September 1785.

Only a few days after his return to America, Franklin was
called before a Congress still worried about the accounts of
the Paris mission.[4] A congressional committee, appointed to
study the matter, noted a deficit of £100,000. When Franklin
was asked about this discrepancy, he replied gravely that "I
was taught when a boy to read the scriptures and to attend to
them, and it is there said: muzzle not the ox that treadeth out
his master's grain." [5] The matter was never cleared up, although "it was generally rumored, in congressional circles,

that Franklin had by no means been muzzled." [6] This story may be apocryphal—no primary records have been found to date the tale as an accurate one which occurred on a specific day during Franklin's lifetime. Yet it sounds so much like something Franklin would have done. Even if false, it has the ring of legend about it; that is, while the words may not tell of a real episode, they sum up an attitude then current about Franklin. As late as 1812, those who had been Franklin's contemporaries were still talking about Franklin's accounts. In that year Gouverneur Morris wrote to John Randolph of Roanoke that Franklin "had shared in the plunder with Deane and Beaumarchais." [7]

In spite of the gossip about his career in France, Franklin continued to be a popular public figure in Pennsylvania. His home state made him president of the Council, and the Assembly chose him as president of the state itself. Two years later, Pennsylvania named him a delegate to the new Constitutional Convention then convening in Philadelphia. Old, tired, and not well, Franklin took little part in the debate out of which came a new charter for the United States.

No matter the state of his health, his zeal for land continued unabated. The year after the Constitutional Convention, four days after Christmas 1788, he wrote to Charles Thomson, enclosing a letter to be forwarded to Cyrus Griffin, President of the American Congress. Franklin wished Thomson to read the enclosure to be certain there was "nothing improper in it, or that . . . you would wish changed or amended." Ben complained to his friend that he had not been properly rewarded for the time he had spent in France. "I must own I did hope," Franklin wrote, "the Congress would at least have been kind enough to have shewn their approbation of my conduct by a grant of some small tract of Land in their Western Country, which might have been of use and some honour to my Posterity." That phrase must have been indelibly burned into his memory; he had used it ten years earlier in his notation on the memo and packet Bancroft had forwarded him from Walpole. Franklin went on to add, "And I cannot but still think they will do some thing of the kind for me, whenever they shall be pleased to take my services into consideration." He complained that both Arthur Lee and John Jay had been rewarded for their European tour of duty; they had received good jobs. "But how different is what has happened to me!" [8] With less than a year and a half to live, the hope of receiving western lands still burned as brightly within Franklin's bosom as it had fifty years previously when he first began his speculative efforts.

A letter of the following year clearly showed Franklin's continuing involvement in other kinds of endeavors. Since early in the Revolutionary War, Ben and Robert Morris had been linked in certain kinds of commercial enterprises. On 2 November 1789 Franklin wrote Morris that "I should be glad if it might suit you to spare half an hour some day this week, to settle between us the loss that accrued on the sale of my funds in France, for the payment of the bills I furnished you with. The sooner the better, as I find myself growing weaker daily, and less fit for business." [9] The old man had little time left. His health progressively deteriorated and the ravages of age took their toll. Weakened, in pain, and confined to his bed, Benjamin Franklin died on 17 April 1790.

Much of the account just set forth has not previously been assembled in this form. The story has involved. treason, breaches of security, lackadaisical administration, privateering, misplaced trust, war profiteering, clandestine operations, spy apparatus, intrigue, double-dealing. Most of it was secret—at least, those involved hoped it would remain hidden from the public view. Very little of this story has been told by those writers who have given us the Parson Weems version of American history. Even in modern times historians have shown us only bits and pieces of the actions of the principal characters in this study. It is unfortunate, for it was a dramatic story and well worth the recounting.

A summation of the material set forth in these pages may be helpful here. Long before the Revolutionary War, Franklin became convinced that there were immense riches to be had through control of western lands. He and George Whitefield hoped for a chance to establish a new colony in the Ohio valley. Franklin and Henry Bouquet thought of ways to begin a colony on the Scioto River. Oddly enough, while dreaming of becoming a proprietor himself, Franklin was in the forefront of a movement in Pennsylvania to have the Crown withdraw such rights from the Penn family. His public language at the time argued against the wisdom of proprietary holdings. Privately, he sought to gain them for himself.

Then came the Proclamation Act of 1763 which prohibited further English settlement west of the mountains. While he thought about ways to get around this new law, Franklin continued to increase his land holdings. He bought tracts in Quebec and invested in Nova Scotia acreages. Several Americans who believed they could make money in the West in spite of the 1763 law formed a company for that purpose on 29 March 1766. This was the Illinois Company. Franklin was soon asked to become a member. For two years Ben and his partners sought a large land grant on the Illinois River. The goal was seen to be hopeless early in 1768 and the effort was abandoned. These men then organized a "Suff'ring Traders" Company to seek repayment for losses suffered by Indian traders during western uprisings. This new organization was later named the Indiana Company inasmuch as Franklin and his friends sought a grant in that area.

This effort also came to nought. Still eager to become a proprietor, Franklin helped set up in England another group consisting of certain of the men with whom he had worked in the past but now bringing in large numbers of British as well. This enterprise was called the Walpole Associates and was set up in the spring of 1769. That same year, on 27 December, the investors reformed themselves into the Grand Ohio Company. They asked for a vast charter grant, which they planned to call Vandalia, in the vicinity of the present state of West Virginia.

In the effort to achieve success in their strivings, the group used any and every method which looked promising. They misrepresented, they lied, they presented falsified petitions, they used secret memberships to squeeze every ounce of influence from men in public positions of responsibility, they abandoned members who were no longer of use and took in new ones whom they thought to be more serviceable. They staged matters so that ratification by Britain of an Indian treaty was made contingent upon official acceptance of private and self-serving speculative arrangements with the tribes. The Vandalia cohorts adopted much of the apparatus of clandestine operations: code names, mail runners, coded messages, and other devices.

Other financial and political activities of Franklin caused the British government to become reluctant to grant the Vandalia charter so long as Ben was a partner. Franklin publicly resigned from the organization although a private agreement with Thomas Walpole actually allowed him to retain both his interest in the company and his shares of stock.

The Boston Tea Party, the Coercive Acts, Lexington and Concord—all made the already apprehensive British government refuse to proceed with the Vandalia grant until peace should return once again. Franklin, who had by now returned to America, helped form an American branch of the Vandalia Company. The English had refused, but perhaps the American Continental Congress might grant them title to the western area they had so long sought. Memberships in the organization were given to influential congressmen. In spite of his best efforts, nothing concrete had been accomplished by the time Franklin sailed for France late in 1776. Arriving on the continent, Franklin continued to work for a grant in the American West. He brought into the action his landlord, Chaumont, and certain members of the French government. He interested heads of wealthy banking houses in such an

American investment. Franklin reestablished contacts with previous Vandalia partners in England such as Thomas Walpole and Samuel Wharton. He used Silas Deane and the contacts that man had. Throughout the war, Franklin did what he could to forward his speculative goals. While seeking title for a tract in the back country from the American Congress, Franklin kept his shares in the English branch of the Vandalia Company current just in case Britain won the war. He could then begin again to push the government of Great Britain toward granting a charter to establish the colony.

Ben refused to give up his ephemeral proprietorship in the West. His vision of becoming a land baron never dimmed. Upon his return home after the war, Franklin continued to lobby with influential friends and with the Congress for a grant of lands. He managed to sustain this effort almost until he lay down upon his deathbed. He spent fifty years on this project, without success.

Pursuit of western lands alone, however, was not enough to keep Ben Franklin fully occupied. His range of interests was extremely wide. During much of his life he followed his own rules, which were not necessarily those upheld by society at large. When he returned from England to America in 1775, he found himself thrust into the forefront of the colonial revolutionary movement. He was burdened with too much work and the new government "committeed" him too often. Already elderly, the necessarily long hours put an undue burden upon his health, which he resented. He had lived in Pennsylvania only for a few months since 1757. His English and continental friends, honors, contacts, and interests had made him more cosmopolitan than American. Nor was he at all convinced that the colonies would win in their struggle in any case. Should the American forces lose the fight, the United States would be no place for him to be found by the British army in mop-up operations. By mid-1776 Franklin was considering ways to extricate himself from the geography of North America.

When Congress considered the plight of America, it decided to send agents abroad to seek foreign alliances. Franklin made the right suggestions and was named as a commissioner to France. He arrived in that country late in 1776 and immediately began to widen the area of his interests. With some forethought he had prepared for his trip abroad. As a congressional agent, he had the prestige in Paris that came both from his title, and from the fact that he represented a far-off and attractive area. Stationed in France, Americans could not blame him for poor leadership if the uprising in the colonies collapsed, whereas they could retaliate against those who had served in the American Congress. Furthermore, if the American cause failed, he would be safer from British retribution in Paris than he could ever be if he had stayed in the United States. And finally, if France became an American ally, he would receive much credit for having helped persuade them to take such a position.

At Passy, Franklin could return to the leisurely life style he had earlier maintained while residing in England. He still had contacts in Britain. Indeed, it had been Ben and Ben alone who had written the orders for Silas Deane the preceding March telling Deane to get in touch with Edward Bancroft when he got to France. Franklin had fastened that British spy upon the Paris mission like a lamprey upon the side of a fish. Ability to communicate with people in England might be important. Ben might allow himself to consider doing what he could in a quiet way to help bring peace again between colonies and mother country.

Franklin had not been long in France when, with Chaumont, Robert Morris, Silas Deane, and others, he began to exploit the rich possibilities of trading in scarce goods with American merchants. The men soon learned how extremely lucrative this endeavor was. Franklin and Deane named Jonathan Williams, Jr., as head of the American commercial agency at Nantes so as to control and profit from the imports and exports of that port and to control the profitable sale of prize ships that were auctioned there.

At the American headquarters in Franklin's home at Passy, Ben gave free run of the place to several British spies: Carmichael, Lupton, Hynson, Bancroft. When Arthur Lee came over to France from England as one of the three co-equal commissioners with Deane and Franklin, he quickly pointed out that Bancroft was a spy. When he brought these charges to Franklin's attention, Bancroft "boldly and indignantly" denied them, "a feat that scarcely could have succeeded if it had not been countenanced by Franklin." [10] Time after time, Franklin defended the spies within his home, turning suspicion away from them and toward others whose only crime was that they feared treason within the American embassy.

In spite of repeated warnings from many quarters, Franklin established no security system over the state papers in his control, but allowed them to be rifled at will and their secrets passed on to the British government in Whitehall. In Berlin, Lee's private papers were stolen. Publicly uninterested himself in security measures, Franklin used the theft of Lee's papers to begin the process of discrediting the Virginian so he might eventually be recalled.

It was during Lee's absence that there occurred the Hynson episode, where for months Deane and Franklin supported that suborned sea captain until he could transfer months of accumulated dispatches for America to the British Secret Service. When the affair became public, William Lee noted that Franklin would use every "finesse" to "conceal the Truth." In America, Thomas Paine charged that for this act of treachery Silas Deane had been paid £200,000.

Franklin continued to exacerbate relations with Arthur Lee. He froze Lee out of embassy business and refused to share correspondence with him. Franklin made certain that Lee did not possess a key to certain locked files although he allowed his spy friend Bancroft to have one. Franklin and

Deane spent commission funds at a fantastic rate, without retaining vouchers or receipts. When Lee criticized this practice, he was excoriated in no uncertain terms. Franklin and
Deane then mounted a concerted effort to convince the
American Congress that Lee was unreliable. Even worse,
they implied that he seemed to be going insane, and on that
account could not be trusted with delicate matters.

The records are clear that throughout 1777 Franklin met
repeatedly with British couriers and with agents of the Secret
Service. That he also carried on an extensive correspondence
with several untrustworthy friends and acquaintances in Britain throughout the war is denied by no one. Between his arrival in France and the end of 1778, Ben received at least
twenty visitors from England with whom he met in clandestine ways. Even Lord North referred to Franklin by his old
code name of "Moses."

Franklin and Deane, at the end of 1777, called for a meet-
ing between themselves and the British spy Paul Wentworth.
Their request was given to Carmichael who passed it on to
Hynson who forwarded it to England. Only days later,
Wentworth arrived in Paris for a group of meetings which
would last from December 1777 into early January 1778.
Wentworth laid before Franklin and Deane the rewards that
would be theirs if they were willing to declare themselves
openly in favor of an end to the war and a reconciliation of
America with the mother country. As early as November
1777 Franklin had been reported as fearful that France might
make a treaty with the United States. Franklin may well have
wanted to explore to the fullest the ramifications of spon-
soring reconciliation before he severed all links with the
mother country. Wentworth, at any rate, felt there still
might be hope that England could use Franklin, for he wrote
Eden of "72['s] cordial affection" for Britain.

At the same time, Franklin was engaged in preliminary
discussions with the French over the forthcoming treaty. He
saw no need of insisting that they recognize the sovereignty

or independence of the United States. To others he intimated that he would prefer that this issue not be formalized by treaty. When Arthur Lee insisted that the wording of the document specify America's independence, Franklin reacted furiously. On the commercial treaty, Franklin was willing to bind all exported goods of the United States while France would commit but one item. Again Lee objected. Franklin responded by snidely insulting Lee as a troublemaker who caused unnecessary delays and difficulties.

It was during this winter of 1777–1778 that Franklin persuaded Lee to hire a British spy as his private secretary, since he had none. Franklin then used this example of Lee's "naïvete" to discredit him with the French Ministry. Soon, at the request of Gérard, the Congress recalled the thoroughly burned Lee.

That Franklin continued to exploit commercial transactions of the United States for personal profit was attested by the agent Wentworth in a report to Eden. After his midwinter meetings with Franklin and Deane, Wentworth wrote that *"They are deeply concerned in the Cargoes going out."* Private gain seemed as important as appointed duties.

Before the Americans in Paris could sign the French alliance, Silas Deane received word that he had been recalled by the Congress. Knowing full well of his dismissal, Franklin allowed him to stay on with all the accoutrements of a commissioner, spending in just the last few days of his stay in Paris some £1,700. Arthur Lee, after repeated requests, finally got hold of some of the Mission account books. He marked several items as unjust, exorbitant, or unsatisfactory, and refused to approve them. "Thou shalt not muzzle the ox that treadeth out the corn."

Even after the signing of the French treaties, Franklin continued to call for additional visits from British agents, the most notable of whom was William Pulteney. After his first visit to France, Pulteney returned for a second time because one of his agents reported that Ben, while unwilling to expose

himself to public censure in America, still remained affection-
ately involved with England and "woud be happy on reasonable terms" to make some sort of accommodation with the
British government. Pulteney was told that Franklin was
willing to have his sentiments expressed to Lord North himself. And so Pulteney and Franklin met again. What came of
it we do not know, but a copy of the results were given to
Deane as he left France for America. Franklin later wrote
Deane a distraught letter urging him immediately to burn the
memo he had given him.

George III soon spoke to Lord North about a message Pulteney had sent. After thinking about its import, George III
told North that it meant that "the Old Doctor may wish to
keep a door open," which "can be of no disservice." It was
later reported in America that Franklin had suggested to Pulteney the manner in which to bring the United States back
into the English fold: the best way would be to offer congressional leaders seats in Parliament. Such a bribe "would be
more alluring than any other."

Then John Adams came to Paris as a replacement for the
recalled Silas Deane. Bereft of his partner and ally, Franklin
used the first opportunity to attempt to poison Adams' mind
against the other Americans in France. Lee would soon lose
his reason, Franklin said, because of his "anxious, uneasy temper" which made him "disagreeable" to work with. Ralph
Izard had a like temperament, possessed of "violent and ungoverned passions." Even worse, Franklin continued, neither
"was liked by the French."

Unpersuaded by all this, Adams carefully watched all his
countrymen living in the French capital. It did not take him
long to make up his mind. While agreeing with Franklin that
Lee was captious, he also believed that Lee was a man of
sound sense and undoubted worth and patriotism. He enjoyed the company of Izard and found him entirely different
than Franklin had represented him. Adams also became convinced that the situation at Nantes was intolerable and joined

with Lee in "requiring the settlement of Mr. Williams' accounts." When they were found to be unsatisfactory, Franklin reluctantly accepted the inevitable and finally joined with
his fellow commissioners, Adams and Lee, in relieving Williams of his duties at Nantes. He also soon had to cooperate in
firing John Ross, Robert Morris' agent in that port city.
Franklin was not at all happy with these developments.

To his cousin Sam, John Adams observed that Franklin's
financial system was rotten to the core. Huge amounts of
money had been spent carelessly, no one knew how. Huge
debts remained to be paid, yet no records had been maintained listing expenditures. For the first time since the first
American had arrived in Paris in 1775, Adams tried to
straighten out the accounts and succeeded in ordering them
to some extent.

Another British agent may have contacted Franklin after
Adams' arrival, the mysterious Charles de Weissenstein. His
message, Franklin claimed to Adams, bore "infallible" marks
of having come from George III himself. The note from the
agent promised, as Wentworth had months earlier, various
perquisites and rewards if Franklin would do what he could
to settle the conflict raging between America and England.
Franklin did nothing about the offer save to report it to the
French police. He did give to Adams "many other hints"
which made his suspicious listener even more concerned
about "some mysterious intercourse or correspondence between the King and him [Franklin], personally."

Franklin continued to play games with the mission's accounts. When he found it necessary to have an audit conducted, he called on Samuel Wharton and Edward Bancroft
to review the accounts and certify them. It would have been
difficult to have located two more unqualified and dishonest
men than those Franklin had selected for this task. It need
hardly be added that they found the ledger books to be in
good order.

In America, the issue of Deane's activities while in France

had become a matter of public scandal with eager partisans joining happily in the fray either to condemn or defend the recalled commissioner. When Adams learned of one tract Deane had published, he called him a wild boar to be hunted down for the good of mankind. Finally discharged by the Congress, the "wild boar" decided to return to Europe.

In midsummer of 1779 Adams returned to America. He would later be followed by Arthur Lee, in the spring of 1780. By the time Lee sailed, Adams had been sent back by Congress to seek ways to negotiate peace. When that seemed for the time unadvisable, he left for Holland to try to secure a loan for the United States. Franklin argued against such an effort, just as he had earlier done with Arthur Lee and his brother William when they sought loans. Indeed, from the time he sat in Congress in 1775 until the end of the Revolution, Franklin consistently argued against seeking either loans or alliances at European courts. Had his advice been taken, the shaky financial structure of the United States might have collapsed long before Yorktown, and the nation never would have had the advantage of the French alliance which militarily strengthened it so much.

Deane arrived in Paris during the summer of 1780 and Franklin immediately allowed him once again to move in with him. The two men had once found it effective to describe Arthur Lee as insane. John Adams now kept tabs on them, and so they tried the same tactic on him. Deane, Franklin, and Bancroft all claimed that Adams was "actually mad." With Chaumont, these men publicly calumniated the American Congress so often that it became an open scandal among others then in Europe and was so reported by James Searle to a friend in Philadelphia. He also spoke of Franklin's hostility to loans to America and of his engaging in doubtful modes of profiteering.

Perhaps even while still living with Franklin at Passy, Silas Deane arranged to meet with Paul Wentworth again. The two men then worked out a plan whereby Deane wrote a series of letters to acquaintances in America in which he called for reconciliation with England. When he had finished drafting them, he gave the messages to the Secret Service, which delivered them, after they were reviewed by the very highest figures in British government, to a Tory printer in New York, James Rivington, who published them in his newspaper at the end of the year. This public repudiation of the American cause irrevocably finished the career of Silas Deane.

Franklin never condemned this action, continued to loan Deane money and to correspond with him. He allowed Deane to use his home as a mailing address. In 1782 Franklin wrote a letter or certificate of probity for Deane, asserting his belief in his ex-colleague's honesty and uprightness in the public service. William Lee chortled and thought the reason Franklin had written the letter was fear that it might otherwise be learned that he had been as crooked as Deane.

During the peace negotiations with Great Britain, Franklin supported for a time an end to the war and a formalized peace without Britain's acknowledgment of the independence of the United States. He saw to it that his grandson, William Temple Franklin, was made secretary for the American delegation in Paris. Ben seems to have been willing to allow France and Spain to "coop us up within the Allegheny Mountains," [11] and argued with his fellow negotiators, Jay and Adams, not to pit themselves against the course of French diplomacy. Far from being the most "dazzling diplomat in America's history," Franklin was regarded by Jay and Adams as a thorn pressed deeply into their sides as they endeavored to procure from Britain the best peace terms possible. When the negotiations were over, the rumors about Franklin's waffling were so thick that he was forced to ask both Jay and Adams to write him letters of recommendation. After the peace treaty was signed, Franklin continued his pursuit of family and personal advantage until he returned to America, and thereafter until his death.

Silas Deane was recalled in 1778 from his overseas post in France by a suspicious Congress. From time to time thereafter there were murmurings that perhaps the same order should be sent to Benjamin Franklin. Had Franklin been recalled, he, like Deane, might well have been hard put to explain what he had been doing in France. The Congress, however, was insufficiently curious—or courageous. Franklin stayed at his post and was never required to appear before a committee chosen to inquire into the activities of the Paris mission. As was his wish, he carried his honor intact, for the most part, to the grave, and when necessary it has been refurbished by later writers. No clarification of his political and economic efforts during the war was ever exacted of Benjamin Franklin. This does not mean that the historian may not ask of the documents questions that could then have been asked of the man.

If Benjamin Franklin was as patriotic and consistent in his love for America as he has been portrayed as being, why did he maintain long years of association with, and vehemently defend, those then known to be otherwise? If he was the brilliant and discerning diplomat that others have claimed him to be, why was the Paris mission run in such a disorderly fashion? Why was he lethargic when surrounded by chaos that cried out to be put straight? Why did Franklin repeatedly ignore warnings that he should levy strict security measures over the state papers in his possession? Why did he ignore even elementary intelligence precautions in his operations at Passy? Why did he admit Bancroft into his home as an employee and friend? What about the other British spies who moved in and out of Paris, using his home as headquarters? If Franklin felt he could use Bancroft and the other Secret Service agents to relay false information to the British, without being used in return, why did so much reliable intelligence fall into the hands of those who sat in governmental offices at Whitehall? Why did very little that was helpful find its way to America? Why did this diplomat from the United States not see clandestine operations that were obvious to Lee, to Adams, to Vergennes?

If Franklin was the wise and tolerant individual he claimed to be and later writers have portrayed him as being, why did he not exert a more moderating influence on the American squabbles in Paris? Were not the various allegations he made regarding his colleagues bad for morale generally? Was Franklin's "Petition of the Letter Z" really the act of one interested in harmony? Why was he unable or unwilling to promote a spirit of unity among the members of the Paris mission? Why was he so ready to assail the character of those who criticized him, as he did toward John Adams, Arthur Lee, William Lee, and Ralph Izard? Why did he accuse his colleagues—Adams and Lee—of being insane? Why did he continue this even after Congress warned that the situation in Paris was fast becoming a public scandal?

Why did Franklin consistently argue against procuring either loans or treaties from European states that might aid America in its struggle with Great Britain? Why did he belittle those who assiduously sought to gain such advantages? Why did he meet so frequently with Secret Service agents of England at a time when that nation and his own were at war? Where were the advantages to the United States that should have come from such contacts if Franklin were truly dedicated to the cause of America? What was on Franklin's mind when he tricked Lee into hiring a Secret Service agent as secretary so he could discredit the Virginian as unreliable and unstable?

Why was Franklin so interested in locking Jonathan Williams, Jr., into control of the commercial agency at Nantes? Why did he fight so hard to keep him there? What prompted Franklin to allow American funds to be spent so freely? Why did he keep few financial records and allow his papers to remain in such a state of confusion that they could not be properly audited? Why did he not exert control over Silas Deane? Why did he allow Deane to speculate in trade and stocks so freely? Why did Franklin join Deane in part of these endeavors?

What caused Franklin to be so diffident during the peace negotiations? Why was he not more concerned that America might receive limited western boundaries? Why was Franklin so willing under every circumstance to use his influence and position to push his own interests in western land speculation?

Was this great man indeed all he and his biographers have claimed? In spite of the paeans of praise Ben sang of himself and the choruses to those verses performed by later writers, the historical records sound strong dissonant notes when they are listened to carefully. Who has upheld the honor and rectitude of Franklin's career during the revolutionary era? He did, carefully and consistently, as would be expected. So also did several of his congressional advocates, but they were far removed from the scenes and characters of his daily life. Others who supported the uprightness of Franklin's views, men such as Jonathan Williams, Jr., and William Temple Franklin, were related to him and profited from that family connection, and the former himself had a career so devoted to wartime profiteering that his activities would not bear close scrutiny without incriminating him. Good words were said about Franklin by men such as Edward Bancroft and William Carmichael, but they also happened to be agents of William Eden and so their motives are suspect. Silas Deane upheld Franklin as Franklin did Deane. Little substantiation from this quarter can be accepted as valid, inasmuch as Deane was also an agent of the British and now known to have been a calculating traitor to the country of his origin. Finally, Franklin has been supported by biographers of later years. We have learned many things from such writings, but very little that might have been detrimental to Franklin has been included.

Who criticized Franklin during those war years? The most

important of the skeptics were those whose duties called for them to be in close association with him. The earliest man to become suspicious was Arthur Lee, whom even the British admitted to be incorruptible and an extreme zealot for the cause of the United States of America. Another critic was Ralph Izard, whose primary crime in the eyes of Franklin seems to have been a desire to be consulted about American affairs in regard to which he thought he might be useful. An additional finger of accusation was pointed by William Lee, who was forced out of his Nantes appointment by Franklin, his cohorts and relatives, and who had the temerity to fight back. There was also John Adams, neutral at first toward the contending parties in France, but who soon came to condemn Franklin's circle, his activities, and his motives. One might also mark the criticisms of John Jay, who thought Franklin was so dilatory on behalf of America that he shattered a clay pipe because of him. The roll call could be extended.

Basically, the situation was that, among his contemporaries, the great majority of those who were known to be patriots and with whom he came into contact in France criticized Franklin. Those who supported him were either suspect in their own right or far removed from the scene and hence unable to observe what was actually occurring. Lee, for example, charged that Franklin and his comrades were "in trade" for their own benefit at the expense of the interests of the United States. The records show that his charge was correct. Lee asserted that "studied confusion" existed in the records for improperly disbursed public funds. He was right. Even a quick glance at the available evidence supports this particular indictment. Lee rightly charged that Passy was filled with profiteers, traitors, and spies betraying America. The documentary evidence for this is clear. He was on the mark when he stated that his colleagues carried on activities that would not bear the scrutiny of honest men.

Were these charges made in a vacuum? The evidence again would indicate that such was not the case. He had known Franklin since the middle 1760s and had been closely associated with him professionally since 1770. He worked as long and as intimately with Franklin as any other man could claim during Franklin's lifetime. His opinion that Franklin was a scoundrel was therefore either based on imaginary, mistaken, or real evidence. There was real evidence. Therefore Lee's assertions should be seriously considered. Moreover, we know, through the records, much that Lee either did not perceive or understood only dimly.

The view developed in this volume has been suggested, but not thoroughly explored, by earlier writers. One has written that "historians have usually condemned the Lees on the basis of loose and general accusations made by their enemies for obvious reasons. No serious charges have been proved against them, their real offense having been opposition to Franklin. . . . One of their offenses was their insistence that public monies should be accounted for to Congress. Their efforts were of no avail and Franklin, Deane, and Robert Morris received huge sums for which Congress never got an accounting." This author goes on to say that privateering, for example, "should have been a source of considerable profit to Congress, [but] that body never derived any advantage from it. In fact, the public suffered seriously because vessels, money, and men" were diverted by Franklin and his partners into privateering. The trouble between Franklin and the Lee brothers originated primarily as a result of Ben's insistence "on taking the privateering business out of the hands of the agents appointed by Congress and retaining control of it" for his own private purposes. The same writer also noted that "a more honest agent" than Benjamin Franklin "would have had difficulty in dealing with Chaumont and the French ministers, as John Adams certainly did." [12] Another historian calculated that Franklin and Deane in France disposed of more than nineteen million livres for which they never gave Con-

gress an account.[13] For observing these things, Arthur Lee
has been excoriated!

Many years ago, Carl Van Doren, a fine writer, published
a very extensive and well rounded biography of Benjamin
Franklin. An uncritical evaluator of his subject, even Van
Doren felt compelled to state at one point that "If Deane had
been a peculator, and Franklin indifferent if not worse, then
Lee would have been in fact the unhappy and mistreated vic-
tim he always thought he was." [14] Van Doren did not then
know that Deane was a "peculator"—one who steals or mis-
uses money or property entrusted to him, particularly public
funds. That was set forth by historians only long after Van
Doren wrote his book. Because he did not believe Lee had
been mistreated, he derided him and always found a way to
gloss over every instance of Franklin's improper conduct toward Lee. More information is available today than was used
by Van Doren. A logical syllogism could be made from the
above quotation; we know that:

> Deane was a peculator.
> Franklin was indifferent if not worse.
> Therefore: Lee was an unhappy and mistreated man.

A Frenchman, Capefigue, who published the memoirs of
Louis XVI, may indeed not have been far from the mark
when he described Ben as "one of the great charlatans" of his
age and suggested that he fit into French society so well because there everything "qui est charlatinisme" succeeded.[15]

What is the explanation for the peculiar activities of Franklin during his time in Paris? There are several possible solutions. (1) He was an ignorant man. As such, he simply was
not intelligent enough to know what was going on around
him and too stupid to perform his duties properly. Such an
answer flies in the face of all we know about the native
shrewdness, the inborn intellect of this man that manifested
itself in so many realms of human endeavor and brought him

well deserved praise for his accomplishments over the course
of years. (2) He was not perceptive. This is another possibility, yet it must be repudiated in the same manner and for the
same reasons as the preceding charge. The evidence is clear
that in all ways Franklin was not only intelligent, but perceptive. (3) Benjamin Franklin was either feeble or lazy—that is,
unable or unwilling to perform the labor necessary to run a
first-rate diplomatic mission. Lacking leadership from him,
others seized the opportunity and misused and abused their
positions for their own advantage. Something might be made
of this possibility. Franklin was an old man even when he
reached France and his health often was not the best. He
suffered seriously from colds, influenza, and gout. Such health
problems may well have made him too feeble, or brought him
into patterns of laziness, neither of which he was able to shake
off. Yet if this was indeed the answer, it is strange that for one
hundred years students of Franklin's career have marveled at
the vitality, the energy, the recuperative powers, the wide-
spread and multiform activities in Paris that would have sent
many a younger man to a sickbed.

Many will immediately reach for another, and for them, a
very real solution. (4) Benjamin Franklin was a thoroughgoing patriot in all his ways and the totality of the material in
this study, from the author's conjectures to the evidence and
suspicions of men as diverse as John Adams and Ralph Izard,
is totally misleading. They will prefer to believe that, without
exception, all the records on which this text has been based
have been wrongly interpreted. They may feel that, of the
possibilities listed above, no biographer (including this one)
has ever suggested that Ben Franklin was ignorant, unpercep-
tive, feeble, or lazy. They may be convinced that the suggestions of self-interest and profiteering are simply not credible.
And this may be true, in spite of the fact that from the time
of the second President of the United States to the work of
modern scholars, whose works have been quoted herein, the
suspicions have not been laid to rest that Franklin's wartime

activities were not as open as he would have had others believe.

There is another possibility. (5) Benjamin Franklin knew, or suspected what was going on at the Paris mission but did not care. For reasons of his own, he saw fit to ignore the situation. Perhaps what he noted in others upon occasion made him uneasy, but he drifted along on a tide of his own making and did nothing to stop the misuse of his home and headquarters. When criticized, his very unease made him react with defensive alacrity and hostility toward those making charges. He had more status, more of a reputation, more ability, than any of his colleagues in Europe, and he resented having to answer to them, or to explain his reasons for doing what he wished. Silas Deane he could dominate, the others he could not. For that reason he felt most comfortable with Deane and chose to work solely with him until Deane was recalled, and after that time Franklin worked alone.

There can be little doubt that Benjamin Franklin was one of the great men of history, surely one of the chiefest in America's pantheon. The years of his life, although illustrious ones, were in many ways as bitter as the taste of dust. He was a real man with all the contradictions within him that real life entails. Renown of many sorts came to him because of the exercise of his native talents and through hard work and utter dedication to his own advancement. His business, his investments, his salaries all made him one of the richer men in America long before the outbreak of the Revolution. Franklin was not satisfied. He wished not only wealth but social status, and in his day that could come only through possession of landed estates. For years he sought success in land ventures, but achievement of this goal proved permanently elusive.

To maintain his ability to participate in such endeavors he had to hold onto his political positions both in America and England, and this sometimes necessitated his saying things that hurt imperial ties between Britain and the colonies. In the black days of 1775 and 1776, concern about land was replaced by Franklin's worries about his own safety if the rebel-lion were to collapse. When the opportunity arose, he left for France. There he continued to do what he could to forward the possibilities of an American land grant.

While in France during the war, Franklin was asked to come out openly on behalf of reunion with the mother coun-try. Never able himself to quite make that step, in spite of many temptations, he watched his colleague Silas Deane do so. Now Franklin saw the fury which was vented upon Deane for his act of public treason. Ben became more and more concerned about being able to take his honor intact to the grave. Old, tired, still desirous of keeping contact with as many camps as possible, he played a difficult role during the peace negotiations. He had to function sufficiently well not to be repudiated by his colleagues. He wished to do nothing, however, that would arouse the ire of Vergennes, in whose country he had spent so many pleasant years. Nor did he want to be "too much an American" and adhere to demands upon the English that they might not desire to grant. It was a tortuous path to follow, but Franklin managed. In the few short years left him, Franklin continued to let it be known that he ought to be rewarded for his foreign service by a tract of western land. Then, with his hope still unrealized, Benja-min Franklin was gathered to his fathers.

His motives during the war years might be summarized in the following way. Benjamin Franklin wanted to win the American Revolution. No matter who lost—the United States, France, England—Benjamin Franklin wanted to win. In some ways he did. His honor remained intact. He gained new renown. He was rewarded by a grateful nation with ad-ditional positions of public responsibility. His secrets gener-ally remained hidden. That he did not win completely, that baronial estates in the back country of America never became either his or his heirs', was something Franklin could not have foreseen.

CHAPTER NOTES

CHAPTER ONE

[1] See Samuel Flagg Bemis, *The Diplomacy of the American Revolution* (Bloomington, 1961), pp. 45–47, 61–65.

[2] "The Papers of Dr. Benjamin Rush," *The Pennsylvania Magazine of History and Biography*, XXIX (1905), 28. Cited hereafter as *PMHB*.

[3] Richard Henry Lee, *The Life of Arthur Lee* (2 vols., Boston, 1829), I, 393–94. Cited hereafter as Lee, *Lee*.

[4] Quoted in Margaret A. Miller, "The Spy-Activities of Doctor Edward Bancroft," *Journal of American History*, XXII, 2 (1928), 162–63.

[5] See Appendix A.

[6] The phrase is Franklin's, used years earlier in an entirely different context. See Benjamin Franklin to Samuel Rhoads, London, 8 July 1765, in Albert H. Smyth, ed., *The Writings of Benjamin Franklin* (10 vols., New York, 1905–7), IV, 387–88. Cited hereafter as Smyth, *Writings*.

[7] Phillips Russell, *Benjamin Franklin: The First Civilized American* (New York, 1926), p. 253; Bernard Faÿ, *Franklin, The Apostle of Modern Times* (Boston, 1929), pp. 393, 403; Verner W. Crane, *Benjamin Franklin and a Rising People* (Boston, 1954), p. 173; Paul C. Phillips, *The West in the Diplomacy of the American Revolution* (New York, 1913), p. 62; quoted in J. Henry Smythe, Jr., ed., *The Amazing Benjamin Franklin* (New York, 1929), p. 1; Carl Van Doren, *Benjamin Franklin* (New York, 1952), p. 593.

[8] Thomas Perkins Abernethy, "The Origin of the Franklin-Lee Imbroglio," *The North Carolina Historical Review*, XV (January 1938), 41.

[9] Malcolm R. Eiselen, *Franklin's Political Theories* (Garden City, N.Y., 1928), p. 29.

[10] Stated by Edward Thornton as quoted in S. W. Jackman, "A Young Englishman Reports on the New Nation: Edward Thornton to James Bland Borges, 1791–1793," *William and Mary Quarterly*, 3d series, XVIII (January 1961), 121.

[11] Quoted in Charles Warren, "A Young American's Adventures in England and France during the Revolutionary War," Massachusetts Historical Society *Proceedings*, LXV (1936), 252.

[12] George Chalmers, *Second Thoughts: or, Observations upon Lord Abingdon's Thoughts on the Letter of Edmund Burke, Esq. To the Sheriffs of Bristol. By the author of the Answer to Mr. Burke's Letter* (London, 1777).

[13] John Adams to William Tudor, Quincy, Massachusetts, 5 June 1817, as quoted in *American Historical Review*, XLVII (July 1942), 806–7.

[14] "My curiosity will at least be employed in observing his invention and his artifice." Entry dated 27 October 1782, in John Adams' *Diary*, in *The Works of John Adams*, ed. Charles Francis Adams (Boston, 1865), III, 300. Hereafter cited as Adams, *Works*.

[15] Arthur Lee to Sam Adams, London, 8 February 1774, Lee, *Lee*, I, 240.

[16] Arthur Lee to Richard Henry Lee, Chaillot, 15 February 1778, *ibid.*, II, 134.

[17] *Ibid.*, II, 148.

[18] Richard Deacon, *A History of the British Secret Service*, (London, 1969), pp. 92–93.

[19] These matters will be treated at length in later pages. For this reason no documentation is given here.

[20] See Charles Maclean Andrews, "A Note on the Franklin-Deane Mission to France," *Yale University Library Gazette*, XII (1928), 59, 65.

[21] Jonathan Williams, Jr., to Benjamin Franklin, Nantes, 30 October 1777, Franklin Papers, American Philosophical Society Library, XXXVII, 117, Philadelphia, Pennsylvania. Hereafter cited as APSL.

[22] Samuel Flagg Bemis, "British Secret Service and the French American Alliance," *American Historical Review*, XXIX (April 1924), 474. Hereafter cited as Bemis, "British Secret Service."

[23] In an introduction to a nineteenth-century edition of the papers of Britain's chief of intelligence services during the American Revolution, his spy-master career is simply not mentioned. See *The Journal and Correspondence of William, Lord Auckland* (4 vols., London, 1861–1862).

[24] See Deacon, *British Secret Service, passim.*

[25] The work in which the charge appeared was in the introduction to Marshall's collection of Franklin's papers, issued in 1817. See Paul Leicester Ford, ed., *Franklin Bibliography: A List of Books Written by or Relating to Benjamin Franklin* (Brooklyn, 1889), p. li and *passim.*

[26] Bemis, "British Secret Service," p. 474.

CHAPTER TWO

[1] "OBSERVATIONS on my Reading History in Library, May 9, 1731," in Leonard W. Labaree and William B. Willcox, eds., *The Papers of Benjamin Franklin* (15 vols. to date, New Haven, 1959), I, 192. Hereafter cited as Labaree, *Papers*. See also Part Three in Leonard W. Labaree,

ed., *The Autobiography of Benjamin Franklin* (New Haven, 1964), p. 161. Hereafter cited as *Autobiography*. The *Autobiography* was written in three sections: in 1771 at the home of Jonathan Shipley, bishop of St. Asaph's; in 1784 at Passy, France; and in 1788 at home in Philadelphia.

[2] *Autobiography*, p. 209; Labaree, *Papers*, V, 58; VI, 430; VIII, 279n; X, 311n.

[3] *Autobiography*, p. 128.

[4] William Franklin, Ben's first illegitimate child, was brought into the Franklin home and raised there. He later became governor of New Jersey and, during the war, a staunch Loyalist. Phillips Russell, *Benjamin Franklin: The First Civilized American* (New York, 1926), p. 114, affirms that Franklin had a daughter and cites a letter of John Foxcroft to Franklin, 2 February 1772, in which John refers to his wife as "your daughter." See also Sydney George Fisher, *The True Benjamin Franklin* (Philadelphia, 1906), pp. 104, 365–76, for additional corroboration. For the possible name of her mother, a maid in his home named Barbara, see the anonymous anti-Franklin pamphlet, *What is Sauce for a Goose is also Sauce for a Gander* (Philadelphia, 1764), pp. 6–7.

[5] These figures are given in Carl Van Doren, *Benjamin Franklin* (New York, 1952), pp. 188–89.

[6] Adams, *Works*, I, 319–20.

[7] *Autobiography*, pp. 185.

[8] *Ibid.*, pp. 209–10.

[9] For the best available study of Franklin's part in the work of provincial legislation, see William S. Hanna, *Benjamin Franklin and Pennsylvania Politics* (Stanford, 1964), *passim*.

[10] Benjamin Franklin to Thomas Clap, New York, 20 August 1753, Labaree, *Papers*, V, 21–22.

[11] *Ibid.*, V, 457–59.

[12] Benjamin Franklin to George Whitefield, New York, 2 July 1756, *ibid.*, VI, 468–69.

[13] For studies of the colonial agents and their role, see Ross J. S. Hoffman, *Edmund Burke, New York Agent* (Philadelphia, 1956), Jack Sosin, *Agents and Merchants* (Lincoln, 1966), Ella Lonn, *The Colonial Agents of the Southern Colonies* (Chapel Hill, 1945), Edward P. Lilly, *The Colonial Agents of New York and New Jersey* (Washington, 1936), James J. Burns, *The Colonial Agents of New England* (Washington, 1935), and Mabel P. Wolff, *The Colonial Agency of Pennsylvania, 1712–1757* (Philadelphia, 1933).

[14] Quoted in J. Philip Gleason, "A Scurrilous Colonial Election and Franklin's Reputation," *William and Mary Quarterly*, 3d series, XVIII (January 1961), 75.

[15] Van Doren, *Franklin*, pp. 288, 360. His home in London was on Craven Street.

[16] *The Interest of Great Britain Considered*, Labaree, *Papers*, IX, 59–100. The quotation is from page 90.

¹⁷ Labaree, *Papers*, IX, 41.

¹⁸ Benjamin Franklin to Isaac Norris, London, 16 September 1758, Labaree, *Papers*, VIII, 157–58.

¹⁹ See David L. Jacobson, "John Dickinson's Fight Against Royal Government," *William and Mary Quarterly*, 3d series, XIX (January 1962), 81–83; "Remarks on a Late Protest Against the Appointment of Mr. Franklin an Agent for This Province," in Smyth, *Writings*, IV, 273–85.

²⁰ This conversation, attributed to an unnamed British official, is recorded only in a letter from Joseph Galloway to Benjamin Franklin, Philadelphia, 20 October 1766, II, 49 APSL.

²¹ The complete text of the Proclamation of 1763 may be found in Clarence W. Alvord and Clarence E. Carter, eds., *The Critical Period, 1763–1765* (Springfield, 1905), pp. 39ff.

²² John Baynton and Samuel Wharton to Benjamin Franklin, Philadelphia, 3 November 1764, I, 105 APSL.

²³ Benjamin Franklin to Richard Jackson, Philadelphia, 1 May 1764, Labaree, *Papers*, XI, 186–87.

²⁴ *Colonial Records of Nova Scotia*, XXXV, 94–101, Department of Lands and Forests, Halifax, Nova Scotia. See also the *Loyalist Transcripts*, XL, 329–93, New York Public Library. Hereafter cited as NYPL. See also Council Minutes, 30 April 1765, Public Archives, Halifax, Nova Scotia, and "Franklin's Answer to the Report," Smyth, *Writings*, V, 509.

²⁵ Henry Bouquet to Benjamin Franklin, 22 August 1764, I, 94 APSL; same to Joseph Galloway, Annapolis, 24 April 1763, J. P. Morgan Library.

²⁶ Henry Bouquet to Benjamin Franklin, 27 August 1764, I, 96 APSL.

²⁷ John Baynton to his daughter, as quoted by Clarence W. Alvord and Clarence E. Carter, eds., *The New Regime, 1765–1767* (Springfield, 1916), p. 337.

²⁸ William Franklin to Benjamin Franklin, 30 April 1766, II, 17 APSL. See also "Heads of Tribes," 1766, L (ii), 47 APSL.

²⁹ Benjamin Franklin to William Franklin, London, 10 May 1766 and 12 September 1766, in John Bigelow, ed., *The Complete Works of Benjamin Franklin* (10 vols., New York, 1887–1889), IV, 416, 417. Hereafter cited as Bigelow, *Complete Works*.

³⁰ This practice worked so well that it was enlarged upon in later and more desperate days.

³¹ The paper from which the above account was taken was probably drawn up by Johnson, for it is appended directly after a letter of his advocating such a colony in the Shelburne Papers, Vol. 48, American Series, *Papers & Proposals Relative to America* [sic], William L. Clements Library, Ann Arbor, Michigan. Hereafter cited as WLCL. Other copies may be consulted in the Historical Society of Pennsylvania and at APSL.

³² "Papers relating to a proposal of Messʳˢ Baynton & Co," England and America, Bancroft Transcripts, Vol. II, NYPL.

³³ Clarence E. Carter, ed., *The Correspondence of General Thomas Gage with the Secretaries of State, 1763–1775* (2 vols., New Haven, 1931), I, *pas-*

sim to p. 180; also Shelburne to Gage, 13 September 1766, *Calendar of Home Office Papers*, II, 79.

³⁴ Benjamin Franklin to William Franklin, London, 25 November 1767, Bigelow, *Complete Works*, IV, 423–24.

³⁵ George Croghan to Benjamin Franklin, 27 January 1767, Shelburne Papers, Vol. 48, American Series, *Papers & Proposals Relative to Amarica* [sic], pp. 135–43, WLCL.

³⁶ Samuel Wharton to Benjamin Franklin, Philadelphia, 30 September 1767, Shelburne Papers, Vol. 50, p. 105, American Series, WLCL.

³⁷ Samuel Hazard, ed., *Pennsylvania Archives* (12 vols., Philadelphia, 1853–1860), 1st series, IV, 281.

³⁸ Benjamin Franklin to William Franklin, London, 25 November 1767, Smyth, *Writings*, V, 65.

³⁹ As quoted by Wharton in Samuel Wharton to Benjamin Franklin, Philadelphia, 27 December 1767, XLVIII, 129 APSL.

⁴⁰ Samuel Wharton to William Franklin, Philadelphia [probably late Spring 1768], XLVIII, 147 APSL.

⁴¹ As quoted in Nicholas B. Wainwright, *George Croghan: Wilderness Diplomat* (Chapel Hill, 1959), pp. 265–66.

⁴² Samuel Wharton to Benjamin Franklin, Philadelphia, 2 December 1768, XLIX, 77 APSL.

⁴³ The Earl of Hillsborough to Thomas Gage, Whitehall, 24 March 1769, Gage Papers, December 1768 to March 1769, English Series, No. 14, WLCL.

⁴⁴ The Earl of Hillsborough to Sir William Johnson, Whitehall, 13 May 1769, Edmund B. O'Callaghan and Berthold Fernow, eds., *Documents relative to the colonial history of the State of New York* (15 vols., Albany and New York, 1856–1887), II, 938.

CHAPTER THREE

¹ Benjamin Franklin to Jane Mecom, London, 30 December 1770, "Letters of Samuel Cooper to Pownall and Franklin," Harkness Collection, II, NYPL.

² As quoted in Verner W. Crane, *Benjamin Franklin and a Rising People* (Boston, 1954), p. 147; and Verner W. Crane, *Benjamin Franklin's Letters to the Press, 1758–1775* (Chapel Hill, 1950), p. 248.

³ It is not known when Franklin adopted this cover name but he was later called "Moses" both in speculative circles and by the highest figures within government itself. See Benjamin Franklin to Thomas Walpole, London, 12 January 1774, and the memorandum he entered upon it, Passy, 14 July 1778, in Harkness Collection of Autograph Letters, NYPL. See also Lord North to William Eden, London, 29 September 1777, Auckland Manuscripts, British Museum Additional Manuscripts, series 34,414, folio 195. Hereafter cited as BM Add MSS.

⁴ Benjamin Franklin to Samuel Cooper, London, 30 September 1769, Smyth, *Writings*, V, 231.

⁵ This letter is quoted by Willis Steell, *Benjamin Franklin of Paris, 1776–1785* (New York, 1927), p. 38. I have not found it elsewhere.

⁶ Arthur Lee to Sam Adams, London, 8 February 1774, Lee, *Lee*, I, 240.

⁷ Arthur Lee to Richard Henry Lee, London, 12 July 1770, Lee Papers, Alderman Library, University of Virginia.

⁸ Samuel Wharton to George Croghan, London, 4 September 1770, Croghan Papers, Letters W, Historical Society of Pennsylvania, Philadelphia, Pennsylvania. Hereafter cited as HSP.

⁹ Samuel Wharton to George Croghan, London, 21 July 1771, *ibid.*

¹⁰ For Franklin's Massachusetts appointment, see Thomas Cushing to Benjamin Franklin, Boston, 6 November 1770, Archives, Massachusetts Historical Society, Boston, Massachusetts. Lee hoped that perhaps Ben might soon leave for America and he could then take over the top office. Three years went by, and although Franklin sometimes talked of leaving, he did not do so. Finally, Lee wrote Sam Adams, 11 June 1773, that "Dr. Franklin frequently assures me that he shall sail for Philadelphia in a few weeks; but I believe he will not quit us till he is gathered to his fathers." Quoted in Sparks, *Works*, VIII, 59.

For Franklin's earlier appointments as agent for Georgia and New Jersey, see "Ordinance of Appointment," 11 April 1768, in Allen D. Candler, ed., *The Colonial Records of the State of Georgia: Statutes, Colonial and Revolutionary, 1768–1773* (Atlanta, 1911), XIX, 12–14; the New Jersey Committee of Correspondence to Benjamin Franklin, 7 December 1769, LII, 68 APSL; and Frederick Ricord and William Nelson, eds., *Documents Relating to the Colonial History of the State of New Jersey* (36 vols., Newark, 1881–1914), X, 135.

¹¹ Samuel Wharton to George Croghan, London, 3 February 1773, Croghan Papers, Letters W, HSP.

¹² Quoted in Julian P. Boyd, *Anglo-American Union: Joseph Galloway's Plans to Preserve the British Empire, 1774–1778* (Philadelphia, 1941), p. 39.

¹³ An undated memorandum by Franklin, L (ii), 50 APSL.

¹⁴ William Strahan to William Franklin, London, 3 April 1771, XLVIII, 139a APSL.

¹⁵ Samuel Wharton to George Croghan, London, 21 July 1771, Croghan Papers, Letters W, HSP.

¹⁶ Thomas Gage to Lord Hillsborough, 1 October 1771, Clarence E. Carter, ed., *The Correspondence of General Thomas Gage with the Secretaries of State, 1763–1765* (New Haven, 1931), I, 310.

¹⁷ Benjamin Franklin to Joseph Galloway, London, 6 February 1772, Franklin Manuscripts, Yale University Library.

¹⁸ Board of Trade, *Report of the Lords Commissioners for Trade and Plantations on the Petition . . . for a grant of lands on the River Ohio, in North America; for the purpose of erecting a new government* (London, 1772), p. 32.

¹⁹ Benjamin Franklin to William Franklin, London, 17 August 1772, Smyth, *Writings*, V, 410.

[20] Samuel Wharton to Joseph Galloway and Thomas Wharton, London, 9 April 1773, III, 2 APSL; Thomas Wharton to George Croghan, Philadelphia, 18 June 1773, Croghan Papers, Letters W, HSP.

[21] Benjamin Franklin to Thomas Cushing, London, 5 February 1771, Sparks, *Works*, VII, 502.

[22] Benjamin Franklin to Committee of Correspondence, London, May 1771, Sparks, *Works*, VII, 521.

[23] Thomas Hutchinson to "Dear Sir," Boston, 23 December 1773, Massachusetts Historical Society, Boston.

[24] Georgia Committee of Correspondence to Benjamin Franklin, Savannah, 14 March 1774, Franklin Papers, 234–42, 244, LC. See also Kenneth Coleman, *The American Revolution in Georgia, 1763–1789* (doctoral thesis, University of Wisconsin, 1952), pp. 138–39, since published under the same title by the University of Georgia Press.

[25] See Benjamin Franklin's memorandum entered on the back of a letter from himself to Thomas Walpole, London, 12 January 1774, Harkness Collection, NYPL. The rough draft of this letter is in Franklin Papers, 2d series, Miscellaneous Manuscripts, X, 2307, LC.

[26] Benjamin Franklin to Thomas Cushing, London, 15 February 1774, Smyth, *Writings*, VI, 186.

[27] Benjamin Franklin to Thomas Cushing, London, 15 February 1774, Smyth, *Writings*, VI, 190–91.

[28] Smyth, *Writings*, X, 270.

[29] Benjamin Franklin to Thomas Cushing, London, 30 June 1774, XLV, 85 APSL.

[30] Samuel Wharton to George Croghan, London, 4 May 1774, Croghan Papers, Letters W, HSP.

[31] Benjamin Franklin to Thomas Cushing, London, 25 July 1774, Crane, *Franklin's Letters to the Press*, p. 265.

[32] Benjamin Franklin to Joseph Galloway, London, 25 February 1775, Smyth, *Writings*, VI, 313.

[33] Samuel Wharton to Thomas Wharton, London, 31 January 1775, Thomas Wharton Manuscripts, Wharton Papers, HSP.

[34] Benjamin Franklin to William Franklin, London, 7 September 1774, XLV, 91 APSL.

[35] Thomas Wharton to George Croghan, Philadelphia, 23 August 1774, "Selections from the Letter-books of Thomas Wharton," 444–48, HSP; same to Samuel Wharton, Philadelphia, 23 September 1774, *ibid.*, 448–51.

[36] George Croghan to Thomas Wharton, 1774, "Letters of Colonel George Croghan," *PMHB, XV* (October 1891), 431.

[37] Samuel Wharton to George Croghan, London, 17 April 1775, Croghan Papers, Letters W, HSP.

[38] Samuel Wharton to Thomas Wharton, London, 31 January 1775, Thomas Wharton MSS, Wharton Papers, HSP.

[39] Samuel Wharton to Benjamin Franklin, Portsmouth, 17 April 1775, IV, 50 APSL.

40 Samuel Wharton to Joseph Wharton, Sr., London, 7 August 1775, Thomas Wharton MSS, Wharton Papers, HSP.

41 George Morgan to W[illiam] F[ranklin] for B[enjamin] F[ranklin], Philadelphia, 8 August 1775, IV, 62 APSL.

42 Quoted by William Franklin to Benjamin Franklin, Perth Amboy, 14 August 1775, IV, 66 APSL.

43 Ibid.

44 Resolution, ca. 1775, L (ii), 52 APSL.

CHAPTER FOUR

1 G. S. Greene and L. B. Clarke, *The Greenes of Rhode Island* (New York, 1903), pp. 169–70.

2 Edmund Cody Burnett, *The Continental Congress* (New York, 1964), pp. 118–19.

3 Worthington Chauncey Ford, ed., *Journals of the Continental Congress* (34 vols., Washington, 1904), VI, 1067; IX, 1077. See also Burnett, *Continental Congress*, pp. 118–19.

4 Edmund Cody Burnett, ed., *Letters of Members of the Continental Congress* (8 vols., Gloucester, Mass., 1963), I, 265–66. Hereafter cited as Burnett, *Letters*.

5 *Ibid.,* I, 274.

6 Pontleroy's report of his journey through New England and the middle colonies is located in Archives des Affaires Étrangères, Correspondences Politiques, Angleterre, vol. 471, ff. 7–9; 124–25. Hereafter cited as Arch. Aff. Étr. For reports of other spies see also vols. 450, ff. 392, 410; vol. 451, ff. 23, 115, 140, 218; and vols. 474, 475 *passim*.

7 This report may be seen in *Lettres inédites du général de La Fayette au vicomte de Noailles, écrites des camps de l'armée américaine durant la guerre de l'indépendance des États-Unis* (Paris, 1924).

8 Friedrich Kapp, *Life of John Kalb* (New York, 1870), p. 63. See also Frank Monaghan, *French Travellers in the United States, 1765–1932* (New York, 1961). For Kalb's instructions see Bibliothèque Nationale, MSS Français, Nouvelles Acquisitions, no. 9435, ff. 352–53. For his report, see *ibid.,* ff. 365–78.

9 The quotation is translated from Henri Doniol, ed., *Histoire de la participation de la France à l'établissement des Etats-Unis d'Amérique* (Paris, 1884–1892), I, 377 (hereafter cited as Doniol). See also Arch. Aff. Étr., vol. 313, no. 45. Also see Doniol, I, 267–69; Samuel Flagg Bemis, *The Diplomacy of the American Revolution* (Bloomington, 1961), pp. 22–23; Charlemagne Tower, Jr., *The Marquis de La Fayette in the American Revolution with some Account of the Attitude of France Toward the War of Independence* (2 vols., Philadelphia, 1895), I, 82ff.

10 Doniol, I, 377; William Graham Sumner, *The Financier and the Finances of the American Revolution* (2 vols., New York, 1891), I, 157.

11 Peter Force, ed., *American Archives: Consisting of a Collection of Au-

thentick Records, State Papers, Debates and Letters and Other Notices of Public Affairs, the Whole Forming a Documentary History of the Origin and Progress of the North American Colonies; of the Causes and Accomplishments of the American Revolution; and of the Constitution of the Government of the United States to the Final Ratification Thereof (9 vols., Washington, 1837–1853) 4th series, IV, 261–62; VI, 771–82. Cited hereafter as Force, American Archives.

[12] Ibid., 4th series, VI, 771–82.

[13] Deane Papers, V, 412–13.

[14] Sumner, The Financier, I, 174–75.

[15] Worthington Chauncey Ford, ed., The Letters of William Lee (3 vols., Brooklyn, 1891) I, 234–35. Hereafter cited as Ford, Letters of Lee.

[16] Francis Wharton, ed., The Revolutionary Diplomatic Correspondence of the United States (6 vols., Washington, 1889), II, 268. (Hereafter cited as Wharton, Revolutionary Diplomatic Correspondence.) In my account of this French trading firm, I have been aided by the efforts of one of my students, Jack Allen, "Emanuel de Pliarne" (unpublished seminar paper, 1969, University of South Florida).

[17] Adams, Works, II, 5.

[18] Ibid., III, 3–4.

[19] Wharton, Revolutionary Diplomatic Correspondence, I, 5–9, and Committee of Secret Correspondence to Silas Deane, Philadelphia, 3 March 1776, in Connecticut Historical Society Collections (Hartford, 1870), II, 367–68.

[20] Quoted by Samuel Wharton to George Croghan, London, 4 September 1770, Croghan Papers, Letters W, HSP.

[21] Quoted by Burnett, Continental Congress, p. 113. See also the interesting account by William Renwick Riddell, "Benjamin Franklin's Mission to Canada and the Causes of its Failure," PMHB, XLVIII (1924), 111–58.

[22] Smyth, Writings, VI, 454. Italics added.

[23] Benjamin Franklin to Lord Richard Howe, Philadelphia, 30 July 1776, Smyth, Writings, VI, 458–62.

[24] Adams, Works, III, 75–76.

[25] Benjamin Franklin to Arthur Lee, Paris, 21 March 1777, Smyth, Writings, VII, 31–35.

[26] Lee, Lee, I, 354.

[27] "Excerpts from the Papers of Dr. Benjamin Rush," PMHB, XXIX (1905), 29.

[28] Notice of both the September election and the special October session soon reached the British Secret Service. See the letters giving the details in Auckland Papers, 16 and 22 October 1776, BM Add MSS 34,413, ff. 169, 173.

[29] William S. Stryker, ed., "Extracts from American Newspapers, 1776–1777," Documents Relating to the Revolutionary History of the State of New Jersey (3 vols., Trenton, 1901), I, 532.

[30] Roger Burlingame, *Benjamin Franklin: Envoy Extraordinary* (New York, 1967), p. 137.

[31] Ambrose Serle to the Earl of Dartmouth, New York, 3 December 1776, in Benjamin Franklin Stevens, comp., *Facsimiles of Manuscripts in European Archives Relating to America, 1773–1783* (25 vols., London, 1889–1898). These volumes are not paginated, but include consecutively numbered facsimile documents. This is number 2048. Hereafter this will be cited as Stevens, *Facsimiles*, followed by the document number.

[32] Edward E. Hale and Edward E. Hale, Jr., *Franklin in France* (2 vols., Boston, 1888), I, 67. Hereafter cited as Hale, *Franklin*. I have been aided in some portions of this account of Franklin's preparations to leave America by the efforts of a former student, Ernest Guthrie, "Why They Were Chosen" (unpublished seminar paper, University of South Florida, 1970).

CHAPTER FIVE

[1] George Bancroft, *History of the United States* (1866 ed.), IX, 286, quoted in Claude H. Van Tyne, "Influences which Determined the French Government to Make the Treaty With America in 1778," *American Historical Review*, XXI (1916), 531.

[2] For a part of this tale, see the very interesting work by Francis Paul Renaut, *L'espionnage naval au XVIIIᵉ siècle* (Paris, 1936).

[3] Ralph Izard to Henry Laurens, Paris, 6 October 1777, in Anne Izard Deas, comp., *Correspondence of Mr. Ralph Izard of South Carolina from the Year 1774 to 1804 With a Short Memoir* (New York, 1844), p. 353.

[4] "Account of the Money issued for His Majesty's Secret and Special Service," Stevens, *Facsimiles*, 2024.

[5] "Report of E. Smith," 3 March 1777, Auckland Papers, BM Add MSS 34,413, f. 294; John Vardill to William Eden, 19 March 1777, in *ibid.*, 34,413, f. 326.

[6] See Charles R. Ritcheson, *British Politics and the American Revolution* (Norman, 1954), p. 234.

[7] One of the early works on Eden, by a descendant, was published as *The Journal and Correspondence of William, Lord Auckland* (4 vols., London, 1861–1862). Perhaps ashamed of Eden's work with the Secret Service, the editor saw fit to ignore completely this important aspect of his ancestor's life. For information on Eden's activities, consult Auckland Papers, BM Add MSS 34,412; 34,413; 34,414; and 34,415. For background, see Alan Valentine, *Lord North* (2 vols., Norman, 1967). A recent and very adequate study is Alan S. Brown, "William Eden and the American Revolution" (Ph.D. thesis, The University of Michigan, 1953).

[8] William Eden to Lord North, August, 1775, Stevens, *Facsimiles*, 456.

[9] Anthony Todd to William Eden, 27 October 1777, Auckland Papers, BM Add MSS 34,414, f. 265.

[10] Paul Wentworth to William Eden, 12 December 1777, 1 and 4 January 1778, 3 April 1778, Stevens, *Facsimiles*, 315, 328, 768, 343.

[11] Edward Bancroft to Joseph Priestly, 8 May 1790, *Deane Papers*, V, 534.

[12] Edward Bancroft, *An Essay on the Natural History of Guiana in South America, Containing a Description of Many Curious Productions in the Animal and Vegetable Systems of that Country, together with an Account of the Religion, Manners and Customs of Several Tribes of its Indian Inhabitants, Interspersed with a Variety of Literary and Medical Observations in Several Letters from a Gentleman of the Medical Faculty during his Residence in that Country* (London, 1769).

[13] Thomas Perkins Abernethy, *Western Lands and the American Revolution* (New York, 1959 [1st ed., 1937]), pp. 143–44.

[14] Wharton, *Revolutionary Diplomatic Correspondence*, I, 640. Italics added.

[15] *Ibid.*, I, 640–41.

[16] Bancroft, *History of the United States*, X, 62, 64, was perhaps the earliest to hint at Bancroft's spy activities. After the publication of the Stevens, *Facsimiles*, Paul Leicester Ford, in his *Edward Bancroft's Narrative of the Objects and Proceedings of Silas Deane, as Commissioner of the United Colonies to France; made to the British Government in 1776* (Brooklyn, 1891), was the first to pinpoint the man's dual role.

[17] Edward Bancroft, "Memorial to the Marquis of Carmarthen, Foreign Secretary in 1784, written 17 September 1784," PRO: Foreign Office 4: 3. The complete text of this memorial is included as Appendix A of this book.

[18] The complete text of his instructions covered much. He was to report to London:

> The progress of the Treaty with France, and of the assistance expected, or commerce carryed on or in any of the ports of that Kingdom.
> The same with Spain, and of every other Court in Europe.
> The agents in the foreign islands in America and the means of carrying on the Commerce with the Northern Colonys.
> The means of obtaining credit—effects and money; and the channells and agents used to supply them; the secret moves about the Courts of France and Spain, and the Congress agents, and tracing the lines from one to the other.
> Franklin's and Deane's correspondence with the Congress, and their agents; and the secret, as well as the ostensible letters from the Congress to them. Copys of any transactions, committed to papers, and an exact account of all intercourse and the subject matter treated of, between the Courts of Versailles and Madrid, and the agents from Congress.

To the British ambassador in France, Lord Stormont, Bancroft was to report:

> Names of the two Carolina ships, masters both English and French, description of the ships, and cargoes; the time of sailing, and the port bound to.

The same circumstances respecting all equipments in any port in Europe together with the names of the agents imployed.

The intelligence that may arrive from America, the captures made by their privateers, and the instructions they receive from the deputys. How the captures are disposed of.

[19] "Engagement of Dr. Edwards to correspond with P. Wentworth and Lord Stormont, and the means of conducting that Correspondence," 13 December 1776, Auckland Papers, BM Add MSS 34,413, f. 107.

[20] Robert Morris to Silas Deane, 20 December 1776, with postscript dated 8 January 1777, *ibid.*, f. 111.

[21] Memorandum, 26–28 September 1776, *ibid.*, f. 169.

[22] Auckland Papers, BM Add MSS 34,413, f. 171.

[23] *Ibid.*, f. 173.

[24] *Ibid.*, ff. 34, 174–88, 189, 318–22, 330, and 415.

[25] Burnett, *Letters*, I, 274.

[26] Works on Beaumarchais are legion. For further reading see Paul Frischauer, *Beaumarchais* (New York, 1935); Louis de Loménie, *Beaumarchais and His Times* (New York, 1857); Georges Lemaître, *Beaumarchais* (New York, 1949); René Dalsème, *Beaumarchais* (New York, 1949); René Pomeau, *Beaumarchais* (Paris, 1962); Elizabeth Kite, *Beaumarchais and the War of American Independence* (2 vols., Boston, 1918); and, for an older work, Michel Frérés, "Life and Character of Beaumarchais," *North American Review*, LXXXIV (January 1857), 132–42.

[27] See Claude H. Van Tyne, "French Aid before the Alliance of 1778," *American Historical Review*, XXXI (October 1925), especially 37–40, and John J. Meng, "A Footnote to Secret Aid in the American Revolution," *American Historical Review*, XLIII (July 1938), 791–95.

[28] Beaumarchais was so deeply influenced by Lee that he has been described, by Doniol, as "séduit" (seduced) by Lee. Beaumarchais often referred to Lee in his correspondence, calling him "le sieur L."

[29] Beaumarchais to Vergennes, Paris, 23 September 1775, Loménie, *Beaumarchais and His Times*, p. 266. Doniol stated that this first message was so foolish as not to be worth reprinting.

[30] The notes of 7 December 1775 and 29 February 1776 were sent to the king through Vergennes. They are reprinted in full in Kite, *Beaumarchais and the War of American Independence*, II, 21–90.

[31] For one view of the origin of this aid see Edward S. Corwin, "The French Object in the American Revolution," *American Historical Review*, XXI (1916), 33–61.

[32] Orlando Stephenson, "The Supply of Gunpowder in 1776," *American Historical Review*, XXX (January 1925), 280.

[33] For the agreement of Lee and Beaumarchais to send supplies to America, see Arthur Lee to Committee of Foreign Affairs, 6 October 1777, Auckland Papers, printed in Stevens, *Facsimiles*, 271; Lee, *Lee*, I, 54–55; Jacques Barbeu-Dubourg to Benjamin Franklin, 20 June 1776, in Force, *American Archives*, 4th series, VI, 771–82; and Lyon G. Tyler, "Arthur

Lee, A Neglected Statesman," *Tyler's Quarterly Historical and Genealogical Magazine*, XIV (April 1933), 198–216.

[34] Loménie, *Beaumarchais and His Times*, p. 273.

[35] See Wharton, *Revolutionary Diplomatic Correspondence*, II, 97–98. A lengthy quarrel ensued with Beaumarchais billing Congress for the supplies shipped to America while Arthur Lee contended that the original arrangements called for French aid to be free. For Lee's view see Auckland Papers, BM Add MSS 34,414, f. 223v.

[36] Edward Bancroft to Silas Deane, 25 June 1776, *Deane Papers*, I, 143.

[37] Julian P. Boyd, "Silas Deane," *William and Mary Quarterly*, XVI (July 1959), 186–87n.

[38] Arthur Lee to Silas Deane, London, 28 July 1776, Stevens, *Facsimiles*, 467.

[39] Silas Deane to Vergennes, 22 August 1776, Force, *American Archives*, 5th series, I, 1105.

[40] Deane to Gerard, 22 August 1776, *Deane Papers*, I, 221–22.

[41] Julian P. Boyd comes to the same conclusion in his "Silas Deane," pp. 186–87.

[42] Silas Deane to the Committee of Secret Correspondence, 18 August 1776, *Deane Papers*, I, 195–218; "Narrative &c. Dr. Bancroft's Information of Silas Deane's Mission to the French Court and his first Proceedings there," 14 August 1776, Public Record Office, America and the West Indies, vol. 448, f. 257. Hereafter cited as PRO.

[43] Silas Deane to John Jay, Paris, 3 December 1776, Wharton, *Revolutionary Diplomatic Correspondence*, II, 212–16.

[44] Thomas Perkins Abernethy, "The Origin of the Franklin-Lee Imbroglio," *The North Carolina Historical Review*, XV (January 1938), 42.

[45] Sydney George Fisher, *The True Benjamin Franklin* (Philadelphia, 1906), p. 298.

[46] William Lee to Samuel Thorpe, Bruxelles, 17 January 1783, in Ford, *Letters of Lee*, III, 915–16.

[47] Julian P. Boyd, ed., *The Papers of Thomas Jefferson* (17 vols., Princeton, 1950–to date), XII, 13.

[48] Boyd, "Silas Deane," 321n.

[49] Beaumarchais to Aranda, Paris, 10 October 1776, in J. F. Yela Utrilla, *España ante la independencia de los Estados Unidos* (2 vols., Lerida, 1925), I, 99–108. See also II, 7–21.

[50] See C. J. Stillé, "Beaumarchais and the Lost Million," *PMHB*, XI (1887), 1–36; Wharton, *Revolutionary Diplomatic Correspondence*, I, 371–86; Loménie, *Beaumarchais and His Times*, chapter XIX; and Kite, *Beaumarchais and the War of American Independence*, II, 184–212.

[51] Burton J. Hendricks, *The Lees of Virginia: a biography of a family* (Boston, 1935), 299.

[52] Paul Wentworth to the Earl of Suffolk, 23 November 1776, Stevens, *Facsimiles*, 131. See also Deane to Morris, 11 April 1777, Robert Morris MSS, LC.

53 Quoted in Hendricks, *Lees of Virginia*, 309.

54 Quoted in *ibid.*, 310.

55 See Beaumarchais to Committee of Secret Correspondence, 18 August 1776, Force, *American Archives*, 5th Series, I, 1021–23.

56 Robert Morris to Silas Deane, Philadelphia, 27 February 1777, *Deane Papers*, II, 14.

57 Hendricks, *Lees of Virginia*, 311.

58 Brissot de Warville, *New Travels in the United States, 1788* (London, 1794), p. 387.

59 Abernethy, *Western Lands and the American Revolution*, p. 173.

60 Lord North to George III, 30 January 1778, Fortescue, IV, 2181.

61 Deane, we know, used the cover name "Benson" at least as early as May 1777. At that time another of Eden's spies looked through Deane's closets and found there some letters addressed to him as "Benson." See Arch. Aff. Étr., États-Unis, vol. 410, f. 16; Paul Wentworth to Earl of Suffolk, 16 November 1777, Stevens, *Facsimiles*, 218. See also *ibid.*, 162.

62 See for example, the copy of Samuel Wharton to Silas Deane, London, 21 [24?] February 1778, Official Correspondence, American Affairs, 1777–1781, BM Add MSS 24,321, f. 6.

63 Samuel Wharton to Silas Deane (copy), 13 March 1778, Official Correspondence, American Affairs, 1777–1781, BM Add MSS 24,321, f. 10.

64 See Wharton to "Benson" (copy), London, 21 April 1778, and 28 April 1778, Official Correspondence, American Affairs, 1777–1781, BM Add MSS, 24,321, ff. 12 and 14. In this section of the records, half of each folio, vertically, has been destroyed, making it extremely difficult to decipher the writing and the intent of the sentences.

65 George III to Lord North, 2 and 3 February 1778, in John Fortescue (ed.), *The Correspondence of King George the Third, from 1760 to December 1783, Printed from the Original Papers in the Royal Archives at Windsor Castle* (6 vols., London, 1927), IV, no. 2186. Hereafter cited as Fortescue, followed by the document number.

CHAPTER SIX

1 Carl Van Doren, *Secret History of the American Revolution* (New York, 1941), p. 61.

2 Richard B. Morris, *The Peacemakers: The Great Powers and American Independence* (New York, 1965), p. 133.

3 Bigelow, *Complete Works*, VI, 58.

4 *Ibid.*, pp. 358–59.

5 *Ibid.*, p. 360.

6 Arch. Aff. Étr., Angleterre, 9 November 1774, vol. 507, no. 84 and vol. 511, no. 29.

7 Benjamin Franklin to Ralph Izard, Passy, 29 January 1778, Bigelow, *Complete Works*, VII, 244.

8 Benjamin Franklin to Silas Deane, Nantes, 7 December 1776, Misc. MSS, APSL, and *Deane Papers*, I, 411–12.

⁹ Lord Stormont dutifully reported his arrival. See Lord Stormont to [?], Paris, 20 December 1776, Hardwicke Papers, BM Add MSS 35,511, f. 124.

¹⁰ Juliana Ritchie to Benjamin Franklin, Paris, 12 January 1777, V, 13½ APSL.

¹¹ Benjamin Franklin to Juliana Ritchie, Paris, 19 January 1777, XLV, 112 APSL.

¹² William Alexander to Benjamin Franklin, Dijon, 1 March 1777, V, 82 APSL.

¹³ *Autobiography*, pp. 149–50.

¹⁴ As quoted by Roger Burlingame, *Benjamin Franklin: Envoy Extraordinary* (New York, 1967), p. 141.

¹⁵ Bemis, "British Secret Service." See also "Information obtained by Lt. Col. Smith during the six weeks of his intercourse with Capt. Hynson, in February and March, 1777," 27–28 March 1777, Stevens, *Facsimiles*, 610.

¹⁶ He used the pseudonym of "William Bolton." See William Bolton to Jerro. Bently, 29 October 1777, Stevens, *Facsimiles*, 282, and William Bolton to Jean Tourville, Paris, 1 November 1777, *ibid.*, 288.

¹⁷ George Lupton to William Eden, Paris, 28 January 1778, Auckland Papers, BM Add MSS 34,415, f. 90.

¹⁸ George Lupton to William Eden, Paris, 27 June 1777, *ibid.*, 34,414, f. 25.

¹⁹ Paul Wentworth to William Eden, Paris, 1 January 1778, *ibid.*, 34,415, 141.

²⁰ Benjamin Franklin to Aruthur Lee, 21 March 1777, Passy, Smyth, *Writings*, VII, 35.

²¹ "Conference with Franklin," Paris, 15 March 1779, notes by William Lee in Ford, *Letters of Lee*, II, 537.

²² American Commissioners to Vergennes, Paris, 23 December 1776, Smyth, *Writings*, VI, 477.

²³ Gérard to Deputies, Versailles, 6 January 1777, XLVII, 70 APSL.

²⁴ BF to Bernard, Frères & Co., Paris, 20 December 1776, IV, 128 APSL.

²⁵ Stormont to Ld Weymouth, Paris, 15 January 1777, PRO: FO, France, vol. 547; same to same, Paris, 2 April 1777, *ibid.*, vol. 548; and same to same, Paris, 12 November 1777, *ibid.*, vol. 551.

²⁶ Silas Deane to Committee of Secret Correspondence, 1 December 1776, Wharton, *Revolutionary Diplomatic Correspondence*, II, 203–10.

²⁷ Edward Bancroft to Benjamin Franklin, 14 September 1778, in Lee MSS, Harvard University Library, quoted in Thomas Perkins Abernethy, "The Commercial Activities of Silas Deane in France," *American Historical Review*, XXXIX (April, 1934), 482.

²⁸ The Commissioners were to contact such courts as Spain, Portugal, Berlin, Tuscany, and so forth. See Congressional instructions, 16 October 1776, Auckland Papers, BM Add MSS 34,413, ff. 171, 174–88, and *passim*.

²⁹ Sparks, *Works*, VIII, 206n.

³⁰ Benjamin Franklin to Arthur Lee, Passy, 21 March 1777, Sparks, *Works*, VIII, 206–7.

³¹ Arthur Lee to Floridablanca, 17 March 1777, Wharton, *Revolutionary Diplomatic Correspondence*, II, 290–91.

³² Arthur Lee to Benjamin Franklin and Silas Deane, Vitoria, 12 March 1777, V, 106 APSL.

³³ Quoted by William Bell Clarke, *Lambert Wickes, Sea Raider and Diplomat: The Story of a Naval Captain of the Revolution* (New Haven, 1932), p. 161.

³⁴ "Report of what is rep'd respecting Hynson," 4 March 1777, Auckland Papers, BM Add MSS 34,413, f. 299.

³⁵ Joseph Hynson to William Eden, 11 February 1777, *ibid.*, f. 207.

³⁶ Samuel Nicholson to Joseph Hynson, 9 February 1777, *ibid.*, f. 198.

³⁷ Joseph Hynson to John Vardill, 11 February 1777, Auckland Papers, BM Add MSS 34,413, f. 204.

³⁸ Joseph Hynson to Isabella Cleghorn, 6 February 1777, and her reply, 13 February 1777, *ibid.*, f. 197 and v; ff. 213–14.

³⁹ Elizabeth Jamp to Joseph Hynson, 12 February 1777, *ibid.*, f. 209.

⁴⁰ Joseph Hynson to Robert and Elizabeth Jamp, 14 February 1777, Auckland Papers, BM Add MSS 34,413, ff. 214, 219.

⁴¹ John Walcot to Anthony Todd, 15 February 1777, *ibid.*, f. 224.

⁴² Joseph Hynson to Col. Smith, 17 February 1777, *ibid.*, f. 231, and "Report of what is rep'd respecting Hynson," 4 March 1777, *ibid.*, f. 299.

⁴³ Sam Nicholson to Joseph Hynson, 17 February 1777, *ibid.*, f. 233.

⁴⁴ Isabella Cleghorn to Joseph Hynson, 13 February 1777, *ibid.*, f. 213.

⁴⁵ Edward Smith to [?], 20 February 1777, *ibid.*, f. 238.

⁴⁶ Edward Smith to John Vardill, 23 February 1777, *ibid.*, f. 244.

⁴⁷ Sam Nicholson to Joseph Hynson, 28 February 1777, Auckland Papers, BM Add MSS 34,413, f. 278.

⁴⁸ Joseph Hynson to Isabella Cleghorn, 28 February 1777, *ibid.*, f. 274.

⁴⁹ Andrew Limozin to Arthur Lee, Le Havre de Grace, 18 April 1778, *Deane Papers*, II, 458–60.

⁵⁰ "Report of E. Smith," 3 March 1777, Auckland Papers, BM Add MSS 34,413, f. 294.

⁵¹ John Vardill to William Eden, 19 March 1777, Auckland Papers, BM Add MSS 34,413, f. 326.

⁵² Hugh Elliot to the Earl of Suffolk, 10 June 1777, PRO: FO, Prussia, vol. 128.

⁵³ See letters of Joseph Hynson to Edward Smith, 28 March, 3 April, and late April 1777, Auckland Papers, BM Add MSS 34,413, ff. 332, 382, 482.

⁵⁴ Clarke, *Lambert Wickes*, p. 182.

⁵⁵ William Carmichael to C. W. F. Dumas, 28 April 1777, Wharton. *Revolutionary Diplomatic Correspondence*, II, 308–09.

⁵⁶ "Information obtained by Lt. Col. Smith during the six weeks of his intercourse with Capt. Hynson, in February and March, 1777," 28 March 1777, Auckland Papers, BM Add MSS 34,413, ff. 341–59.

[57] PRO: FO, France, vol. 550, and Stevens, *Facsimiles*, 471, and see Clarke, *Lambert Wickes*, p. 163.

[58] John Vardill to William Eden, 6 April 1777, Auckland Papers, BM Add MSS 34,413, f. 386, and Lord Stormont to William Eden, 16 April 1777, *ibid.*, f. 401.

[59] Diary entry, Lee, *Lee*, I, 366–67.

[60] Carlting was but one of the many cover names under which Wentworth received messages from his field agents. Other aliases he used were William Duncan, William Gordon, John Gibson, Robert Montgomery, Pierre Richard, Louis Chaurette, Georges Simone, Fred Samson, William Simpson, Alexander Selkirk, Jean de Trouville, Robert Alexander, and many more. "Names by which Mr. P. W. receives Letters," Auckland Papers, BM Add MSS 34,414, f. 551.

[61] P. Le Maître [William Carmichael] to George Carlting [Paul Wentworth], 24 April 1777, Miscellaneous American Papers, BM Add MSS 24,322, f. 20. Italics added.

[62] Edward Bancroft to Paul Wentworth, Paris, 24 April 1777, Auckland Papers, BM Add MSS 34,413, f. 402. The document is dated only "24 April" and someone later added the year "1778." This was clearly a mistake, for the endorsement added at the time of its receipt reads "copy of two letters from Dr B to Mr W., Paris, 24 April 1777."

[63] This story is summarized in Ford, *Letters of Lee*, I, 213–14n. Also see wrapper for papers received from Elliot at Berlin, 10 July 1777, Stevens, *Facsimiles*, 1481; "Narrative of the Abstraction of Arthur Lee's papers at Berlin," 11 July 1777, Stevens, *Facsimiles*, 1468; the list of Lee's papers, 11 July 1777, Stevens, *Facsimiles*, 1469. Note also PRO: FO, Prussia, vol. 128.

[64] Abernethy, "Commercial Activities of Deane," p. 483.

[65] Charles Thomson to Silas Deane, Philadelphia, 26–28 September 1776, Auckland Papers, BM Add MSS 34,413, f. 169.

[66] Silas Deane to President of Congress, 20 May 1777, *Deane Papers*, II, 365–67.

[67] Silas Deane and Benjamin Franklin to the Committee of Secret Correspondence, 4 May 1777, Wharton, *Revolutionary Diplomatic Correspondence*, II, 277.

[68] Silas Deane to John Hancock, 20 May 1777, Auckland Papers, BM Add MSS 34,413, f. 462.

[69] George Lupton to William Eden, 28 May 1777, Auckland Papers, BM Add MSS 34,413, f. 472.

[70] John Vardill to William Eden, 29 May 1777, *ibid.*, f. 475.

[71] Silas Deane to Joseph Hynson, *ibid.*, f. 4. See also same to same, 28 June 1777, in *ibid.*, f. 29.

[72] Silas Deane to Joseph Hynson, 10 September 1777, *ibid.*, f. 149.

[73] *Deane Papers*, V. 307–08.

[74] Silas Deane to Joseph Hynson, 10 September 1777, Auckland Papers, BM Add MSS 34,413, f. 149.

⁷⁵ William Carmichael to Joseph Hynson, 19 September 1777, and Simeone Deane to Joseph Hynson, 21 September 1777 in *ibid.*, ff. 160, 172; Silas Deane to Joseph Hynson, 27 September 1777, *ibid.*, f. 193.

⁷⁶ Silas Deane to Jonathan Williams, Jr., 19 October 1777, *Deane Papers*, II, 196.

⁷⁷ Silas Deane to Joseph Hynson and John Folger, 7 October 1777, *Deane Papers*, II, 174–77.

⁷⁸ William Carmichael to Joseph Hynson, undated, Auckland Papers, BM Add MSS 34,414, f. 20.

⁷⁹ Auckland Papers, BM Add MSS 34,414, ff. 230, 231, 210.

⁸⁰ Report by William Eden, 20 October 1777, *ibid.*, f. 239.

⁸¹ Silas Deane to Jonathan Williams, Jr., 24 October 1777, *Deane Papers*, II, 199. Italics added.

⁸² Silas Deane to Joseph Hynson, 26 October 1777, Auckland Papers, BM Add MSS 34,414, f. 261.

⁸³ "First Intelligence respecting Benson's journey to Dover," in Auckland Papers, BM Add MSS 34,414, f. 556.

⁸⁴ Joseph Hynson to Nicholas Noel [Edward Smith], Paris, 23 November 1777, *ibid.*, ff. 383 and same to same, 25 November 1777, *ibid.*, ff. 385–87. Italics added.

⁸⁵ Joseph Hynson to Col. Edward Smith, 17 December 1777, *ibid.*, f. 380ff.

⁸⁶ Joseph Hynson to Edward Smith, 10 December 1777, Auckland Papers, BM Add MSS 34,414, ff. 406–07.

⁸⁷ William Bolton [William Carmichael] to M. Jean Trouville [Paul Wentworth], Paris, 1 November 1777, *ibid.*, f. 300.

⁸⁸ Memo by William Eden, December 1777, Stevens, *Facsimiles*, 312. For the foregoing account of the Hynson affair, I am greatly indebted to and have drawn heavily from the scholarly work of one of my students, Michael P. Pfeifer, "John Vardill and Joseph Hynson: Spy Activities in 1777" (unpublished M. A. paper, University of South Florida, 1970).

⁸⁹ *Deane Papers*, III, 369–70. Italics added.

⁹⁰ Quoted in Clarke, *Silas Deane*, 149–50.

⁹¹ William Lee to Arthur Lee, Frankfurt sur le Main, 30 April 1778, Ford, *Letters of Lee*, II, 425–26.

CHAPTER SEVEN

¹ George Lupton to William Eden, Paris, 27 June 1777, Auckland Papers, BM Add MSS 34,414, f. 27.

² Thomas Walpole to Ben Franklin, London, 1 February 1777, V, 47 APSL.

³ Thomas Walpole to Ben Franklin, London, 10 February 1777, V, 53 APSL.

⁴ Thomas Walpole to Ben Franklin, London, 5 March 1777, V, 91 APSL.

[5] Edward Bancroft to Benjamin Franklin, 4 March 1777, V, 89 APSL.

[6] Ralph Izard to Henry Laurens, Paris, 6 October 1777, in Anne Izard Deas, comp., *Correspondence of Mr. Ralph Izard of South Carolina from the Year 1774 to 1804 With a Short Memoir* (New York, 1844), p. 353.

[7] Paul Wentworth to Silas Deane, Paris, 12 December 1777, Auckland Papers, BM Add MSS 34,414, f. 529.

[8] Quoted by Roger Burlingame, *Benjamin Franklin: Envoy Extraordinary* (New York, 1967), pp. 138–39 and Alfred O. Aldridge, *Benjamin Franklin, Philosopher and Man* (Philadelphia, 1965), 277.

[9] See, for example, "Port News," Auckland Papers, BM Add MSS 34,414, f. 291.

[10] See Martin Gaston, "Commercial Relations between Nantes and the American Colonies," *Journal of Economic and Business History*, IV (August, 1932).

[11] Abernethy, "Commercial Activities of Deane," 479.

[12] Robert Morris to Silas Deane, Philadelphia, 31 January 1777, quoted in Thomas Perkins Abernethy, "The Origin of the Franklin-Lee Imbroglio," *The North Carolina Historical Review*, XV (January 1938), 43.

[13] *Ibid.*, p. 45.

[14] Sydney George Fisher, *The True Benjamin Franklin* (Philadelphia, 1906), pp. 293–94.

[15] Robert Morris to Silas Deane, Philadelphia, 29 June 1777, *Deane Papers*, II, 77.

[16] Fisher, *The True Benjamin Franklin*, p. 289. Italics added.

[17] Helen Augur, *The Secret War of Independence* (New York, 1955), p. 198.

[18] Abernethy, "The Origin of the Franklin-Lee Imbroglio," pp. 43–44.

[19] Fisher, *The True Benjamin Franklin*, p. 294.

[20] Benjamin Franklin to Jonathan Williams, Jr., Paris, 22 December 1777, *Deane Papers*, II, 282. Italics added.

[21] William Lee to Benjamin Franklin, 25 August 1777, XLIV, 17 APSL.

[22] George Lupton to William Eden, Paris, 17 July 1777, Auckland Papers, BM Add MSS 34,414, f. 56.

[23] Abernethy, "The Origin of the Franklin-Lee Imbroglio," p. 47.

[24] Benjamin Franklin to Jonathan Williams, Jr., Paris, February [?] 1778, Smyth, *Writings*, VII, 113.

[25] William Lee to Francis Lightfoot Lee, Nantes, 9 August 1777, *Deane Papers*, II, 98.

[26] Abernethy, "The Origin of the Franklin-Lee Imbroglio," p. 47.

[27] *Ibid.*, pp. 47–48.

[28] William Lee to Francis Lightfoot Lee, 11 November 1777, *Deane Papers*, II, 218.

[29] William Lee to Richard Henry Lee, Frankfurt, 15 October 1778, Ford, *Letters of Lee*, II, 493.

[30] William Lee to Benjamin Franklin, 13 March 1778, *ibid.*, pp. 397–98.

[31] Arthur Lee to Sam Adams, 4 October 1777, Auckland Papers, BM Add MSS 34,414, f. 207.

[32] Arthur Lee to Richard Henry Lee, Paris, 4 October 1777, *ibid.*, f. 211.

[33] *Ibid.*

[34] Diary entry for 30 December 1777, Lee, *Lee*, I, 373.

[35] Jonathan Williams, Jr., to Benjamin Franklin, Nantes, 30 October 1777, XXXVII, 117 APSL.

[36] Silas Deane to Benjamin Harrison [?], Paris, 20 December 1777, Stanislaus Vincent Henkels, (catalog) *The Confidential Correspondence of Robert Morris* (Philadelphia, 1917), pp. 66–67.

[37] *Ibid.*, p. 1.

[38] Arthur Lee to Richard Henry Lee, 9 January 1778, quoted in Burton J. Hendricks, *The Lees of Virginia: a biography of a family* (Boston, 1935), p. 308.

[39] Fisher, *The True Benjamin Franklin*, p. 287.

[40] Smyth, *Writings*, V, 550–51.

[41] *Ibid.*, p. 286.

[42] Silas Deane to Jonathan Williams, Jr., Paris, 13 January 1778, *Deane Papers*, II, 327.

[43] Benjamin Franklin to Arthur Lee, Passy, 4 April 1778, Smyth, *Writings*, VII, 132.

[44] Benjamin Franklin to Joseph Reed, Passy, 7 April 1780, *ibid.*, VIII, 44.

[45] Diary entry for 10 April 1778, Adams, *Works*, III, 123.

[46] Silas Deane to President of the Congress, 12 October 1778, Wharton, *Revolutionary Diplomatic Correspondence*, III, 18.

[47] Benjamin Franklin to Samuel Cooper, Passy, 12 December 1780, Hale, *Franklin*, I, 44n.

[48] Undated letter quoted in George Larkin Clark, *Silas Deane: A Connecticut Leader in the American Revolution* (New York, 1913), p. 156.

[49] Arthur Lee to Richard Henry Lee, 15 February 1778, Lee, *Lee*, II, 134–35.

[50] Arthur Lee to Sam Adams, 19 September 1779, *Deane Papers*, IV, 99–100. No other evidence has been found to shed light on Lee's fears that his colleagues wanted him committed.

[51] Arthur Lee to Richard Henry Lee, 15 February 1778, Lee, *Lee*, II, 134–35.

[52] The lack of references is not particularly surprising. Not only did these events happen a long time ago, but, as reported in "The Double-Cross System," *Newsweek*, LXXVIII, 21 (22 November 1971), 58: "Few countries are more zealous in guarding yesterday's secrets than Britain." Even George III caused papers to be destroyed. To North he said at one time: "I send the two letters to shew what a curious correspondent I have got. You will commit them to the Flames." George III to Lord North, 13 June 1778, Fortescue, IV, 2380.

[53] Benjamin Franklin to Thomas Walpole, London, 12 January 1774, Harkness Collection, NYPL. The rough draft of this letter is in Franklin Papers, 2nd ser., Misc., X, 2307, LC.

[54] Letter and note are in the Harkness Collection, NYPL.
[55] Paul Wentworth to William Eden, Paris, 8 January 1778, Auckland Papers, BM Add MSS 34,415, f. 18.
[56] [Lord North] to [William Eden], 29 September 1777, *ibid.*, 34,414, f. 195.
[57] For a signed letter by Lord North compare *ibid.*, f. 209.
[58] Stevens, *Facsimiles*, 234.
[59] Aldridge, *Philosopher and Man*, 301.
[60] Beaumarchais to Vergennes, 8–9 March 1777, Arch. Aff. Étr., Angleterre, vol. 522, f. 47.
[61] *Ibid.*, f. 130.
[62] Auckland Papers, BM Add MSS 34,414, ff. 298–300.
[63] Hendrick, *Lees of Virginia*, p. 285.
[64] Joseph Hynson to Edward Smith, 10 December 1777, Auckland Papers, BM Add MSS 34,414, ff. 406–7.
[65] Julian P. Boyd, "Silas Deane: Death by a Kindly Teacher of Treason," *William & Mary Quarterly*, 3d Series, XVI (July 1959), II, 332n.
[66] For Eden's instructions, see "Minutes arranged with Mr. Wentworth," 6 December 1777, Stevens, *Facsimiles*, 484.
[67] *Ibid.*, 277.

CHAPTER EIGHT

[1] Paul Wentworth to William Eden, Paris, 6 January 1778, Auckland Papers, BM Add MSS 34,415, f. 37.
[2] William Lee to Richard Henry Lee, 4 February 1778, Ford, *Letters of Lee*, II, 355.
[3] Paul Wentworth to Silas Deane, Paris, 12 December 1777, Auckland Papers, BM Add MSS 34,414, f. 529.
[4] *Ibid.*, f. 530.
[5] Paul Wentworth to Silas Deane, Paris, 15 December 1777, *ibid.*, f. 530v.
[6] For information on Wentworth's meeting with Deane, see Paul Wentworth to William Eden, Paris, 17 December 1777, Auckland Papers, BM Add MSS 34,414, ff. 433–42; same to same [undated] *ibid.*, ff. 423–25; same to same, 22 December 1777, *ibid.*, ff. 448–53 and ff. 454–59.
[7] Beaumarchais to Vergennes, 17 December 1777, Arch. Aff. Étr., Angleterre, vol. 526, f. 270.
[8] Deane-Gérard notes, 16 December 1777, *Deane Papers*, II, 273.
[9] See Carl Van Doren, *Benjamin Franklin* (New York, 1952), p. 590; and Claude H. Van Tyne, "Influences Which Determined the French Government to Make the Treaty With America in 1778," *American Historical Review*, XXI (1916), 528–41.
[10] Lee later wrote: "Mr. Deane will not deny that when we were settling the treaty here, he had a private conference, upon matters, unknown to one of your Commissioners at least, with a Mr. Paul Wentworth, the corrupt

and corrupting instrument of Lord Mansfield. I was informed of this some time after, and desired to know of Mr. Deane the subject of this conference, who told me, it was only general professions of wishes to accommodate." Ingraham, *Papers in Relation to Deane*, p. 151n. E. D. Ingraham (ed.), Papers in Relation to the Case of Silas Deane (Philadelphia, 1855), 151n.

¹¹ Paul Wentworth to William Eden, 3d Private Dispatch, 17 December 1777, Paris, Auckland Papers, BM Add MSS 34,414, ff. 433–42.

¹² Lord North to George III, 30 January 1778, Fortescue, 2181.

¹³ Paul Wentworth to William Eden, 22 December 1777, Auckland Papers, BM Add MSS 34,414, ff. 448–59. Italics in original.

¹⁴ *Ibid.*, 25 December 1777, ff. 460–66.

¹⁵ Paul Wentworth to William Eden, Paris, 25 December 1777, Auckland Papers, BM Add MSS 34,414, ff. 463–66.

¹⁶ Diary entry for 22 December 1777, Lee, *Lee*, I, 366.

¹⁷ *Ibid.*

¹⁸ Paul Wentworth to William Eden, Paris, 22 December 1777, Auckland Papers, BM Add MSS 34,414, ff. 448–53.

¹⁹ Digges to Lee, 30 August 1778, quoted by Arthur Lee, *Extracts from a Letter written to the President of Congress . . . in answer to a Libel . . . by Silas Deane* (Philadelphia, 1780), pp. 69–73.

²⁰ Paul Wentworth to William Eden, Paris, 7 January 1778, Auckland Papers, BM Add MSS 34,415, f. 18.

²¹ Paul Wentworth to William Eden, Paris, 8 January 1778, *ibid.*, BM Add MSS 34,415, f. 18.

²² Paul Wentworth to William Eden, 6 January 1778, *ibid.*, BM Add MSS 34,415, f. 40.

²³ Paul Wentworth to William Eden, Paris, 7 January 1778, *ibid.*, f. 47. The following extracts are taken from this source unless otherwise stated.

²⁴ Paul Wentworth to William Eden, Paris, 8 January 1778, Auckland Papers, BM Add MSS 34,415, ff. 18–23.

²⁵ The same might be said for a visit Franklin had at about this time with James Hutton, a Moravian clergyman from England. For further details about this meeting, see chapter nine.

²⁶ Sydney George Fisher, *The True Benjamin Franklin* (Philadelphia, 1906), p. 295.

²⁷ Thomas Perkins Abernethy, "The Origin of the Franklin-Lee Imbroglio," *The North Carolina Historical Review*, XV (January 1938), 49–50.

²⁸ Helen Augur, *The Secret War of Independence* (New York, 1955), pp. 199–200.

²⁹ Arthur Lee to the Committee for Foreign Affairs, 1 June 1778, Wharton, *Revolutionary Diplomatic Correspondence*, II, 600–03.

³⁰ Benjamin Franklin to Whom it may concern, Passy, 8 August 1779, LIV, 55 APSL.

³¹ William Lee to Richard Henry Lee, Frankfurt, 10 February 1779, Ford, *Letters of Lee*, II, 522.

³² William Lee to Committee for Foreign Affairs, Paris, 12 September 1778, *ibid.,* p. 473.

³³ "Conference with Franklin," Paris, 15 March 1779, *ibid.,* p. 537.

³⁴ William Lee to Richard Henry Lee, Paris, 12 September 1778, *ibid.,* pp. 478–79.

³⁵ Thomas Perkins Abernethy, *Western Lands and the American Revolution* (New York, 1959 [1st ed., 1937]), p. 484.

³⁶ Quoted from Julian P. Boyd, "Silas Deane," *William and Mary Quarterly,* XVI (July 1959), 336–37.

³⁷ Abernethy, *Western Lands and the American Revolution,* p. 208. The fact that a copy of this letter was preserved by Franklin may be an indication of who the initial author may have been.

³⁸ Paul Wentworth to William Eden, Paris, 8 January 1778, Auckland Papers, BM Add MSS 34,415, f. 18.

³⁹ Abernethy, *Western Lands and the American Revolution,* p. 208.

⁴⁰ Arthur Lee to Committee for Foreign Affairs, 9 September 1778, Wharton, *Revolutionary Diplomatic Correspondence,* II, 704–05.

CHAPTER NINE

¹ Ralph Izard to Henry Laurens, 16 February 1778, Wharton, *Revolutionary Diplomatic Correspondence,* II, 497–501.

² Ralph Izard to Benjamin Franklin, 17 June 1778, in *ibid.,* 618–26.

³ See Bancroft to Wentworth, 22–28 January 1778, in Stevens, *Facsimiles,* 492; Wentworth, "Intelligence from Mr. Edwards," with outline of treaties of commerce & alliance, dated 6 February, the paper itself dated 4 March 1778, Stevens, *Facsimiles,* 1881.

⁴ Quoted by Paul Wentworth to William Eden, Paris, 8 January 1778, Auckland Papers, BM Add MSS 34,415, f. 18.

⁵ Lee, *Lee,* II, 378, 381.

⁶ *Ibid.,* pp. 124, 162.

⁷ Arthur Lee to Theodoric Bland, 13 December 1778, *Deane Papers,* III, 80.

⁸ See Richard Henry Lee and James Lovell to the American Commissioners, 14 May 1778, Wharton, *Revolutionary Diplomatic Correspondence,* II, 574–75.

⁹ Sydney George Fisher, *The True Benjamin Franklin* (Philadelphia, 1906), p. 303.

¹⁰ See Lyon G. Tyler, "Arthur Lee, A Neglected Statesman," *Tyler's Quarterly Historical and Genealogical Magazine,* XIV, 3 (January 1933), 135–38 for a well stated argument defending Lee's conduct during the war.

¹¹ Ralph Izard to Benjamin Franklin, 17 June 1778, Wharton, *Revolutionary Diplomatic Correspondence,* II, 618–26.

¹² Stormont to [?], 16 March 1778, Hardwicke Papers, BM Add MSS 35,513, f. 168. In October 1779 Stormont succeeded the late Earl of Suffolk as Secretary of State for the Northern Department, thus becoming

part of the chain of command of the Secret Service. Before 1779 he may have taken the place of Eden, for much of the spy correspondence is directed to him after Eden leaves with the Carlisle Commission for America. See *ibid.*, 35,517, f. 238.

[13] Fortescue, IV, 2201.

[14] Stevens, *Facsimiles*, 394. For a full account of the Carlisle Commission, see Alan S. Brown, *William Eden and the American Revolution* (Ph.D. thesis, University of Michigan, 1953), *passim*.

[15] Benjamin Franklin to James Hutton, Passy, 12 February 1778, Smyth, *Writings*, VII, 101; Paul Wentworth to William Eden, Paris, 6 January 1778, Auckland Papers, BM Add MSS 34,415, f. 37; Benjamin Franklin to James Hutton, Passy, 1 February 1778, Franklin Papers, 401 LC, and for Hutton's official authorization, see James Hutton to [Lord North?], 3 December 1777, Fortescue, *Correspondence*, III, 2093.

[16] Benjamin Franklin to David Hartley, Passy, 12 February 1778, Smyth, *Writings*, VII, 101–4. See also David Hartley to Benjamin Franklin [copy], London, [?] February 1778, Official Correspondence, American Affairs, 1777–1781, BM Add MSS 24,321, f. 4.

[17] Benjamin Franklin to David Hartley, Passy, 26 February 1778, Smyth, *Writings*, VII, 107–9.

[18] Quoted in Frederick B. Tolles, "Franklin and the Pulteney Mission: An Episode in the Secret History of the American Revolution," *Huntington Library Quarterly*, XVII (1953–1954), 42. I am indebted to Tolles for the chronology of the Pulteney mission, and for his insight on a number of points.

[19] Quoted in Tolles, "Franklin and the Pulteney Mission," p. 43. The identifications of the code letters and words in this letter were made by Tolles, an insight with which I concur.

[20] Benjamin Franklin to William Pulteney, Passy, 30 March 1778, Smyth, *Writings*, VII, 124. Also see Fortescue, IV, 2250.

[21] William Alexander to William Pulteney, 19 March 1778, quoted in Tolles, "Franklin and the Pulteney Mission," pp. 46–47.

[22] William Alexander to William Pulteney, 26 March 1778, quoted in Tolles, "Franklin and the Pulteney Mission," p. 47.

[23] Stevens, *Facsimiles*, 411.

[24] Fortescue, IV, 2250–2251.

[25] The proposals were as follows: "(1) The present Governments to remain. But the King to name a Governor out of these. (2) Judges and all civil officers to be named by them; care being taken of the rights of patent officers. Courts of Admiralty for prizes only. (3) No negatives on acts of Assembly, except such as effect the trade of G B, or the trade with any other Colony. But no negative as to acts for the prohibition of Negroes, or for establishing paper currency, if not made a legal tender in private payments. All acts to be transmitted for due notification. Acts prohibiting luxury's affecting all countrys equally to pass without negative. (4) No appeals to privy Council except in prize cases from courts of Admiralty in time of

war. (5) Congress to subsist, its powers to be defined. The King to name a President. (6) No taxes to be imposed, nor no military force kept up without consent of Assemblys. Officers to have commissions from his Majesty subject to being removed on address of Assembly. (7) The ungranted lands and quit Rents to be given to the Colonys upon an Equivalent. (8) To have a free trade from all places but not to interfere with the grant to exclusive companys now subsisting. No officers of Customs to subsist. (9) To have Representatives to Parliament. (10) Mutual amnesty—Mutual restitution; Mutual compensation for wanton damage. (11) Immediate Cessation of hostilities by Sea and Land. (12) The King is and shall be the only superior Governor, and to have power of War and peace, and alliances after the present general pacification. (13) All judicial proceedings and acts of Government and new grants of lands, and other legal instruments to run as formerly in his name. (14) Forces to be annually voted for defence of colony's, and paid by them. Officers to have commissions from the King, and removeable as above on address. (15) A contribution to be so settled as to increase with their growth. (16) All Bounties, Drawbacks, and prohibitions in their favour to cease. (17) The expence of their own Civil Government to be paid by them. (18) All hostile resolutions of theirs to be annulled." "Copy of the propositions discussed between Dr. Fr. and Mr. P. in March and April 1778," Stevens, *Facsimiles*, 68.

²⁶ William Pulteney to Benjamin Franklin, 29 March 1778, in Wharton, *Revolutionary Diplomatic Correspondence*, II, 523.

²⁷ Benjamin Franklin to William Pulteney, Passy, 30 March 1778, Smyth, *Writings*, VII, 124–25.

²⁸ See Benjamin Franklin to David Hartley, Passy, 26 February 1778, *ibid.*, p. 109. See also his letter to Sam Adams, Passy, 2 March 1778, *ibid.*, p. 114, and to James Hutton, Passy, 24 March 1778, *ibid.*, p. 122, in which Franklin said that as of that date *"we can treat, if any Propositions are made to us."* (Italics in original.)

²⁹ Benjamin Franklin to Joseph Reed, Passy, 19 March 1780, Smyth, *Writings*, VIII, 43–44.

³⁰ George III to Lord North, 8 April 1778, W. Bodham Donne (ed.), *The Correspondence of King George III with Lord North*, 1768–1783 (2 vols., London, 1867), II, 170.

³¹ See Charles M. Andrews, "A Note on the Franklin-Deane Mission to France," *Yale University Library Gazette*, II (April 1928), 59, 65–66.

³² Tolles, "Franklin and the Pulteney Mission," p. 51, believes Pulteney offered a bribe but that surely Franklin must have "indignantly spurned" it.

³³ William Eden to Sir Henry Clinton, 10 October 1778, Clinton Papers, WLCL.

³⁴ This episode is related in Tolles, "Franklin and the Pulteney Mission," p. 56.

³⁵ William Alexander to William Pulteney, 21 June 1778, quoted in *ibid.*, p. 52.

³⁶ *Ibid.*, pp. 52–57.

³⁷ Silas Deane to Simeon Deane, Paris, 15 January 1778, *Deane Papers*, II, 333.

³⁸ "Mr. Deane's Narrative," in Ingraham, *The Case of Silas Deane*, p. 65.

³⁹ *Ibid.*, p. 165.

⁴⁰ "Certificate as to the Probity of Silas Deane in the Public Service," Passy, 1778, LVI (i), 20 APSL.

⁴¹ Arthur Lee to Benjamin Franklin and Silas Deane, Chaillot, 31 March 1778, VIII, 212 APSL.

⁴² Benjamin Franklin to Arthur Lee, Passy, 1 April 1778, Smyth, *Writings*, VII, 129–30. See also XLV, 120 APSL.

⁴³ Arthur Lee to Benjamin Franklin, Chaillot, 2 April 1778, Smyth, *Writings*, VII, 130–31. See also IX, 4 APSL.

⁴⁴ Benjamin Franklin to Arthur Lee, Passy, 4 April 1778, Smyth, *Writings*, VII, 133. See also XLV, 121 APSL.

⁴⁵ See Report of Committee for Foreign Affairs, 28 March 1779, Papers of the Continental Congress, No. 25, vol. I, ff. 83ff; Henry Laurens to Richard Henry Lee, 31 August 1779, *Deane Papers*, IV, 87–90; and Arthur Lee, Memorial of Arthur Lee to the Congress, 1 May 1779, in Bigelow, *Complete Works*, VIII, 46–57.

⁴⁶ Benjamin Franklin to Arthur Lee, Passy, 3 April 1778, Smyth, *Writings*, VII, 132.

⁴⁷ Benjamin Franklin to Arthur Lee, Passy, 4 April 1778, *ibid.*, 132–37.

⁴⁸ Roger Burlingame, *Benjamin Franklin: Envoy Extraordinary* (New York, 1967), p. 140.

CHAPTER TEN

¹ Diary entry, 10 April 1778, Adams, *Works*, III, 123.

² Diary entry, 13 April 1778, *ibid.*, p. 129.

³ Ralph Izard to Benjamin Franklin, Paris, 25 April 1778, IX, 78 APSL.

⁴ William Lee to Arthur Lee, Frankfurt, 30 July 1778, and same to same, 18 October 1778, Ford, *Letters of Lee*, II, 469, 504.

⁵ Arthur Lee to [?], 1 June 1778, *Deane Papers*, III, 37.

⁶ Lee, *Lee*, II, 148.

⁷ Arthur Lee to John Page, 27 May 1778, *ibid.*, p. 130.

⁸ Diary entry, 21 April 1778, Adams, *Works*, III, 138.

⁹ Diary entry, 13 April 1778, Adams, *Works*, III, 129.

¹⁰ Diary entry, [copy] John Adams to Jonathan Williams, Jr., Passy, 25 May 1778, *ibid.*, p. 165.

¹¹ Wharton, *Revolutionary Diplomatic Correspondence*, IV, 245; Adams, *Works*, III, 131; Hale, *Franklin*, I, 233.

¹² Diary entry, 21 April 1778, Adams, *Works*, III, 138.

¹³ Diary entry, 3 May 1778, *ibid.*, p. 151.

¹⁴ *Ibid.*, 25 May 1778, *ibid.*, p. 167.

¹⁵ *Ibid.*, 13 April 1778, *ibid.*, p. 131.

¹⁶ Thomas Perkins Abernethy, *Western Lands and the American Revolution* (New York, 1959 [1st ed., 1937]), p. 212.

[17] Diary entry, 5 June 1778, Adams, *Works*, III, 176.

[18] Sydney George Fisher, *The True Benjamin Franklin* (Philadelphia, 1906), p. 304.

[19] The letter is reproduced in Stevens, *Facsimiles*, 835; accompanying documents are reprinted as nos. 836 and 837.

[20] Diary entry, 9 July 1778, Adams, *Works*, III, 178.

[21] See dinner seating plan, XLIX, 78 APSL.

[22] Diary entry, 9 July 1778, Adams, *Works*, III, 178.

[23] Willis Steell, *Ben Franklin of Paris, 1776–1785* (New York, 1927), pp. 87–88.

[24] John Adams to Henry Laurens, Passy, 27 July 1778, Adams, *Works*, VII, 21.

[25] Quoted by George Larkin Clark, *Silas Deane: A Connecticut Leader in the American Revolution* (New York, 1913), p. 239.

[26] John Adams to Arthur Lee, Passy, 10 October 1778, Adams, *Works*, VII, 58.

[27] Arthur Lee to John Adams, Chaillot, 12 October 1778, *ibid.*, pp. 58–59.

[28] John Adams to James Lovell, Passy, 20 February 1779, *Deane Papers*, III, 378.

[29] Arthur Lee to Theodoric Bland, Paris, 13 December 1778, Lee, *Lee*, I, 163.

[30] Adams, *Works*, VII, 60.

[31] Silas Deane to Benjamin Franklin, Aix, 8 April 1778, IX, 22 APSL.

[32] Certificate, 31 March 1778, LVI (i), 20 APSL; *Deane Papers*, III, 303.

[33] James Lovell to Sam Adams, 3 August 1779, *Deane Papers*, IV, 42.

[34] See Report of the Committee of Foreign Affairs, 24 March 1779, Papers of the Continental Congress, no. 25, I, 83ff; Henry Laurens to Richard Henry Lee, 31 August 1779, *Deane Papers*, IV, 87–90; Benjamin Franklin to John Jay, 4 October 1779, Bigelow, *Complete Works*, VIII, 129.

[35] Ingraham, *Papers relating to the Case of Deane*, 56.

[36] William Graham Sumner, *The Financier and the Finances of the American Revolution* (New York, 1891), I, 172; see also Wharton, *Revolutionary Diplomatic Correspondence*, I, 301.

[37] Quoted in Clark, *Silas Deane*, pp. 139–40. But William Lee said "The League of Sam. Wharton, Jno. Ross, Dr. Bancroft, young and old Jon.a Williams, seem to have no other contest, but who shall take to himself the best share of the public money that is intrusted to Dr. Franklin, in which sport they are most eminently assisted by Mr. Chaumont, who has young Moylan of Phila. as his agent at L'Orient, and young Williams at Nantes. . . . I must say that in my opinion, it will be impossible for the American affairs to be properly conducted in France, while Dr. F. continues sole minister, commercial agent, agent for prizes, treasurer. . . ." William Lee to Samuel W. Stockton, Ford, *Letters of Lee*, III, 812.

[38] *Journals of the Continental Congress*, XII, 1181, 1192, 1200, 1202.

[39] "Mr. Deane's Narrative," 21 December 1778, *Deane Papers*, III, 186–87.

[40] *Ibid.,* p. 195.

[41] Adams, *Works,* III, 187, 191.

[42] Wharton, *Revolutionary Diplomatic Correspondence,* IV, 245, 293; Adams, *Works,* III, 131; Hale, *Franklin,* I, 233.

[43] *Journal of Congress,* XII, 1011–12.

[44] William Lee to Ralph Izard, 2 March 1779, Ford, *Letters of Lee,* II, 535n.

[45] Benjamin Franklin to James Lovell, Passy, 17 October 1779, Bigelow, *Complete Works,* VIII, 147.

[46] Abernethy, *Western Lands and the American Revolution,* p. 231.

[47] Benjamin Franklin to Arthur Lee, Passy, 18 February 1779, *Deane Papers,* III, 376. Franklin had already written to Adams for the papers he had, promising to keep them in order. Benjamin Franklin to John Adams, Passy, 22 January 1789, XLV 140 APSL.

[48] Arthur Lee to Benjamin Franklin, Chaillot, 21 February 1779, *ibid.,* p. 379.

[49] Benjamin Franklin to Arthur Lee, Passy, 13 March 1779; Arthur Lee to Benjamin Franklin, Chaillot, 19 March 1779; Benjamin Franklin to Arthur Lee, Passy, 27 March 1779, *ibid.,* 401–3, 404–5, 405.

[50] Arthur Lee to Sam Adams, Paris, 22 May 1779, *ibid.,* pp. 463–65.

[51] Diary entry, 20 June 1779, Adams, *Works,* III, 218.

[52] Diary entry, 2 July 1779, *ibid.,* p. 225.

[53] Benjamin Franklin to the President of the Congress, 16 March 1780, Bigelow, *Complete Works,* VIII, 203–4; *Journals of the Continental Congress,* XIX, 187, XX, 475–76, 738; Abernethy, *Western Lands and the American Revolution,* p. 274.

[54] Edmund C. Burnett, Letters of Members of the Continental Congress (8 vols., Washington, D.C., 1921–1936), V, 425–26.

[55] *Journals of the Continental Congress,* XVIII, 1114–15, XIX, 13–14, 316, XXI, 900. See also Ingraham, *Case against Silas Deane,* pp. 89ff.

[56] See Richard B. Morris, *The Peacemakers: The Great Powers and American Independence* (New York, 1965), pp. 196–98.

[57] Benjamin Franklin to John Adams, 2 October 1780, Smyth, *Writings,* VII, 262–63.

[58] Silas Deane to Robert Morris, Williamsburgh, 17 April 1780, *Deane Papers,* IV, 124–27.

[59] Silas Deane to Joseph Wharton, Williamsburgh, 10 May 1780, *ibid.,* p. 147.

[60] Silas Deane to Samuel Wharton, Paris, 30 August 1780, *ibid.,* p. 209.

[61] William Lee wrote his brother that "Your former minister, Mr. Silas Deane . . . since his return to France . . . lives at Passy with your minister [Franklin], and seems to be his favorite and prime councillor." William Lee to Arthur Lee, Anvers, 10 December 1780, Ford, *Letters of Lee,* III, 835.

[62] Silas Deane to John Jay, Paris, 23 August 1780, *Deane Papers,* IV, 196.

[63] See J. Holker to Benjamin Franklin, 16 April 1780, XVIII, 47 APSL;

Edward Bancroft to Benjamin Franklin, 25 August 1781, XXII, 125 APSL; J. Holker to W. T. Franklin, 4 September 1781, CIII, 95 APSL; Benjamin Franklin to Jonathan Williams, Jr., Passy, 27 December 1780, Bigelow, *Complete Works*, VIII, 344–45.

⁶⁴ Silas Deane to John Shee, Paris, 4 September 1780, *Deane Papers*, IV, 220.

⁶⁵ Silas Deane to John Jay, Passy, November 1780, *ibid.*, p. 262.

⁶⁶ Benjamin Franklin to Charles W. F. Dumas, Passy, 18 January 1781, *ibid.*, pp. 274–75.

⁶⁷ Quoted in William B. Reed, ed., *The Life and Correspondence of Joseph Reed* (Philadelphia, 1847), II, 455–57.

⁶⁸ [Benjamin Franklin and Samuel Wharton], *Plain Facts* (Philadelphia, 1781), a copy of which is located at the Illinois Historical Survey, Urbana.

⁶⁹ The king said to North that he had thus far read only two of the letters, "upon which I form the same opinion of too much appearance of being concerted with this Country." He then noted: "The extract from Franklin is very material." He did not say "the report *on*," but "from." That extract stated, according to the king, that "should France not supply America amply I think it has the appearance that this long contest will end as it ought by the Colonies returning to the Mother Country." Either Franklin or the king was an optimist. See George III to Lord North, 19 July 1781, Fortescue, V, 3374.

⁷⁰ Fortescue, V, 200, 255–56, 260; Wharton, *Revolutionary Diplomatic Correspondence*, I, 565.

⁷¹ Elkanah Watson, *Men and Times of the Revolution*, quoted in *Deane Papers*, IV, 546.

⁷² *Ibid.*, IV, 400–402, 543–44; V, 15, 192; Sumner, *The Financer and the Finances of the American Revolution*, I, 233.

⁷³ Silas Deane to Paul Wentworth, Grand, 4 February 1782, *Deane Papers*, V, 59–60.

⁷⁴ Silas Deane to Barnabas Deane, Ghent, 31 January 1782, *ibid.*, p. 34.

⁷⁵ Benjamin Franklin to Robert R. Livingston, Passy, 4 March 1782, *ibid.*, p. 70.

⁷⁶ Given at Passay, the 18th, of December, 1782, by B. Franklin, Minister Plenipotentiary from the United States of America, at the Court of France, printed in *Deane Papers*, V, 116–17.

⁷⁷ William Lee to Samuel Thorpe, Bruxelles, 17 January 1783, Ford, *Letters of Lee*, III, 915.

⁷⁸ Silas Deane to Barnabas Deane, 5 April 1783, *Deane Papers*, V, 153.

⁷⁹ Deane met often with Edward Bancroft, sometimes secretly and sometimes openly. He also saw Paul Wentworth periodically and endeavored to maintain a correspondence with him, although he wrote more letters to the British agent than he received. See Silas Deane to Paul Wentworth, Ghent, 31 January 1782, *Deane Papers*, V, 21; same to same, Grand, 4 February 1782, *ibid.*, pp. 59–60; same to same, 8 February 1782, *ibid.*, p. 70; same to same, 6 March 1782, *ibid.*, pp. 71–72; same to E. Edwards [Ban-

croft], Ghent, 17 March 1782, *ibid.*, p. 77; same to same, Ghent, 23 March 1782, *ibid.*, p. 79; same to same, Ghent, 11 April 1782, *ibid.*, p. 83; same to same, Ghent, 10 February 1782, *ibid.*, p. 130; same to same, 14 April 1782, *ibid.*, p. 84, and *passim.*

[80] Silas Deane to E. Edwards [Bancroft], Ghent, 10 February 1783, *Deane Papers*, V, 130; Edward Bancroft to Barnabas Deane, Philadelphia, 18 October 1783, *ibid.*, p. 212; Silas Deane to Simeon Deane, London, 30 April 1783, *ibid.*, p. 294; same to Barnabas Deane, London, 17 March 1786, *ibid.*, p. 475.

[81] Silas Deane to Edward Bancroft, Ghent, 10 February 1783, *Deane Papers*, V, 130, and *passim.*

[82] Benjamin Franklin to Charles Thomson, Philadelphia, 29 December 1788, "The Charles Thomson Papers," *Collections of the New York Historical Society for the Year 1878* (New York, 1879), pp. 245–47.

CHAPTER ELEVEN

[1] Richard B. Morris, *The Peacemakers: The Great Powers and American Independence* (New York, 1965), p. 192.

[2] Benjamin Franklin to Lord Shelburne, Paris, 18 April 1782, in Carl Van Doren, ed., *Benjamin Franklin's Autobiographical Writings* (New York, 1952), p. 520.

[3] *Ibid.*, pp. 523–24.

[4] Benjamin Franklin to Lord Shelburne, 18 April 1782 [copy], sent to Vergennes, 4 May 1782, in Ministère des Affaires Étrangères, Paris, Correspondance politique, États-Unis 21: 23, 57.

[5] Richard Jackson to Lord Shelburne, 1782, Shelburne Papers, WLCL, 72: 9–10.

[6] George III to Lord Shelburne, 21 August 1782, Fortescue, VI, 3894.

[7] Herbert E. Klingelhofer, ed., "Matthew Ridley's Diary During the Peace Negotiations of 1782," *William and Mary Quarterly*, XX (January 1963), 112.

[8] Quoted in Morris, *The Peacemakers*, p. 246.

[9] Diary entry, Adams, *Works*, III, 43n, 48–51.

[10] John Adams to Robert Livingston, Paris, 8 November 1782, Adams, *Works*, VIII, 4.

[11] Quoted in Morris, *The Peacemakers*, p. 356.

[12] In April 1783 Shelburne was forced out of the government and replaced by a coalition government composed of Lord North and Shelburne's old enemy, Charles James Fox. The North-Fox coalition lasted from April 1783 until December of that year. In December, William Pitt the Younger became Prime Minister for the first time.

[13] Commission by Benjamin Franklin and John Jay, 1 October 1782, in Wharton, *Revolutionary Diplomatic Correspondence*, V, 789; Benjamin Vaughan to Lord Shelburne, 31 July 1782, Massachusetts Historical Society *Proceedings*, 2d Series, XVII (1903), 414n; Adams, *Works*, I, 373n.

[14] Lee's statement is quoted in Morris, *The Peacemakers*, p. 355.

[15] Benjamin Franklin to the President of the Congress, Passy, 12 March 1781, Sparks, *Works*, IX, 1–6.

[16] Diary entry, 11 January 1783, Adams, *Works*, III, 355.

[17] Diary entry, 27 October 1782, *ibid.*, p. 300.

[18] John Jay to Robert R. Livingston, Paris, 18 September 1782, in Henry P. Johnston, ed., *The Correspondence and Public Papers of John Jay* (New York, 1890), II, 347.

[19] Bemis, *Diplomacy*, 207; Thomas Pownall to Benjamin Franklin, 13 May 1782, XXV, 70 APSL; Lord Shelburne to Richard Oswald, 21 May 1782, PRO, FO: 27, 2; Thomas Walpole to Charles James Fox, 27 May 1782, *ibid.*; Richard Oswald to Lord Shelburne, 2 June 1782, *ibid.*; *Journals of the Continental Congress*, XXIII, 596–603; Bigelow, *Complete Works*, IX, 348.

[20] Klingelhofer, "Matthew Ridley's Diary, Diary During the Peace Negotiations of 1782," p. 108.

[21] *Ibid.*, p. 100.

[22] John Adams to Robert Livingston, Paris, 11 November 1782, Adams, *Works*, VIII, 9.

[23] Sydney George Fisher, *The True Benjamin Franklin* (Philadelphia, 1906), p. 338.

[24] This conversation is recorded in Morris, *The Peacemakers*, p. 310. Professor Morris has done a fine job of telling the entire story of the peace negotiations in magnificent detail with thorough documentation.

[25] This delightful story is told by Durand Echeverria, *Mirage in the West: A History of the French Image of American Society to 1815* (New York, 1960), p. 50.

[26] Morris, *The Peacemakers*, p. 304.

[27] Jonathan Williams, Jr., to Benjamin Franklin, Nantes, 6 December 1782, Franklin Papers, Miscellaneous, III, 70 HSP.

[28] See extract of a letter in Franklin's handwriting given to Vergennes from Thomas Cooper to Benjamin Franklin, 5 May 1782, in Ministère des Affaires Étrangères, Paris, Correspondance politique, États-Unis 24: 183, and the reply, Benjamin Franklin to Cooper, Passy, 26 December 1782, Bigelow, *Complete Works*, X, 62–63.

[29] I am again indebted for this quotation to Morris, *The Peacemakers*, p. 446.

[30] Van Doren, *Benjamin Franklin's Autobiographical Writings*, pp. 433–34.

[31] "Certificate as to the Probity of Silas Deane in the Public Service," Passy, 1778, LVI (i), 20 APSL.

[32] Letter written by Franklin on behalf of Deane, printed in *Deane Papers*, V, 116–17.

[33] Benjamin Franklin to John Jay, Passy, 10 September 1783, Johnston, *Papers of Jay*, III, 72.

[34] John Jay to Benjamin Franklin, Passy, 11 September 1783, *ibid.*, p. 73.

CHAPTER TWELVE

[1] The information about these men has been drawn from a variety of sources, including Lewis Einstein, *Divided Loyalties: Americans in England during the War of Independence* (Boston, 1933), *passim;* Carl Van Doren, *Secret History of the American Revolution* (New York, 1941), *passim;* Boyd, "Silas Deane," Part III, *William and Mary Quarterly* (October 1959), *passim;* and Mark Mayo Boatner III, comp., *Encyclopedia of the American Revolution* (New York, 1966), *passim.*

[2] Benjamin Franklin to Thomas Mifflin, President of the Congress, Passy, 26 December 1783, Smyth, *Writings,* IX, 141.

[3] Benjamin Franklin to Chaumont, Passy, 2 May 1784, LIV, 125 (vii), APSL.

[4] Thomas Barclay, on 9 July 1785, had forewarded to the Congress "sundry accounts" of Ben Franklin and the Paris mission's banker, Ferdinand Grand, which he had settled. This file was sent to the Committee for Foreign Affairs, which in turn passed it to the Treasury Board. *Journals of the Continental Congress,* XXIX, 725.

[5] The biblical reference was drawn from Deuteronomy 25: 4 and is quoted by the Apostle Paul in I Corinthians 9:9.

[6] Quoted by Moncure D. Conway, *The Life of Thomas Paine* (New York, 1893), I, 147. Conway also tells the story of Franklin before the Committee of Congress and states that it was quoted from the manuscript diary of a Mr. Rickman, "recently" found by one Dr. Clair Grece (see p. 146). The story is not set forth in the papers of the Continental Congress and I could find neither the diary of Rickman nor any account of its being found by Grece.

[7] Gouverneur Morris to John Randolph, Washington, 20 January 1812, quoted in Conway, *The Life of Thomas Paine,* I, 140.

[8] Benjamin Franklin to Charles Thomson, Philadelphia, 29 December 1788, "The Charles Thomson Papers," *Collections of the New York Historical Society for the Year 1878* (New York, 1879), pp. 245–47.

[9] Benjamin Franklin to Robert Morris, 2 November 1789, Smyth, *Writings,* X, 48.

[10] Boyd, "Silas Deane," part II, pp. 336–37.

[11] Benjamin Franklin to Robert R. Livingston, Passy, 12 August 1782, in Sparks, *Works,* IX, 386.

[12] Thomas Perkins Abernethy, "The Origin of the Franklin-Lee Imbroglio," *The North Carolina Historical Review,* XV (January 1938), 51–52 *passim.*

[13] William Graham Sumner, *The Financier and the Finances of the American Revolution* (New York, 1891), I, 214.

[14] Carl Van Doren, *Benjamin Franklin* (New York, 1952), p. 584.

[15] Quoted in Hale, *Franklin,* I, 82.

APPENDIX

———•◆•———

Edward Bancroft's Memorial to the Marquis of Carmarthen, Foreign Secretary in 1784, written 17 September 1784. Public Record Office: Foreign Office 4: 3.

In the month of June 1776, Mr. Silas Deane arrived in France, and pursuant to an instruction given him by the Secret Committee of Congress, wrote to me in London, requesting an interview in Paris, where I accordingly went, early in July, and was made acquainted with the purposes of his Mission, and with every thing which passed between him, and the French Ministry. After staying two or three weeks there, I returned to England, convinced, that the Government of France would endeavour to Promote an Absolute Separation, of the then United Colonies, from Great Britain; unless a speedy termination of the Revolt, by reconciliation, or Conquest, should frustrate this project. I had then resided near ten years, and expected to reside the rest of my Life, in England; and all my views, interests and inclinations were adverse to the independancy of the Colonies, though I had advocated some of their Claims, from a persuasion, of their being founded in Justice. I therefore wished, that the Government of this Country, might be informed, of the Danger of French interference, though I could not resolve to become the informant. But Mr. Paul Wentworth, having gained some general Knowledge of my Journey to France, and of my intercourse with Mr. Deane, and having induced me to believe, that the British Ministry were likewise informed on this Subject, I at length Consented to meet the then Secretaries of State, Lords Weymouth and Suffolk, and give them all the information in my power; which I did, with the most disinterested views; for I not only did not ask, but expressly rejected, every Idea of, any reward. The Declaration of Independancy, was not then known in Europe, and I hoped, that Government, thus informed of the Danger, would prevent it, by some accomodation with the Colonies, or by other means. It had been my original intention to stop after this first Communication; but having given the first notice of a beginning intercourse, between France and the United Colonies, I was urged on, to watch and disclose the progress of it; for which purpose, I made several Journeys to Paris, and maintained a regular Correspondence with Mr. Deane, through the Couriers of the French Government. And in this way, I became *entangled* and obliged to proceed in a kind of Business, as repugnant to my feelings, as it had been to my original intentions. Being thus devoted to the Service of Government, I consented like others, to accept such Emoluments, as my situation indeed required. And in Feb'y 1777, Lord Suffolk, to whom by Ld Weymouths Consent, my Communications were then made, formally promised me, in the King's Name, a Pension for Life of £200 pr an. to Commence from the Christmas preceeding. This was for Services *then rendered;* and as an inducement for me to go over and reside in France, and continue my services there, until the Revolt should terminate, or an Open rupture with that nation ensue, his Lordship farther promised, that when either of these Events should happen, my permanent pension of £200 pr an. should be increased to £500 *at least.* Confiding in this promise, I went to Paris, and during the first year, resided in the same House with Dr. Franklin, Mr. Deane etc., and regularly informed the Government of every transaction of the American Commissioners; of every Step and Vessel taken to supply the revolted Colonies, with Artillery, Arms etc.; of every part of their intercourse with the French and other European Courts; of the Powers and instructions given by Congress to the Commissioners, and of their correspondence with the Secret Committees etc. and when the Government of France at length determined *openly* to support the Revolted Colonies, I gave notice of this determination, and of the progress made in forming the two Treaties of Alliance and Commerce, and when these were signed, on the Evening of the 6th of Feb'y, I at my own Expence, by a special Messenger, and with unexampled dispatch, conveyed this intelligence to this City, and to the King's Ministers, within 42 hours, from the instant of their Signature, a piece of information, for which many individuals here, would, for purposes of Speculation, have given me more than all that I have received from Government. Afterwards, when that decisive measure, of sending Count D'Estaign with the fleet from Toulon, to Commence Hostilities at the Delaware and New York, was adopted, I sent intelligence of the direct object and Plan of the Expedition. I had originally explained to Lord Suffolk my Determination to quit this business, whenever an Open War with France, should destroy, what had been my principal inducement to meddle with it; I mean, the hope of preventing a Separation of the revolted Colonies: And as this war now appeared unavoidable, I requested that the King's Ministers would, as soon as practicable, provide other Sources of information, and permit me to withdraw myself. This request however was never granted. But to fullfill the promise made by my Lord Suffolk my permanent Pension was increased to 500 £ per an. and regularly entered, in Book Letter A. payable to Mr. P. Wentworth for the use of Edwd. Edwards; the name, by which, for greater Secrecy, it had been long before agreed to distinguish me. In June 1780, the King's Ministers, reflecting that this Pension had been given as the reward of *Antecedent* Services, and that it would be unreasonable, to require a longer Continuance of them, without a farther recompense, agreed to allow me an additional yearly sum of £500, *so long as I should reside in France;* and they encouraged me to expect that this last Sum, or at least a Considerable part of it, would be ultimately added to my permanent pension, in case Government should be satisfied with my future services. I accordingly received from his Majesties Treasury the Stipulated annual allowance of £1000, until the month of April 1782; when the Change of Ministers, with Mr. Burkes Bill, created some difficulty on this Subject. But the matter being Explained to my Lord Shelburne, he took care, before his resignation, to secure and pay me through the then Secretary of State, for foreign Affairs, (my Lord Grantham), a full years Sallary, though the last quarter was not then due. In June 1783, I came to London, and informed Lord North (to whom my latter information had by particular direction been addressed) of my intention of going to America, where I offered my Services, in promoting measures and dispositions, favourable to the interests of this Country, as well as in giving information of the State of things there, and of the views and proceedings of Congress etc. I likewise reminded him, of the Encouragement which I had received to expect that the second 500 £ pr. an. or at least a part of it would be made permanent like the first, adding, that if my services in America, were accepted, it would as I presumed, in any case, be thought reasonable, to Continue to me, at least while there, the same allowance as had been made me in France. With this Proposition, his Lordship appeared to be satisfied, but at a subsequent interview, he referred me to Mr. Fox for a decision respecting it, as well as for the payment of a quarter Sallary, then due, alledging, that Mr. Burke's Bill, had made it absolutely necessary, to provide for me, through that Department. I accordingly saw and conversed with Mr. Fox respecting my situation and propositions, which he promised to consider of; but as I had not foreseen any difficulty, or delay, and had already agreed, and Paid for, my Passage to Philadelphia, I was obliged to follow the Ship to the Downs, on the 12th of August 1783, before any decision was made, and indeed, whilst Mr. Fox was out of Town. I however informed him, by Letter, on the evening of my departure, that he might expect the Continuation of my Services to Government whilst in America, and requested that the quarters Salary, then due, might be paid to Mrs. Bancroft. She accordingly soon after received £250 for that Quarter; since which nothing has been paid for my account. On my part, I have endeavoured, as far as practicable, whilst absent, in America, to render myself useful to the British nation and Government. Great Events indeed did not occur for Communication, and the ill temper produced in America by the Proclamation, respecting the intercourse from thence to the West Indies, did not allow me to do all I had hoped, in promoting sentiments and dispositions favourable to this Country; though I endeavoured it, and I think with some little Success, in particular Channels and Connections; and I have endeavoured, occasionally, to vindicate the late measures of this Government, in Newspapers, particularly under the Signature of Cincinnatus, against the Publications of Common Sense.

One years Salary was due to me at midsummer last, which I request the payment of: what it shall be, must depend on the King's pleasure, and that of his Ministers: I make no Claim beyond the permanent pension of £500 pr an. for which the Faith of Government has been often pledged; and for which, I have sacrificed near eight years of my Life, and my pursuits in it; always avoiding any Kind of appointment, or emolument from, as well as any sort of Engagement to, any Government in the United States; in the full determination, of remaining to the end of my Life, a faithful Subject to my natural, and most Gracious Sovereign.

                                        In Dr. Bancroft's Sept. 17, 1784.

St. James's 16th Sept'r 1784

BIBLIOGRAPHY

Manuscript Collections

Auckland, Lord William Eden, Papers, Additional Manuscripts, British Museum, London.

Bancroft, George, Transcripts, England and America, New York Public Library, New York City, New York.

Clinton, Henry, Papers, William L. Clements Library, University of Michigan, Ann Arbor, Michigan.

Colonial Records of Nova Scotia, Department of Lands and Forests, Halifax, Nova Scotia.

Croghan, George, Papers, Cadwalader Collection, Historical Society of Pennsylvania, Philadelphia, Pennsylvania.

Council Minutes, Public Archives, Halifax, Nova Scotia.

Franklin, Benjamin, Manuscript Collection, J. P. Morgan Library, New York City, New York.

———, Manuscript Collection, Yale University Library, New Haven, Connecticut.

———, Papers, American Philosophical Society Library, Philadelphia, Pennsylvania.

———, Papers, Historical Society of Pennsylvania, Philadelphia, Pennsylvania.

———, Papers, Library of Congress, Washington, D.C.

Hardwicke, Lord, Papers, Additional Manuscripts, British Museum, London.

Harkness Collection of Autograph Letters, New York Public Library, New York City, New York.

Lee, Arthur, Papers, Alderman Library, University of Virginia, Charlottesville, Virginia.

Loyalist Transcripts, New York Public Library, New York City, New York.

Manuscript Division, Massachusetts Historical Society, Boston, Massachusetts.

Manuscrits Français, Nouvelles Acquisitions, Bibliothèque Nationale, Paris.

Ministère des Affaires Etrangères, Correspondance politique, Angleterre, Paris.

Ministère des Affaires Etrangères, Correspondance politique, Etats-Unis, Paris.

Miscellaneous American Papers, Additional Manuscripts, British Museum, London.

Miscellaneous Manuscript Collection, American Philosophical Society Library, Philadelphia, Pennsylvania.

Morris, Robert, Papers, Library of Congress, Washington, D.C.

Public Record Office, Colonial Office Papers, London, England.

Public Record Office, Foreign Office Papers, London, England.

Shelburne, William Petty, Lord, Papers, William L. Clements Library, University of Michigan, Ann Arbor, Michigan.

Wharton, Thomas, Letter Book, 1773–1784, Historical Society of Pennsylvania, Philadelphia, Pennsylvania.

Early Tracts and Printed Accounts

[Anonymous]. *What is Sauce for a Goose is also Sauce for a Gander.* Philadelphia, 1764.

[Board of Trade]. *Report of the Lords Commissioners for Trade and Plantations on the Petition of the Honourable Thomas Walpole, Benjamin Franklin, John Sargeant, and Samuel Wharton, esquires, and their associates: For a Grant of Lands on the River Ohio, in North America; for the Purpose of erecting a new Government.* London, 1770.

Chalmers, George. *Second Thoughts: or, Observations upon Lord Abingdon's Thoughts on the Letter of Edmund Burke, Esq. To the Sheriffs of Bristol; By the author of the Answer to Mr. Burke's Letter.* London, 1777.

BIBLIOGRAPHY

[Franklin, Benjamin and Samuel Wharton]. *Plain Facts: Being an Examination into the Rights of the Indian Nations.* Philadelphia, 1781.

Hutchinson, Thomas. *The History of the Colony and Province of Massachusetts-Bay.* Lawrence S. Mayo, ed. 3 vols., Cambridge, 1936.

Lee, Arthur. *Extracts from a Letter written to the President of Congress by the Honourable Arthur Lee in answer to a Libel by Silas Deane.* Philadelphia, 1780.

Warville, Brissot de. *New Travels in the United States, 1788.* London, 1794.

[Wharton, Samuel and Edward Bancroft.] *View of the Title of Indiana, & tract of Country on the River Ohio. Containing Indian Conferences of Johnson Hall in May, 1765, The Deed of the Six Nations to the Proprietors of Indiana—the Minutes of the Congress at Fort Stanwix in October and November. 1768—the Deed of the Indians, settling the boundary line between the English and Indian Lands—and the Opinion of Counsel on the Title of the Proprietor of Indiana.* Philadelphia, 1776.

Published Documents

Adams, John. *The Works of John Adams.* Charles Francis Adams, ed. 10 vols., Boston, 1850–1856.

Alvord, Clarence W. and Clarence E. Carter, eds. *The Critical Period, 1763–1765.* Springfield, 1905.

[Anonymous]. *Lettres inédites du général de La Fayette au vicomte de Noailles, écrites des camps de l'armée américaine durant la guerre de l'indépendance des États-Unis.* Paris, 1924.

Bigelow, John, ed. *The Complete Works of Benjamin Franklin.* 10 vols., New York, 1887–1889.

Boyd, Julian P., ed. *The Papers of Thomas Jefferson.* 17 vols., Princeton, 1950–.

Burnett, Edmund C., ed. *Letters of Members of the Continental Congress.* 8 vols., Washington, D.C., 1921–1936.

Candler, Allen D., ed. *The Colonial Records of the State of Georgia: Statutes, Colonial and Revolutionary, 1768–1773.* Atlanta, 1911.

Carter, Clarence E., ed. *The Correspondence of General Thomas Gage With the Secretaries of State, 1763–1775.* 2 vols., New Haven, 1931.

"Charles Thomson Papers." New York Historical Society *Collections.* New York, 1879.

Crane, Verner W., ed. *Benjamin Franklin's Letters to the Press, 1758–1775.* Chapel Hill, 1950.

Deas, Anne Izard, comp. *Correspondence of Mr. Ralph Izard of South Carolina from the Year 1774 to 1804 With a Short Memoir.* New York, 1844.

Doniol, Henry, ed. *Histoire de la participation de la France à l'établissement des États-Unis d'Amérique.* 5 vols., Paris, 1884–1892.

Force, Peter, ed. *American Archives: Consisting of a Collection of Authentick Records, State Papers, Debates and Letters and Other Notices of Public Affairs, the Whole Forming a Documentary History of the Origin and Progress of the North American Colonies; of the Causes and Accomplishments of the American Revolution; and of the Constitution of the Government of the United States to the Final Ratification Thereof.* 4th series, 9 vols., Washington, D.C., 1837–1853.

Ford, Paul L., ed. *Edward Bancroft's Narrative of the Objects and Proceedings of Silas Deane, as Commissioner of the United Colonies to France; made to the British Government in 1776.* Brooklyn, 1891.

Ford, Worthington, C., ed. *The Letters of William Lee.* 3 vols., Brooklyn, 1891.

Fortescue, John, ed. *The Correspondence of King George the Third, from 1760 to December 1783, Printed from the Original Papers in the Royal Archives at Windsor Castle.* 6 vols., London, 1927.

Hazard, Samuel, ed. *Pennsylvania Archives.* 12 vols., Philadelphia, 1853–1860.

Hunt, Gaillard, Worthington C. Ford *et al.,* eds. *Journals of the Continental Congress, 1774–1789.* 34 vols., Washington, D.C., 1904–1937.

Ingraham, E. D., ed. *Papers in Relation to the Case of Silas Deane.* Philadelphia, 1855.

Isham, Charles W., comp. *The Deane Papers.* New York Historical Society *Collections.* 5 vols., New York, 1886–1890.

Johnston, Henry P., ed. *The Correspondence and Public Papers of John Jay.* 4 vols., New York, 1890.

Journal and Correspondence of William, Lord Auckland. 4 vols., London, 1861–1862.

Klingelhofer, Herbert E., ed. "Matthew Ridley's Diary During the Peace Negotiations of 1782." *William and Mary Quarterly.* 3rd series, XX (1963).

Labaree, Leonard W. and William B. Willcox, eds. *The Papers of Benjamin Franklin.* 15 vols. to date, New Haven, 1959–.

Lee, Richard Henry, comp. *The Life of Arthur Lee.* 2 vols., Boston, 1829.

"Letters of Colonel George Croghan." *Pennsylvania Magazine of History and Biography.* XV (1891).

O'Callaghan, Edmund B. and Berthold Fernow, eds. *Documents relative to the colonial history of the State of New York.* 15 vols., Albany and New York, 1856–1887.

"Papers of Dr. Benjamin Rush." *Pennsylvania Magazine of History and Biography.* XXIX (1905).

Reed, William B., ed. *The Life and Correspondence of Joseph Reed.* 2 vols., Philadelphia, 1847.

Ricord, Frederick and William Nelson, eds. *Documents Relating to the Colonial History of the State of New Jersey.* 36 vols., Newark, 1881–1914.

Smyth, Albert H., ed. *The Writings of Benjamin Franklin.* 10 vols., New York, 1905–1907.

Sparks, Jared, ed. *The Works of Benjamin Franklin.* 10 vols., Boston, 1840.

Stevens, Benjamin F., comp. *Facsimiles of Manuscripts in European Archives Relating to America, 1773–1783.* 25 vols., London, 1889–1898.

Stryker, William S., ed. "Extracts from American Newspapers, 1776–1777." *Documents Relating to the Revolutionary History of the State of New Jersey.* 3 vols., Trenton, 1901.

Van Doren, Carl, ed. *Benjamin Franklin's Autobiographical Writings*. New York, 1952.

Wharton, Francis, ed. *The Revolutionary Diplomatic Correspondence of the United States*. 6 vols., Washington, D.C., 1889.

The War: Preparation, Prosecution, and Peace

Abernethy, Thomas P. "Commercial Activities of Silas Deane in France." *American Historical Review*. XXXIX (1934).

Abernethy, Thomas P. *Western Lands and the American Revolution*. New York, 1937.

Bemis, Samuel F. "British Secret Service and the French American Alliance." *American Historical Review*. XXIX (1924).

Bemis, Samuel F. *The Diplomacy of the American Revolution*, revised edition. Bloomington, 1961.

Boyd, Julian P. "Silas Deane: Death by a Kindly Teacher of Treason?" *William and Mary Quarterly*. 3rd series, XVI (1959).

Brown, Alan S. "William Eden and the American Revolution." Ph.D. Thesis, University of Michigan, 1953.

Burnett, Edmund C. *The Continental Congress*. New York, 1941.

Clark, George L. *Silas Deane: A Connecticut Leader in the American Revolution*. New York, 1913.

Clarke, William B. *Lambert Wickes, Sea Raider and Diplomat: The Story of a Naval Captain of the Revolution*. New Haven, 1932.

Conway, Moncure D. *The Life of Thomas Paine*. 2 vols., New York, 1893.

Corwin, Edward S. "The French Object in the American Revolution." *American Historical Review*. XXI (1916).

Deacon, Richard. *A History of the British Secret Service*. London, 1969.

Echeverria, Durand. *Mirage in the West: A History of the French Image of American Society to 1815*. New York, 1960.

Einstein, Lewis. *Divided Loyalties: Americans in England during the War of Independence*. Boston, 1933.

Gaston, Martin. "Commercial Relations between Nantes and the American Colonies." *Journal of Economic and Business History.* IV (1932).

Greene, C. S. and L. B. Clarke. *The Greenes of Rhode Island.* New York, 1903.

Henderson, Herbert J., Jr. "Political Factions in the Continental Congress, 1774–1783." Ph.D. Thesis, Columbia University, 1962.

Hendrick, Burton J. *The Lees of Virginia: A Biography of a Family.* Boston, 1935.

Kapp, Friedrich. *Life of John Kalb.* New York, 1870.

Kite, Elizabeth. *Beaumarchais and the War of American Independence.* 2 vols., Boston, 1918.

Meng, John J. "A Footnote to Secret Aid in the American Revolution." *American Historical Review.* XLIII (1938).

Miller, Margaret A. "The Spy-Activities of Doctor Edward Bancroft." *Journal of American History.* XXII (1928).

Monaghan, Frank. *French Travellers in the United States, 1765–1932.* New York, 1961.

Morris, Richard B. *The Peacemakers: The Great Powers and American Independence.* New York, 1965.

Pfeifer, Michael P. "John Vardill and Joseph Hynson: Spy Activities in 1777." M. A. Paper, University of South Florida, 1970.

Phillips, Paul C. *The West in the Diplomacy of the American Revolution.* New York, 1913.

Renaut, Francis P. *L'espionage naval au XVIII⁺ siècle.* Paris, 1936.

Ritcheson, Charles E. *British Politics and the American Revolution.* Norman, 1954.

Sosin, Jack M. *Agents and Merchants: British Colonial Policy and the Origins of the American Revolution, 1763–1775.* Lincoln, 1966.

Stephenson, Orlando. "The Supply of Gunpowder in 1776." *American Historical Review.* XXX (1925).

Stillé, C. J. "Beaumarchais and the Lost Million." *Pennsylvania Magazine of History and Biography.* XI (1887).

Sumner, William G. *The Financier and the Finances of the American Revolution.* 2 vols., New York, 1891.

Tower, Charlemagne, Jr. *The Marquis de La Fayette in the American Revolution with some Account of the Attitude of France Toward the War of Independence.* 2 vols., Philadelphia, 1895.

Tyler, Lyon G. "Arthur Lee, A Neglected Statesman." *Tyler's Quarterly Historical and Genealogical Magazine.* XIV (1933).

Utrilla, J. F. Yela. *España ante la independencia de los Estados Unidos.* 2 vols., Lerida, 1925.

Van Tyne, Claude H. "French Aid Before the Alliance of 1778." *American Historical Review.* XXXI (1925).

Van Tyne, Claude H. "Influences which Determined the French Government to Make the Treaty With America in 1778." *American Historical Review.* XXI (1916).

Wainwright, Nicholas B. *George Croghan, Wilderness Diplomat.* Chapel Hill, 1959.

Wickwire, Franklin B. *British Subministers and Colonial America, 1763–1783.* Princeton, 1966.

Works on Franklin

Abernethy, Thomas P. "The Origin of the Franklin-Lee Imbroglio." *North Carolina Historical Review.* XV (1938).

Aldridge, Alfred O. *Benjamin Franklin: Philosopher and Man.* Philadelphia, 1965.

Andrews, Charles M. "A Note on the Franklin-Deane Mission to France." *Yale University Library Gazette.* XII (1928).

Augur, Helen. *The Secret War of Independence.* New York, 1955.

Burlingame, Roger. *Benjamin Franklin: Envoy Extraordinary.* New York, 1967.

Crane, Verner W. *Benjamin Franklin and a Rising People.* Boston, 1954.

Currey, Cecil B. *Road to Revolution: Benjamin Franklin in England, 1765–1775.* Garden City, 1968.

Eiselen, Malcolm R. *Franklin's Political Theories*. Garden City, 1928.

Faÿ, Bernard. *Franklin: The Apostle of Modern Times*. Boston, 1929.

Fisher, Sydney G. *The True Benjamin Franklin*. Philadelphia, 1906.

Ford, Paul L., ed. *Franklin Bibliography: A List of Books Written by or Relating to Benjamin Franklin*. Brooklyn, 1889.

Gleason, J. Philip. "A Scurrilous Colonial Election and Franklin's Reputation." *William and Mary Quarterly*. 3rd series, XVIII (1961).

Hale, Edward E. and Edward E. Hale, Jr. *Franklin in France*. 2 vols., Boston, 1888.

Hanna, William S. *Benjamin Franklin and Pennsylvania Politics*. Stanford, 1964.

Riddell, William R. "Benjamin Franklin's Mission to Canada and the Causes of its Failure." *Pennsylvania Magazine of History and Biography*. XLVIII (1924).

Russell, Phillips. *Benjamin Franklin: The First Civilized American*. New York, 1926.

Smythe, J. Henry, Jr., ed. *The Amazing Benjamin Franklin*. New York, 1929.

Steell, Willis. *Benjamin Franklin of Paris, 1776–1785*. New York, 1927.

Tolles, Frederick B. "Franklin and the Pulteney Mission: An Episode in the Secret History of the American Revolution." *Huntington Library Quarterly*. XVII (1953–1954).

Van Doren, Carl. *Benjamin Franklin*. New York, 1952.